The
Cognitive
Connection

The Cognitive Connection

Thought and Language in Man and Machine

Howard Levine and Howard Rheingold

PRENTICE HALL PRESS
New York

Published by Prentice Hall Press
A Division of Simon & Schuster, Inc.
Gulf + Western Building
One Gulf + Western Plaza
New York, NY   10023

PRENTICE HALL PRESS is a trademark of Simon & Schuster, Inc.

Registered Trademarks

Apple is a registered trademark of Apple Computer, Inc.
Commodore is a registered trademark of Commodore Business Machines.
UNIVAC is a registered trademark of Remington Rand.
PDP is a registered trademark of Digital Equipment Company.
Rocky's Boots and Robot Odyssey are registered trademarks of The Learning
    Company.
Star is a registered trademark of Xerox Corporation.

Library of Congress Cataloging-in-Publication Data
Levine, Howard, 1947-
    The cognitive connection,

    Bibliography: p.
    Includes index.
    1. Programming languages (Electronic
computers) 2. Linguistics. I. Rheingold,
Howard. II. Title.
QA76.7.L49   1987   005.13   86-15143
ISBN 0-13-139619-6

Manufactured in the United States of America

1 2 3 4 5 6 7 8 9 10

For our mothers,

Constance Levine and Geraldine Rheingold,
who made it all possible.

Acknowledgments

There is at least one false statement in this book. By beginning *The Cognitive Connection* with the previous sentence, we have traded on the paradoxical nature of natural language to insure that the first sentence of our book asserts a truth. For if, as we hope, all the remaining sentences in the book are true, then the book contains no false statements save the first. And in the very process of stating the possibility of falsity, that first sentence assures its own veracity. Such are the strange ways of paradox that had their beginnings in early Greek philosophy and ultimately led, 2500 years later, to the modern computer.

In our own quest for truth we were aided by the following individuals: Rita Aero, Carol Crowell, Donald Day, Robin Eckhardt, Jay Elliot, Joe Esposito, Laura Gould, Eric Hulteen, Milissa Koloski, Jaron Lanier, Gerri Levine, David Lodge, Judy Maas, Connie Moffit, Charles Silver, Randy Smith, Bob Taylor, Gloria Warner, and Judith Watkins. Any falsehoods or errors that remain are the sole responsibility of the authors.

Other books by
Howard Levine and Howard Rheingold

Talking Tech: A Conversational Guide to Science and Technology,
   1983

By Howard Levine

*Life Choices: Confronting the Life and Death Decisions Created by
   Modern Medicine*, 1986 (Simon & Schuster)

By Howard Rheingold

Tools for Thought, 1985 (Simon & Schuster/Prentice Hall Press)
Higher Creativity, (with Willis Harman), 1984

Contents

Introduction *The Paradox of the All-Purpose Machine*   xv

Chapter 1 *Natural Language and Natural Thought*   1
    Language as a Thought Tool   1
    The Language of Science   5
    The Science of Language   12
    The Structure of Language   15
    The Function of Language   24
    From Linguistics to Cybernetics   27

Chapter 2 *Formal Language and Formal Thought*   33
    The Quest for a Calculus of Thought   33
    Boolean Algebra and the Mechanization of Logic   41
    The Quest for a Logic Machine   47
    Metalogic, Paradox, and the Theory of Computability   57

Chapter 3 *Computer Language and Hierarchies*   71
of Abstractions
    Building Cathedrals Out of Bricks   71
    The Binary Basis and the Universal Game   75
      of Twenty Questions
    Gates, Registers, and Adders—Transforming Hardware   87
      into Software
    From the Fundamental Particles of Microcode to the   97
      Cosmos of the Operating System

Chapter 4 *Computer Thought—From Languages*   111
to Programs
    Algorithms: Power Tools for the Mind   111
    Sequence, Selection, and Iteration: Design Tools for 115
      Algorithms
    Computability, Complexity, and Correctness: Adequacy 122
      Conditions for Algorithms
    Information in Space: The Data Structure Concept   127
    The Grand Synthesis: Algorithms + Data Structures   133
      = Programs
    Programming Style: Metaphors and Methodologies   136

Chapter 5 *The Family of Programming Languages*   145
From Programming Code to Programming Language—   145
    FORTRAN
Industrial Strength Computing—COBOL   153
Computing Goes to College—BASIC   161
The Lingua Franca of the Artificial Intelligentsia—LISP   167
Powerful Ideas and Objects to Think With—Logo   176
Structured Programs and Data Structures—Pascal   187
A Language for Creating Languages—FORTH   198

Chapter 6 *The Future of Programming Languages*   209
The Cognitive Connection   209
Alternate Models: Smalltalk and Object-Oriented   215
    Languages
Emerging New Metaphors: Modeling, Simulation, and   221
    Programming by Rehearsal
Iconic Programming: Sketchpad, Pict, Mandala, and   228
    Beyond
PROLOG to the Future: The Ultimate Logic Machine   236
New Cognitive Paradigms   241

Notes   249

Bibliography   261

Index   269

If we could rid ourselves of all pride, if, to define our species, we kept strictly to what the historic and prehistoric periods show us to be the constant characteristic of man and of intelligence, we should not say *Homo sapiens* but *Homo faber*. In short, *intelligence considered in what seems to be its original feature, is the faculty of manufacturing artificial objects, especially tools for making tools.*

Henri Bergson, *Creative Evolution*

Man-computer symbiosis is an expected development in cooperative interaction between men and electronic computers. It will involve very close coupling between the human and the electronic members of the partnership . . . . In the anticipated symbiotic partnership, men will set the goals, formulate the hypotheses, determine the criteria, and perform the evaluations. Computing machines will do the routinizable work that must be done to prepare the way for insights and decisions in technical and scientific thinking. Preliminary analyses indicate that the symbiotic partnership will perform intellectual operations much more effectively than man alone can perform them.

J.C.R. Licklider, "Man-Computer Symbiosis"

Introduction

The Paradox of the All-Purpose Machine

The protean nature of the computer is such that it can act like a machine or like a language to be shaped and exploited. It is a medium that can dynamically simulate the details of any other medium, including media that cannot exist physically. It is not a tool, although it can act like many tools. It is the first metamedium, and as such it has degrees of freedom for representation and expression never before encountered and as yet barely investigated. Even more important, it is fun, and therefore intrinsically worth doing.[1]

Humans have always enjoyed an intimate relationship with artifacts—those inanimate objects we use to mold our environment and that end up changing our lives, often without our knowledge or consent. Today, Marshall McLuhan's dictum that "we shape our tools and thereafter our tools shape us" is particularly applicable to the twentieth-century descendants of *Homo habilis* (the human tool user). For it is our destiny to live in the era of the metatool, the only tool that has no overt purpose.

This relationship between people and tools is more important now than ever before, in part because of the physical power of modern technologies, but mostly because of the intellectual power of modern technology. Networks of telephones, televisions, and communication satellites transfer staggering quantities of information to and from large segments of the world's population every second of every day, and the personal computer revolution has introduced millions of people to a new kind of tool for amplifying the power of minds rather than muscles. Suddenly, the most powerful machines aren't those that extend muscular power or harness inanimate sources of energy but are those that help us generate and disseminate knowledge.

Humankind's most influential tools today are devices for manipulating language and symbols—historically our most important, if least tangible, technology. Ironically, the crowning achievement in the history of technology is the invention of the computer, which isn't even a machine in the generally understood sense of the word. The computer is fundamentally different from all the machines that preceded it, not because it is made of silicon chips or because it can perform huge calculations very quickly, but because it is the first and only machine that has no specific purpose other than to follow instructions—a linguistic rather than a physical capability.

Many people fail to understand the computer's potential as a symbol-processing device because they think those symbols must be restricted to numbers and mathematical operations. This misconception originated in the earliest days of computers when numbers in unprecedented quantities, manipulated at unheard of speeds were the grist for machines with names like ENIAC (Electronic Numerical Integrator and Calculator).

But the role of automatic arithmetician was only the first guise of the device that was called "the general-purpose machine" by one of its inventors. Arithmetic is only one of an infinite number of symbol systems that can be manipulated by a digital computer. When other formal systems such as logic and natural language are emulated by the great automatic imitator, the computer becomes something more than just an electronic equation solver: It becomes anything anyone can clearly imagine it to be (or a reasonable facsimile).

This disparity between the popular image of computer capabilities and their true potential has been noted by Terry Winograd, a leader in the field of artificial intelligence research:

> In the popular mythology the computer is a mathematics machine: it is designed to do numerical calculations. Yet it is really a language machine: its fundamental power lies in its ability to manipulate linguistic tokens—symbols to which meaning has been assigned.[2]

Computers, computer languages, and computer programs are, by their nature, distinctly different and potentially more powerful than any other machine ever invented. The invention of computation, which preceded the invention of the first electronic digital computer by 10 years, was a unique event in the history of technology. Indeed, the existence of computer programs has caused us to rethink what is meant by the words *machine* and *technology*.

For more than 6000 years, machines were devices to control the application of power, either to amplify human or animal energy, as in the case of the five ancient simple machines—the lever, pulley, inclined plane, screw, wheel, and axle—or to channel that power for the modification of a natural substance, such as the spindle for spinning fiber or the plow for digging a furrow. Clearly, as far as ancient civilizations were concerned, machines were material substances themselves, and technology was the study of using machines to transform other material substances.

The invention of the clock and the printing press at the dawn of the Renaissance undermined this strictly materialist view of machines since useful machines no longer had to work solely with material substance to yield something of value to people. Instead, public clocks could provide a city full of people with information that would enable them to better coordinate mechanical and commercial processes, and printing presses could even help disseminate information about other useful machines and processes. The study of technology was no longer constrained to an exclusively material, mechanistic domain; the meaning of technology expanded to include the nonmaterial idea of information.

The introduction of machines that harnessed inanimate sources of energy (coal, water, oil) in order to power other machines precipitated the Industrial Revolution and once again enlarged the definition of machine. This time, the most important machines, steam engines, were no longer the ones that produced goods such as cloth and steel; they were the ones that produced the energy to drive and, in a very important sense, to control the old-fashioned, traditionally muscle-powered machines that worked directly with material. Thus, by the turn of the twentieth century, the concept of technology had expanded to include the notions of machines such as the clock, which provide simple, basic information; the printing press, which could communicate basic information; and control devices such as governors, which could regulate the actions of other machines.

Understanding the computer, a half-material, half-nonmaterial device that produces an intangible product, requires yet another expansion of our concepts of machine and technology. Although computer hardware is certainly made of material substances, the software, without which the computer is useless, is nonmaterial and consists of pure information. In fact, a crucial concept in computer science is that of *virtual machine*—the algorithms (specific instructions) and data structures (encoded information) that totally describe the behavior of a particular computing machine.

Frequently there is no intention of actually building a material version of this virtual machine; you just program a computer to *imitate* the virtual machine. The important point is that the software *is* the computer; the hardware is just one method to realize it physically. The true computer—that which is processed by the computing agent, whether the agent is made of electronic circuits (hardware), neurons (humanware), or marks on a piece of paper (paperware)—is the program (software).

It seems strange at first to refer to a computer program or the language used to create it as a kind of machine, yet the real power of computer technology emerges only when the hardware part of a computer is yoked to the coded instructions that constitute its software. A computer program in operation, together with the machine that follows the program's instructions and the data on which the instructions operate, is a machine for manipulating neither matter nor energy but that invisible, familiar, mysterious entity known as *information.*

Like other conceptual revolutions, the computer revolution can be puzzling at first. Just as we're finally coming to understand the meaning of the paradoxes of modern physics (e.g., how light can be both particle and wave; how matter can be energy and energy can be matter), the nature of computers has presented us with a new series of mind-bending puzzles: How can a language be a machine? Of what use is a machine that deals in neither energy nor matter? And the central paradox of the all-purpose machine: How can computers appear to do so much when, in fact, they actually can do so little?

To the electronic engineer who designs computer hardware, the computer is simply a collection of microscopic switches that transfer and store sequences of electronic signals. To the programmer who composes the instructions that direct the computer's operations, the computer is a machine for decoding sequences of symbols and executing the operations specified by those sequences. The programmer looks at a code, not at a collection of switches. The person who uses the computer, however, experiences neither electronic impulses nor coded symbols, but instead uses a word processor, makes airline reservations, runs an automated assembly line, updates financial records, teaches a child how to multiply, plays chess, paints a picture, composes music, calculates, simulates, synthesizes, analyzes, or does anything else that a programmer can encode in algorithms and data structures.

How is it possible that the concrete description of the engineer and the abstract description given by the end-user both refer to the same machine? How can the one tool be so many tools? One way to attack this riddle is to look for the part of the system that makes the difference between a picture-painting computer and a bookkeeping computer. What part of the machine changes when the user switches from one task to another? The physical components of the computer—the vast numbers of tiny switches—do not change when the machine is transformed from a word processor to a chess player. The *program*, the nonphysical but indispensable ordering of the states of the switches, is what changes.

When you trace the logical path of computer operation through the labyrinth of components that make up the computer system, you discover that computer programs are the machines with which the end-user actually deals. Computers are said to be protean in nature because, like the Greek god, Proteus, they are capable of assuming shape, of becoming any tool that can be unambiguously described. This astonishing capability is not a function of the machinery, but of the instructions to the machinery.

The key to reconciling the engineer's and the computer user's description is to understand how programs direct computers to manipulate information and, in particular, what strings of 1s and 0s on a piece of paper, or a series of impulses denoting on and off states in an electronic circuit, have in common with real-world descriptions such as "move this paragraph," "reserve a seat on flight 744," "shut down the factory if the boiler exceeds 320 degrees," "sum the income column," "drill the multiplication table," "perform a queen side castle," "monitor the house for smoke," or even, "ask seemingly probing questions."

How people write the instructions to cause a computer to carry out these real-world tasks and how the computer translates these instructions into symbols that it can manipulate is the story told in this book. It is a story that has more to do with language than machines, a story about a quest that has more to do with philosophy than arithmetic.

The nature of computer languages is more closely related to the way people think than the way collections of switches are put together. Understanding the basics of computer languages is a prerequisite to using the power of such languages, but understanding the nature of computer languages can lead to something far more useful than an ability to program computers. Computer languages, like natural languages (those that we speak), are tools for extending the power and expanding the scope of thought: Like reading, writing, arithmetic, logic, science, and geometry, computer languages enable us to think new thoughts in new ways and on grander scales.

1

Natural Language and Natural Thought

Language serves not only to express thoughts, but to make possible thoughts which could not exist without it . . . it cannot be denied that all fairly elaborate thoughts require words. I can know, in a sense, that I have five fingers without knowing the word "five," but I cannot know that the population of London is about eight millions unless I have acquired the language of arithmetic.[1]

LANGUAGE AS A THOUGHT TOOL

If it is true that humans and tools shape one another, then the relationship between thought and language is the primary example. The emergence of language made it possible for people to think in new ways, on much grander scales, and with greater effect. Indeed, abstract thought would seem to be impossible without the aid of language. Whereas thought is a necessary condition of language, language is the medium of higher thought.

Without language we would all be prisoners in our own tiny thought worlds, existing as isolated individual minds without a means of communicating our thoughts to one another. Yet language is also the major means of structuring our thoughts, and without it our thought worlds would be greatly impoverished domains. It isn't enough to have a thought; we also need to memorize and remember thoughts, to relate different thoughts to one another, and to perform a variety of transformations on thoughts. Language is the tool that gives us a special ability to manipulate our thought, and hence change our world.

1

Thought, language, and the human species have been coevolutionary partners for millions of years. The long history of this mutually advantageous relationship is indicated by contemporary linguistic evidence that the human brain is biologically predisposed to use language: In a way that science has yet to explain, the ability to create language (and a template for the deep structure of language) appears to be built into our brain structure. It is this biological advantage that has enabled us as humans to create culture.

A classic example of the way thought and language continue to advance each other's development is the history of cardinal (counting) numbers, a case in which the expansion of our ideas about the size of the world seems to have directly increased our effect on the world. In many primitive tribes, people can only count to 3 because their language only provides three numbers. Everything beyond 3 is simply considered to be "many." It isn't just that these people don't have a word for 4—they don't have the *concept* of 4.

The Egyptians, with their pictographic symbols, were somewhat better off. They could count to a few thousand, but they were still incapable of representing (and hence thinking clearly about) extremely large numbers, such as the distance to the moon. This wasn't an ideal situation for a civilization consisting of millions of subjects, covering hundreds of thousands of square miles. It was not until the third century B.C. that Archimedes devised the first system for handling extremely large numbers; the system is similar to our modern idea of exponential notation (e.g., 10^{30} to represent 10 multiplied by itself 30 times). With this discovery (which was as linguistic as it was mathematical since it furnished a notation and linguistic framework for communicating large numbers) it became possible for scientists to think about things such as the mass of the earth and astronomical distances.

Yet even Archimedes reached a point beyond counting, where words for specific numbers had to give way to that old favorite, many. It took 2000 more years before a nineteenth-century German mathematician, Georg Cantor, was able to extend the counting numbers into the realm of Archimedes's many. Cantor demonstrated that there are many manys. There is a hierarchy of infinities, each one larger than the previous one, including at least three levels. Cantor called the three levels of "transfinite" numbers *Aleph-2* (e.g., the cardinality of points in a plane), *Aleph-1* (e.g., the cardinality of points on a line), and *Aleph-0* (e.g., the cardinality of rational numbers), thus providing us with a thought tool to think about numbers beyond infinity.[2]

Yet even our knowledge of transfinite numbers extends only to a certain point, and no further. We are only marginally better off than the primitive tribes people: We can count to more than three infinities, but we have no idea what these numbers represent. Our concepts stop at Aleph-2; after that we once again find ourselves in the zone of the many. Although numbers may be illustrative of the way in which language and thought enrich each other, you don't have to be a mathematician to benefit from this relationship. Just look in your own back yard.

Before spoken language existed, if you wanted to communicate something about a tree, you had to point at an actual tree. This constraint limited conversation about trees to those times when you and your conversational partner were within sight of a tree. In this particular case, a rough sketch in the sand might serve to convey the information. But that would limit the objects of communication to objects that could be translated into pictorial form; it also would mean that you would have to draw skillfully in order to communicate effectively.

When you have a word for "tree," you don't have to point at one or draw one. Also, conversations tend to proceed at a much faster rate when you don't have to sit down and draw a picture for every word. When you have a word for "tree," however, you have more than a convenient symbol for a tall plant with a trunk and branches. You have an *abstraction*, and abstractions are the stuff of reasoning. In fact, the process and products of abstraction are essential elements in both natural and computer languages.

Without abstraction, thought and communication are limited to the world of concrete objects and visible actions. A tree is concrete. You can see it, feel it, run into it in the dark. But when it comes to thinking, the world of the concrete is severely limited. Without abstractions you can't think about the past or the future, and you can't think about things you have never experienced. Without a sense of past and future and the ability to refer to objects and actions that are not physically present, the kinds of higher mental processes we call "reasoning" would not be possible.

Three of the most important aspects of higher thought that flow from the ability to abstract are the concept of time, the use of imagination, and the ability to make generalizations. With these three thinking skills, the descendants of *Homo habilis* have numbered the stars, studied the birth of the universe and projected its death, and created coding systems capable of transmitting the essence of the species' accumulated wisdom to infants. Time, imagination, and generalization also are deeply involved with the use of language.

One of the characteristics that appears to distinguish our species from all others is our ability to think in terms of the past and future. As individuals and as a species, we can plan, foresee, and remember. We are able to study the wisdom of the past, as well as communicate what we know to future generations. All this is possible because human thought can use the symbols provided by language to manipulate the abstraction of experience known as "time."

Just as words free our communications from the constraints of the immediately visible world, they also free us to think about things we have never seen. Our ability to form a mental image of something our external organs have never perceived enables us to consider entirely new possibilities by combining two presently known elements (e.g., to imagine mermaids) or to universalize a known element to an abstract concept (e.g., to use the concept of *a* tree instead of *this* tree or *that* tree). The process of *universalization*, by which examination of individual cases leads to the formalization of general laws, is one of the underpinnings of the scientific method, our society's most powerful thought tool.[3]

Spoken language was a tremendous leap, but it was not the final word (so to speak) in the refinement of symbolic communication systems. The invention of writing, a much more recent development, was also a tremendously liberating event. Although nobody knows exactly when spoken languages originated, the invention of written alphabetic (as opposed to strictly pictographic or hieroglyphic) language is generally attributed to the Phoenicians of approximately 1000 B.C. (The Phoenician port of Byblos is the site where modern scholars think the alphabet originated; the Greek word for rolled book, *biblion*, comes from the name of the port, as do the English words *bible* and *bibliography*.) Just as spoken language is an abstraction for concrete objects, augmenting primitive gesture-based communications by substituting audible words, written language is an abstraction of speech representing spoken language by means of a code made up of visual symbols.

Written language does much more than model the function of audible speech as a medium for conveying information—it augments and extends the power of speech by communicating knowledge across barriers of time and space that are impenetrable by the voice alone.

Before speech, you had to have a tree in sight in order to point to it. With the aid of spoken language, you could only tell somebody about a tree if the person was within hearing distance. With writing, you can communicate information about trees and all manner of other things to people of distant lands and future centuries. Each successive level of abstraction—from gesture to spoken word to written word—has dramatically increased the power and scope of thought and communication.

How far can the thought–augmenting process proceed? Ever since the invention of writing, people who specialized in thinking about thinking, mostly logicians and mathematicians, have tried to build even more precise and powerful tools for thinking and communicating. Geometry, mathematics, logic, science, and, ultimately, computer languages, were the result of those attempts to invent more and more powerful symbol systems.

Although a computer is a kind of machine constructed of circuits and semiconductors, *computation* is more closely related to the development of symbol systems than to the history of physical devices. Thus one of our goals in this book is to clarify the connections between human thought, human language, computation, and computer languages—the symbols and instructions humans can use to command computers to augment their own thinking.

In an important sense, this kind of theoretical quest is a prerequisite to the kind of applied science needed to build a computer. The fact that computers can exist at all and the nature of all human-computer communication systems both depend upon a hierarchy of abstractions—symbol systems built from less sophisticated symbol systems that were originally constructed using even more primitive symbol systems.[4] In fact, some of the intellectual discoveries that led to the modern computer are over 2500 years old, and the completed theory of computation existed for over a decade before the first true electronic digital computer was built.

THE LANGUAGE OF SCIENCE

Truth lay just around the corner like a veiled statue waiting men to uncover it. The causes and effects of everything from comets to heart palpitations could be made known, and, in Descartes' words, men would soon be "the lords and possessors of nature."

This was the epic scale on which Descartes dreamed. He had discovered a wonderful new method for discerning the truth—a method totally different from the ones men had been using. It was to apply the method of mathematics to every area of life. By using logic, step by step, all the secrets of nature could be laid bare. And with knowledge would come control.[5]

Instructions have always been the invisible side of every invention; without them, all inventions would be one-of-a-kind items. The inventor of the wheel, for example, has been given far too much credit. The one who truly deserves accolades for improving the lot of the human race was the first person who *told somebody else* how to build a wheel. Language, a medium for transmitting encoded information, and instructions, a systematic method for conveying information about how to do things, were the factors that allowed our antecedents to build upon the knowledge of others, to increase their store of knowledge with each generation, and, finally, to stop reinventing the wheel. In each case, *symbols*, communicated by either auditory or visual signals, were used to create the abstractions necessary for compressing ever-larger amounts of information into ever-more efficient codes.

With each level of abstraction, language made increasingly more power available. The first level came with the slow evolution of spoken language and the growth of an oral tradition that began with hundreds of thousands of years of prehistoric hunter-gatherer societies and ended up creating agricultural civilization about 9000 years ago. Then the higher-level abstraction of alphabetic writing was invented about 3000 years ago, radically increasing the level of knowledge available to individuals as well as to entire cultures.

But the kind of hyperaccelerated scientific-technological progress that led to the twentieth century didn't begin until humans created the third level of linguistic abstraction—tools for generating and determining the validity of knowledge. Science dominates so much of the modern environment that few people ever think of it as a kind of language or thought tool, or suspect that it was first and foremost a way of thinking about the world and is actually a relatively recent invention.

One person who was interested in thinking systematically about the rules of a new scientific language was René Descartes. On the night of November 10, 1619, Descartes experienced a series of dream visions in which he perceived a set of rules for thinking—a system of instructions people could use to generate knowledge. Descartes' "new method of thought," as set forth in *Discourse on the Method*, the book he started to write upon awakening from his visions, became one of the foundations of what we know now as the *scientific method*.[6]

Until the seventeenth century, there was still quite vigorous debate (sometimes called religious wars) over the question of whether anybody outside the Church even had a *right* to dream up new systems of knowledge. But Descartes, never known for false modesty, felt that the entirety of what passed for education in those days ought to be totally discarded; someone, preferably him, had to think up a new curriculum and new ways to learn about the universe. The whole matter of *how* one would go about creating something more powerful than logic, mathematics, and geometry was Descartes' goal, which made him one of the first Western thinkers to reassert the possibility of creating better methods for discovering and validating knowledge.

This young French mathematician–philosopher's bold claim that he had discovered a powerful way to think carried more than a little clout because he immediately applied the principles of his system to his invention of analytic geometry, one of the most impressive achievements in the history of thought. "Here is a new way to think," he told the world, "and these are the kinds of things I came up with when I tried it myself."

The work of Descartes and other philosopher-scientists around the beginning of the seventeenth century signaled the reawakening in the West of an ancient quest for knowledge-generating systems—a pursuit that had reached its zenith during the age of Euclid and Aristotle but had been dormant in Europe since the fall of Rome. The idea that new knowledge could be created is so fundamental to our current era that most of us probably can't envision a society in which the only knowledge is old knowledge. But European thinkers of Descartes' time were rehashing Greek discoveries that were close to 2000 years old. When European thinkers finally started tinkering with new knowledge systems, however, they did it in a big way.

The Greeks had performed experiments and pursued the limits of pure reason long before the Christian era, and the great Moslem mathematician-scientists not only preserved the thought tools created by the Greeks, but they made their own significant contributions to individual sciences during the middle ages. The invention of a *systematic* kind of science, however, dates back only to seventeenth-century Europe. The work of Descartes, Bacon, Leibniz, Galileo, and Newton fit together to create the rationally based, empirically validated system known as *science*—a knowledge tool that even the Greeks hadn't (entirely) invented first.

The scientific method of formulating a hypothesis on the basis of observations, then testing it by performing an experiment or by observing, then describing the result in terms of mathematical equations is a hybrid of two methods, each with its own long history. The purely theoretical part of the scientific method—the application of mathematical descriptions and the use of logical rules for formulating hypotheses—was, in large part, Descartes' work. The empirical tradition of checking the products of the imagination against the behavior of the natural world converged on modern science from another direction, specifically from the work of Galileo and Bacon.

Descartes lived in an era of sweeping systemic changes. The idea that a central authority was the only legitimate arbiter of knowledge was on its way out, and the idea that individual thinkers could discover the truth was on its way back in, after a very long absence. Descartes, the supreme rationalist, was confident that the nature of the universe could be understood by the mind's use of the proper tools. Descartes proclaimed that he had created a thinking tool of such power and certainty that you didn't have to be Descartes to use it.

His brilliant combination of geometry and algebra in the field of analytic geometry was a paragon of such a tool (which was later used by Leibniz and Newton to create calculus and thus further Descartes' goal of mathematizing science). In his *Discourse on the Method of Rightly Conducting the Reason and Seeking Truth in the Field of Science*, Descartes extended the use of mathematics to all knowledge.

Descartes acknowledged the power of an earlier system of thought—Aristotle's syllogistic logic—but realized that this established system had serious limitations. Syllogistic logic, in which true premises were manipulated according to rules guaranteed to preserve true relationships in order to produce true conclusions, was only useful for teasing out truths that were already contained in the premises. Because Descartes was also interested in ways of directly apprehending the truth, he emphasized intuition, which comprehends abstractions such as the connection between algebra and geometry, as another way of establishing new knowledge.

He sought a clear and distinct system for turning inferences, intuitions, and experiences into knowledge. Being a doubting man, he wanted to guarantee that his knowledge system included a way for individuals to verify its findings for themselves. The system had to be so clear and distinct that he could describe it to others who could then apply it to fields beyond those explored by the author.

Descartes prescribed a set of four rules for extending the power of formal thought beyond the bounds of metaphysics:

> The first rule was never to accept anything as true unless I recognized it to be certainly and evidently such.
>
> The second was to divide each of the difficulties which I encountered into as many parts as possible, and as might be required for an easier solution.
>
> The third was to think in an orderly fashion when concerned with the search for truth, beginning with the things which were simplest and easiest to understand, and gradually and by degrees reaching toward more complex knowledge.
>
> The last was, both in the process of searching and in reviewing when in difficulty, always to make enumerations so complete, and reviews so general, that I would be certain that nothing was omitted.[7]

To us, these "rules" might seem hopelessly general and vague, but they were truly revolutionary back in the days when the main way of learning about a topic was to see what Aristotle or Thomas Aquinas said about it.

In the first rule, Descartes paid homage to Euclid, but went even further: Not only should you start from fundamental premises, but you should always question whether the premise is truly fundamental no matter what Aristotle or the Church might have said (an attitude that was part of the overall philosophical method that has come to be known as Cartesian doubt).

The second rule set forth the analytical approach that is still fundamental to the physical and most of the social sciences. From electron microscopes to psychological tests to atom smashers, science studies phenomena by *taking them apart* and then studying how the pieces fit together.

The third rule is another subtle variation on the rules of classical logic and geometric argument. But Descartes proposed that the deductive method of chaining combinations of axioms together to prove theorems, which worked so well for Aristotle and Euclid, could be extended to the study of the natural world or any other topic. In the way he restated the principle, Descartes emphasized the *hierarchical* nature of knowledge gained in this stepwise manner: You start by understanding the simplest elements and deducing all the compound consequences of their various combinations, then you work your way up to the more complex combinations.

In the fourth rule, Descartes hit upon an idea that had profound impact upon the history of science—the notion that it is possible to discover a way not only of generating knowledge, but also of ascertaining its veracity. *Certainty* was a matter of supreme importance to one of philosophy's greatest doubters, and the quest for certainty, Descartes knew, would have to use the rigorous language of mathematics. This search for certainty about the foundations of formal knowledge didn't end for 300 years, but when it reached its goal, the results would have surprised Descartes himself.

At about the same time that Descartes invented analytic geometry, an influential member of the Elizabethan court was the first person to proclaim that "knowledge is power." Like Descartes, Francis Bacon felt that it was time to go beyond the knowledge of the ancients, to discover a new method for finding truth, and like Descartes he believed that well-trained minds, rather than authorities, could accomplish the task if only they were given the proper tools. The reason that people such as Aristotle came along so infrequently, Bacon believed, was not because most people are constitutionally incapable of original thought, but because so few people had ever been trained to think properly. He had a bold and prophetic proposal: By educating many people around the world in the use of a truly effective "engine for the discovery of truth," Bacon foresaw that it would be possible to create an edifice of knowledge much larger than the scope of any of its individual contributors.

Bacon's version of this "engine"—a set of rules prescribing a system for gaining knowledge—was based on *inductive* reasoning, a kind of logic that worked in exactly the opposite manner as Aristotle's syllogisms or Euclid's proofs. Instead of starting from fundamental axioms and deriving theorems from the relationships between axioms the way a deductive system does, Bacon said we should go to nature herself to find the truth, seeking generalizations by observing many individual cases.[8]

During the decades preceding and following Descartes and Bacon, other thinkers across Europe applied themselves to refining the new method of gaining knowledge. Galileo, Copernicus, Leibniz, and most of all, Newton, met great success when they applied the methods of thinking described by Descartes and Bacon. Mathematical relationships that had been known for centuries were applied to observations in the natural sciences, with spectacular results. When Newton described the laws of motion and gravitation in terms of a set of equations, he proved that the proper use of logic, mathematics, and inductive reasoning could lead to new knowledge of astonishing power.

The new knowledge system could produce physical and political power by furnishing a means of predicting and controlling the physical world. Consequently, the pragmatic, empirical part of science—the part that leads to technology—came to dominate history. But the formal questions about the limits of certainty and the soundness of the foundations of symbolic systems did not go away. Although the empirical side of the scientific endeavor became a dominant historical force, a small group of specialists continued to pursue the search for science's formal foundations.

The empiricists had the advantage of dealing with the tangible, concrete, testable world of phenomena. You can build nuclear bombs and transistor radios with the knowledge gained by applying Bacon's inductive method. But this method, for all its power, was not *certain* enough for the formalists, who were seeking absolute guarantees. Logicians and pure mathematicians wanted to know whether the rules of thumb that worked so well for scientists were actually truths or just strategies that work well most of the time.

For a mathematician, there is a very big difference between something that is guaranteed to be true and something that is true most of the time. Uncertainty is the flaw in a purely inductive system: If you generalize a law from what you have learned from observing 1 million cases, you have no guarantee that the 1 million-first case won't be an exception.

The issue of mathematical certainty remained in the background of human thought while great minds were applying themselves to creating technologies such as steam engines and sciences like chemistry, physics, and biology. Mathematics seemed to be moving into every realm of thought, tidying up centuries worth of metaphysical speculation. But the search for formal certainty seemed to have wandered, unheeded, in the wilderness of obscure philosophy and mathematical journals during the last few centuries while the empiricists have been busy creating the industrial and postindustrial revolutions.

It was only when the machines of industrial society became too complex for humans to control that the engineers and other empirically minded scientists realized the need for a new type of machine—

one that could monitor and control the power-producing machines. This new machine, the computer, is based on the use of precise instructions called *algorithms*—a direct descendant of Descartes' search for "enumerations so complete . . . I would be certain that nothing was omitted." After 300 years of essentially independent development, the work of the empiricists and formalists, which had originally created science, was again joined together to create modern science's most useful thought tool—the computer.

The dominant position of the computer in the world of technology also means that the role of language as a thought tool has come full circle. Language was originally our only thought tool and we used it to create symbol systems that amplified our ability to think. Since the Renaissance, our predominant thought tool has been science, and it has seemed at times that language was no longer an engine of discovery but only a vehicle for description. Modern sociology is littered with laments such as C.P. Snow's, decrying the existence of the two seemingly separate cultures of the sciences and the humanities.

Yet the very success of science has rekindled the need to pay attention to the use of language as a thought tool—this time, as a means for human-computer communication. Just how natural language works and how that understanding may be applied to programming languages are discussed in the remainder of this chapter.

THE SCIENCE OF LANGUAGE

> Linguistic theory is a metatheory dealing with the properties of linguistic descriptions of natural language. In particular, linguistic theory is concerned with whatever such descriptions have in common—with *universals* of linguistic description.[9]

Important as it might be to the human race, language was not a general subject of scientific investigation until relatively recently. In fact, serious scholarly and experimental investigation of the nature of language is even younger than the theory and practice of computation. Professional linguists have concerned themselves with the universality of language for only about 30 years. Before then, linguistics was dominated by the *structural* school, which believed that language was just one more form of behavior—that talking is just like walking. Laboring under this paradigm, structural linguists went all over the world to tape the dialects of obscure tribes. The object of their study was always the particular language, not its relationship to any universal rules. The ultimate goal of linguistics was simply to describe, not to make inferences or generalizations.

By the mid-1950s, however, it had become clear to Noam Chomsky and other linguists, in what became known as the *trans-formational* school of linguistics, that the behaviorist approach could not account for two crucial aspects of language.[10] First, the grammars of every language describe a basic knowledge that appears to be shared by the speakers of all languages. This first discrepancy between structural theory and observed behavior led Chomsky to his notion of a *universal grammar*—a highly restrictive schema to which any human language must conform. It is as if every human brain comes equipped with an innate organizational structure for understanding and creating language, as well as for following some set of general rules that specific languages obey.

Because this theory of language emerged at about the same time (the early 1950s) and the same place (the Massachusetts Institute of Technology) as early work in computer science, the phrase "hardwired" became popularly if not officially associated with this aspect of the language theory. More recent advances in neurophysiology have made it clear that "wiring" is a poor metaphor for brain function. Chomsky, however, was not concerned with the nature of the brain structures responsible for the ability to use language, but only with the idea that such abilities seem to be innate, that they are not learned through some kind of cultural mechanism, but are actually encoded in the genetic instructions.

Chomsky's second point was that our use of language is fundamentally *creative*. Like our ability to count to a number larger than any number we have previously encountered, all speakers of natural languages have the ability to construct an infinite variety of sentences that have never been heard or seen before. Whereas parrots and computers can mimic grammatically correct sentences that have been taught to them, nobody but humans (yet) can endlessly generate new sentences. What is most amazing is the fact that almost all young children are able to master this ability in just a few years.

More than mimicry or even a complex mathematical system for generating permutations, language arises from a generative process that proceeds from a universal set of structural rules. Somehow, every speaker develops a strong intuitive sense of what sounds right—

even if he or she has never heard the sentence before. Chomsky's transformational grammar is an attempt to describe the characteristics of that universal, innate set of rules and to provide a theory of language that accounts for the facts missed by the structuralists. To be sure, transformational grammar has not proceeded without problems, and there is still much debate about the validity of the idea of a universal grammar. But this much is clear: All languages do obey certain structural rules, and if programming languages are to be seen from the perspective of natural language, then a comparison of their structures will play a key role.

Yet looking at linguistic structure alone would be like trying to determine what a person is like solely by looking at X-rays or inspecting organs. Language is much more than a set of rules, much more than a formalism represented by a particular grammar. It is also the medium we use to communicate our feelings as well as our thoughts, to emote as well as to inform. Although language cannot be explained solely in terms of human behavior, neither can it be explained without any reference to the way humans appear to act, feel, and think.

The existentialist credo holds that you *are* what you do, and this is no less true for language. In some fundamental sense, the definition of language must include what *it* does. The ways in which it functions are as essential in defining language as is the way it is structured. Therefore, before we can fully judge whether programming languages are really languages (and if not, how it is that they differ), we must also consider how language *functions*.

Finally, we must turn the analysis around and look at it from the other side: What are the language needs of computers and the people who wish to communicate with them? What does it mean to say that a computer "understands" a programming language? Since the computer is solely an information processor, answering these questions will require a discussion of the concept of information as well as an examination of the structure of languages. Only when we understand the relationship among languages, instructions, and information will we be able to understand fully how humans can communicate with the machine world.

Today, while natural language continues to shape our natural thought, the advent of sophisticated programming languages (themselves a result of the interplay between thought and language) are helping us to shape a new kind of computer-aided thought. Just as natural language is crucial both for our ability to communicate and to think, we need some kind of programming language if we intend to use computers to do some of our thinking for us.

Programming languages are the tools we use to communicate our thoughts to computers. But programming languages do more than communicate our thoughts and intentions to computers. Good programming languages, properly used, provide us with tools to enhance the way we think about solving problems. Just as the language of cardinal numbers enables us to think about bigger and bigger quantities, programming languages with provisions for manipulating data structures and algorithms enable us to think in grander abstractions and generalizations. If computers are the technology with the greatest ability to shape the future of humanity, then programming languages are the thought tools humanity will use to shape the future of computers.

THE STRUCTURE OF LANGUAGE

As is often said, grammar expresses the unconscious logic of the popular mind. *The chief intellectual classifications that constitute the working capital of thought have been built up for us by our mother tongue.* Our very lack of explicit consciousness in using language that we are employing the intellectual systematizations of the race shows how thoroughly accustomed we have become to its logical distinctions and groupings.[11]

When we realize that there are about 2800 individual languages spoken on this planet (750 on the island of Papua, New Guinea, alone) the claim that they all share a common structure is remarkable. Yet, the fact that the child of Masaai parents growing up in Brooklyn will learn to speak English gives us reason to think that all languages must share some common structure.

Although recent work in linguistic theory has not been able to produce an explanation of how that "deep structure" works and how it is related to neurophysiology, it has given us some tools to use in thinking about deep structures: Every language is specified by its *grammar*, which must be capable of generating the infinite set of sentences in that language. This statement focuses on two important aspects of all natural languages. First, their grammars must be *generative*; that is, they must contain functional rules that generate sentences. Second, language must be *open-ended*; in other words, there must be no bounds on its number of legal sentences. All natural languages adhere to these two strictures and, as we'll see, so do all programming languages.

According to modern linguistic theory, a grammar is composed of three components: *Syntax* is the system of rules that explains how the components of the language are put together to form sentences; *semantics* is concerned with the rules for attaching meaning to the sentences of the language; *phonology* addresses the means by which language is turned into recognizable utterances.

Syntax is the collection of all the rules of structure that make any language what it is. These rules tell us how to combine the primitive constituents of the language (words) into well-formed sentences. Just as importantly, the syntax can be put to work in the reverse manner, that is, as a tool for analyzing a putative sentence in order to tell us whether or not it is well formed. This is accomplished through a two-step process.

First, a word string is broken into its component parts (known technically as *tokens*), and a table is created that gives a list of each word in the string, its root, its lexical category, and its syntactic features.

For example, consider the sentence, John saw that oil can leak:

Word	Root	Lexical Category	Features
John		noun	proper name
saw	see	verb (transitive)	past tense
		noun	
that		pronoun	singular
		adjective	demonstrative
		conjunction	
		adverb	
oil		noun	mass
can		verb (auxiliary)	
		verb (transitive)	
		noun	
leak		verb (transitive)	
		verb (intransitive)	
		noun	

Second, the sentence is parsed. If you remember diagramming sentences, you have a good idea of how parsing works. We take the analyzed tokens and reconstruct the sentence in order to show its syntactic structure as illustrated in Figure 1.1.

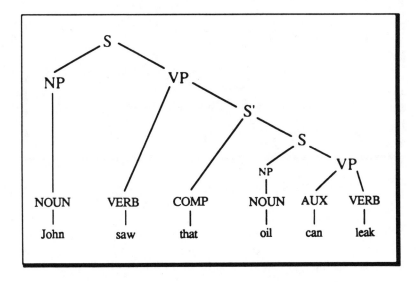

Figure 1.1 Parsed Sentence of Leaking Oil

The parsing of our sentence to show its syntactic structure reflects the fact that the substance oil is capable of leaking. It is the structure of the sentence we utter when we look under the car after failing to tighten the oil filter sufficiently.

But the lexical analysis of the words in the sentence also allows a different parsing, as shown in Figure 1.2.

In this parsing, "oil can" is the subject of the subordinate sentence. This is the structure of the sentence we utter when we purchase a can of oil and later observe a viscous fluid spreading out on our car's back seat.

Parsing works because it is the pictorial representation of a number of syntactic rules:

$$S \quad = \quad NP + VP$$
$$VP \quad = \quad Verb + S'$$
$$VP \quad = \quad Aux + Verb$$

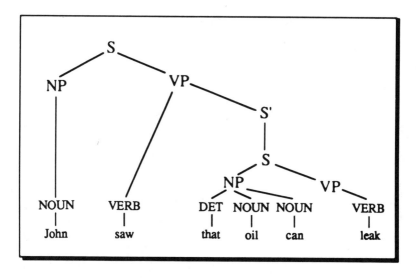

Figure 1.2 Parsed Sentence of Leaking Oil Can

The first rule states that a sentence is composed of a noun phrase and a verb phrase, the second that a verb phrase is composed of a verb plus another sentence, and the third that a verb phrase also can be composed of an auxiliary word and a verb. Any string of words that conform to these rules is syntactically correct, which is why natural language is so prone to syntactic ambiguity.

Such lexical analysis and syntactic parsing is the first step in any program that translates between languages, whether the languages are English and Russian or BASIC and machine code (a string of ones and zeros). The task of lexical analysis is always the same—to break a statement (sentence) into its constituent parts (words) and to provide an analysis of the tokens. Likewise, the task of syntactic parsing is also always the same—to produce the structure that holds the individual tokens together in a coherent syntactic unit.

Syntax tells us if a sentence is well formed but not necessarily if it is meaningful. Using the above rules, we can generate sentences such as

John saw that dog can leak.

or

Mary saw that butter can talk.

It is easy to imagine other well-formed sentences, generated by more complex syntactic rules, that are even more peculiar:

Green ideas sleep furiously.

The equator is purple.

The peanut ate the elephant.

Ironically, the "green ideas" sentence, which was originally proposed by Chomsky as an example of a well-formed but meaningless sentence, has come to have a kind of meaning by association, insofar as it is the single phrase most often cited by Chomskyite linguists when they illustrate this point. The conclusion is that syntax is just a formalism, a system of rules for combining elements. In order to start making sense, syntactic structures need to be interpreted, and that is the role of semantic theory.

Semantics is the part of linguistic theory that attaches meaning to a language's sentences. In order for a semantic system to work, it must contain a dictionary of the words in the language and a set of rules for determining which dictionary entry is proper given the contextual usage. We are all familiar with what a dictionary entry looks like. It is the lexical analysis table with a column added to contain the word's possible meanings. For example, a dictionary listing for *bachelor* looks like this:

Word	Lexical Category	Features	Meanings
bachelor	noun		1. unmarried male 2. awardee of first degree 3. young knight 4. young fur seal

The listing in a programming language's dictionary is quite similar, as this example from the BASIC "dictionary" demonstrates:

Word	Lexical Category	Features (Format)	Meaning
MID$	command	MID$(<string exp1>,n[,m])> = <string exp2>	MID$ replaces a portion of one string with another string.
	function	MID$(X$,I [,J])	Returns a string of length J characters from X$ beginning with the Ith character.

The two examples, bachelor and MID$, demonstrate three important differences between the semantics of natural language and that of programming languages. First, although programming languages, with their limited vocabularies, have adequate dictionaries, they are written in a natural language. When human programmers want to look up the meaning of a command in BASIC, for example, they look in a dictionary written in English or French, not in a dictionary written in BASIC. Contrast this with a natural language dictionary that is written in terms of other words of the same natural language, a situation that can lead to a circularity of definition. It definitely assumes that the language user has some knowledge of the language before approaching the dictionary.

By writing programming language definitions in natural language, we avoid any problems of circularity; but we also discover an area in which the analogy between programming languages and natural languages begins to break down: Programming languages are not semantically rich enough to describe themselves. Furthermore, because programming languages are used for human-machine communication, there is also a "dictionary" for the computer, written in machine language.

Second, although philosophers and linguists have struggled for centuries to give precise meaning to the word "meaning," you don't need a degree in either discipline to realize that what constitutes meaning for a programming language is dramatically different from what constitutes meaning for a natural language. Meaning in a programming language is an exact rule for how to apply a word, as well as the end result of that application. Meaning in natural language is much fuzzier, ranging from exact rules (e.g., the meaning of "add" in a precise mathematical rule) to mere synonyms (e.g., as in "bachelor" is an unmarried male), all the way to metaphor (e.g., as in the famed essay "How Does a Poem Mean?"). It seems safe to conclude that there is a qualitative difference between the meaning of a programming language word and the meaning of a natural language word.

The third difference demonstrates that there is also a quantitative difference between natural and programming languages. The natural language dictionary must allow for one word to have more than one meaning within a single lexical category, whereas, in the programming language dictionary such dual meanings are prohibited.

In the early days of work in artificial intelligence, there were high hopes that computers soon could be used to translate between two natural languages. The idea was simply to equip a computer with a large dictionary and a few rules of grammar, then turn it loose. Unfortunately, the first results of such experimentation put a damper on this enthusiasm, because an attempt to translate the English line "the spirit is willing but the flesh is weak" into Russian and back again into English yielded: "the wine is agreeable, but the meat has spoiled."

Today, language translation programs are somewhat more successful because they are beginning to address a crucial element of natural language semantics: It is context dependent, and users of natural language have internalized a set of rules that allow them to determine which dictionary entries are proper, given the context of discourse. In order to understand natural language, you have to understand a lot of things about the world, from the fact that the sky is blue to the proper form for addressing an unmarried member of the opposite sex.

Consider the word *bachelor*. We normally use it to mean *unmarried male*, and every speaker would immediately understand the sentence, "John had to go to a bachelor party." But bachelor also has other meanings. From the context, we decide which definition is proper in the following examples: "John is studying bachelors for his degree in marine biology"; "John is studying bachelors for his degree in medieval history"; "John is studying bachelors for his bachelors in sociology." Quite clearly, the sentence, "John is studying bachelors for his bachelors" is ambiguous. We don't know what John is studying.

Ambiguity is a feature of the semantics of natural languages that is not shared by the semantics of programming languages. In order for a computer to carry out the instructions in its software, there can be no ambiguity. Each programming language instruction can be interpreted in only one way at the level of machine code. It is tempting to think that programming languages achieve this degree of specificity simply by using natural language words (GOTO, REPEAT, STOP, etc.) that could not be interpreted ambiguously.

This line of thought might seem plausible until we think about the logical connector *and*. To see its contextual dependence in natural language, consider the difference between "Mary got married *and* had a baby" and "Mary had a baby *and* got married," as far as the father of the bride is concerned. In programming languages, *and* is defined as a logical function without any appeal to context: P and Q is true if and only if P is true and Q is true. In natural language, the meaning of *and* has a truth functional component, but its meaning also depends on context.

It is a mistake to think that programming languages have simply appropriated the nonambiguous parts of natural language. In the first place, all natural language locutions have the capacity to be ambiguous; in the second place, programming language words are not the same as their natural language counterparts. They may look identical, but programming language words are precisely defined in a way foreign to natural language words.

In addition to straightforward ambiguities, natural languages also have the capacity to enter into paradoxes. Consider the claim, "I am lying." If it's true, then it must be false, since I can't be both telling the truth and lying. If it's false, then it must be true, since if I'm not lying I must be telling the truth. Although we think of language as an instrument for making ourselves understood, the existence of paradoxes demonstrates that natural languages have built into themselves mechanisms not only for obscuring meaning, but also for making meaning absolutely confusing (i.e., paradoxical). No such confusion is allowed to exist in computer languages. The notions of true and false are simply defined as *primitives*, and any kind of self-reference that would lead to paradox is eliminated.

If the semantics of natural language are not a complete match for the semantics of programming languages, then the analogy seems to break down totally when we turn to phonology—the rules specifying how a written language is turned into recognizable utterances. Put simply, no one speaks in BASIC. Natural language may occasionally appropriate a bit of computer jargon and make it a part of the language (e.g., caught in a loop and debugging), but no one could carry on much of a conversation in Pascal.

Yet, although it is true that not much conversing goes on in programming languages, it cannot be blamed on the phonology. It is not that we don't know the rules for vocalizing a programming language's vocabulary, it is simply that the vocabulary was not designed (think about how strange it sounds to say that the English vocabulary was "designed") for conversation between people, and so there is little conversational interest that can be expressed using it. Look at the following list of programming language primitives from various languages: GOSUB, char, CMOVE. We all know how to pronounce these words; we simply apply the rules of our natural language. What we don't know is how to use these words, and others like them, to express the wide range of our thoughts and feelings.

How important is the fact that programming languages are not spoken? Does it severely limit the ways we can think about them? Is it adequate grounds for deciding that programming languages are not really languages? These issues about the *function* of language will be addressed in the next section.

Like all metaphors, the comparison of natural and computer languages has its limits. Syntactically they are very similar, semantically less so, and phonology really doesn't apply since programming languages are exclusively written. It seems that while programming languages are nowhere near as rich as natural languages, it is also true that the analysis of programming languages does not require any additional tools. Whether programming languages are rich enough to be considered as languages may be debatable, but this is not: Our intuitive understanding of natural language can be applied to our study of programming languages.

THE FUNCTION OF LANGUAGE

> The point is, simply, that language serves many functions, pursues many aims, employs many voices. What is most extraordinary of all is that it commands as it refers, describes as it makes poetry, adjudicates as it expresses, creates beauty as it gets things clear, serves all other needs as it maintains contact. It does all these things at once, and does them with a due regard to rules and canons such that a native speaker very early in life is usually able to tell whether they were well done or botched. I would like to suggest that a man of intellectual discipline is one who is master of the various functions of speech, one who has a sense of how to vary them, how to say what he wishes to say—to himself and to others.[12]

Using language is like riding a bicycle. While we're learning, we must pay careful attention or risk falling into the abyss of misunderstanding. Once we've mastered the skill, we no longer need to pay much attention. In fact, trying to pay close attention (e.g., thinking about whether to use an adverb or an adjective or deciding if a clause is a relative clause) may actually hinder our linguistic performance. Competent language users need only think about what they want to communicate, not how to communicate it (structure) or its proper mode of expression (function).

In fact, the functions of language, just like its structure, are something few of us think about. We may remember a few elementary distinctions from grade school (e.g., declarative vs. interrogatory sentences), but generally we just think of language as our primary means of communicating information. The trouble with this level of analysis is that the word "information" is carrying a lot of baggage. We know, for example, that we often communicate information to other humans that we would never even consider communicating to a computer. Therefore, it is necessary to take the analysis one step further: Exactly what kinds of information do natural languages allow us to communicate?

The linguist and philosopher of language Roman Jakobson has classified the functions of natural languages into six categories: referential, connotative, poetic, phatic, metalingual, and emotive.[13] The most obvious use of language is to formulate and convey information about what is the case or is believed to be the case. Generally speaking, this is the cognitive function of language, which Jakobson has split into two subgroups: referential and connotative.

Referential statements are those that represent facts (e.g., the month is January, pi is equal to 3.14). In the parlance of high school English, they are statements in which we use the predicate to affirm some quality of the subject.

Programming languages have an almost exact analog to referential statements in *assignment statements*—statements that are used to assign values (qualities) to variables and constants (subjects). For example, in Pascal we would note the month like this: Month : = January. In BASIC we would assign pi a value like this: pi = 3.14). In Logo, a correct statement for assigning a name would be: MAKE "NAME MIKE.

Connotative statements are used to give instructions (e.g., knead the bread for 30 strokes; if you're taller than 48 inches, you can ride the bumper cars). In programming languages, there is also a need to give instructions, but they are instructions to the computer. Such instructions are given by *control words*—words that direct the flow of instructions through a program. For example, BASIC instructs the computer to repeat a task a given number of times this way: FOR I = 1 TO 30: KNEAD THE BREAD: NEXT I. Logo makes the basic if-then decision this way: IF X > 48 [RIDE] or, conversely, a Logo statement that would accomplish the same end would be: IF X < 48 [STOP].

Although natural and programming languages share these cognitive functions, it is important to note that the universe of discourse for natural languages is much greater. They can make referential and connotative statements over a much wider range of topics.

Poetic language is not just the language of poetry, it is the patterning of language itself for aesthetic purposes. As such, it is less a function of any individual word and more a function of how those words are put together. Although it may be inconceivable to the computerphobe that a program could be an aesthetic object, programmers, from the novice to the expert, often use the vocabulary of aesthetics. A program, just like a poem, may be focused, streamlined, and beautiful, or it may be vague, cluttered, and ugly.

That programmers view their work partly as art was stated eloquently by Alan Kay, one of the guiding forces behind the personal computer revolution:

> Computers are to computing as instruments are to music. Software is the score, whose interpretation amplifies our reach and lifts our spirit. Leonardo da Vinci called music "the shaping of the invisible," and his phrase is even more apt as a description of software.[14]

The fourth of Jakobson's categories, phatic utterances, includes vocalizations like "uh," "mm," and "aah," which are clearly components of spoken, not written, language. On the written page, we would only expect to see them set within quotes to denote that they are something being said. Their function is to keep the oral channel of communication open, to let a hearer know that we are still interested in communicating and are in the process of forming more thoughts. Although programming languages have no spoken component, there are, curiously, two instances of phatic type functions in programming languages.

First, in large time-sharing computer installations (e.g., installations in which one computer is controlled by many terminals), an operator may continually tap a key to keep the attention of the computer on his or her terminal. In this way, operators ensure that the computer is ready to process information from their terminals as soon as they are ready to input it. Second, small computers and calculators that run on batteries often have an auto shut-off circuit (i.e., to save the batteries, they shut themselves off if no keyboard input is received within a preset time). Tapping a key every few minutes will keep the display on the screen.

Natural language is in its metalingual mode when it is talking about itself, when it is being self-referent. In fact, the previous sentence is metalingual since it is using English to talk about one of the functions of English. Metalingual utterances often lead to paradoxes (e.g., A word is autological if it is self-descriptive—"English" is English, "polysyllabic" is polysyllabic—and heterological if it is not self-descriptive—"French" is not French, "monosyllabic" is not monosyllabic. Is "heterological" autological or heterological?). Because self-reference easily leads toward paradox, programming languages do not have a metalingual function. Instead, they all have a facility such as BASIC's REM command or Pascal and Logo's curly brackets (e.g. {this is a Pascal remark}) that allows us to use natural language in order to comment upon the programming language.

Finally, emotive language is used to either express our own feelings (e.g., I feel great!) or to evoke a feeling response from others (e.g., Ouch!). Because computers have no feelings—yet—the emotive function is totally absent from the current generation of programming languages.

Overall, there is no major gulf between the functions of natural languages and the functions of programming languages. The major difference lies in the scope of information that may be represented. Quite clearly, programming languages have a much more restricted use. This is hardly surprising, since the type of information that computers manipulate is only a small subset of the information that a human brain can process. It turns out, however, that programming languages are extremely good conveyors of the types of information that we use natural language to express. In the final section of this chapter, we'll take a closer look at what information means for humans and machines.

FROM LINGUISTICS
TO CYBERNETICS

Evidently nature can no longer be seen as matter and energy alone. Nor can all her secrets be unlocked with the keys of chemistry and physics, brilliantly successful as these two branches of science have been in our century. A third component is needed for any explanation of the world that claims to be complete. To the powerful theories of chemistry and physics must be added a late arrival: a theory of information. Nature must be interpreted as matter, energy, and information.[15]

Considering how important information is to all life on earth, it is surprising at how late a date the study of information joined the history of ideas. The abstract, intangible nature of information in comparison to the concreteness of matter and the demonstrable effects of energy undoubtedly contributed to the long neglect of the topic. The very concept of information remained vague, ambiguous, and unmeasurable until the day, less than 40 years ago, when a publication in a technical journal elevated information theory to the status of a science.

In 1948, a bright young researcher at Bell Laboratories formulated a mathematically precise definition of information that revolutionized scientific thinking in every field, from communication technology to biology, from thermodynamics to electrical engineering, from computer science to psychology. Claude Shannon was the researcher. He was only 32 at the time, and the publication of "A Mathematical Theory of Information" was more than enough to ensure his immortality in the annals of science.[16] But Shannon was no stranger to epochal discoveries: A decade before, as a 22-year-old graduate student, he made one of the key discoveries that made electronic computation possible.

We will return to the subject of Shannon's earlier discovery, which revealed the connection between Boolean algebra and the behavior of electrical switching circuits, when we examine how information is coded in patterns of electronic switches to form the basic data structures of computing machines. For now, our concern is with Shannon's discovery of how information can be measured, encoded, and predicted by means of mathematical equations.

Shannon's publication of the fundamental theorems of information theory provided a rigorous, precise, and powerful tool for the designers of automatic information-processing systems. On a less visible but no less significant level, the appearance of information theory signaled a shift in the way scientists and the general population think about the world—what science historian Thomas Kuhn would call a *paradigm shift*. According to Kuhn, these shifts in attitudes, perceptions, and beliefs always accompany turns in the direction of scientific thinking and often trigger waves of discoveries in totally unrelated fields.[17]

Three hundred years before Shannon, Isaac Newton demonstrated how the motions of the stars and the fall of an apple can both be measured, predicted, and controlled by the same set of equations. Newtonian mechanics revolutionized physics and triggered similar radical changes in other sciences. The new picture of the universe that emerged from Newton's discoveries initiated a period of scientific progress that led directly to the Industrial Revolution. Newton's scientific revolution depended upon, but went far beyond, the equations themselves because Newton's laws of gravitation and motion empowered the idea, new at the time, that the universe is a huge but predictable machine.

In the Newtonian universe-as-machine-in-motion, the dominant force was *energy*, and all the sciences that followed Newton did remarkable jobs of describing the world as an energy machine. Technologists achieved new heights of ingenuity by inventing machines to take advantage of the energy-machine-like aspect of the world. No paradigm remains fertile forever, however: After the scientific and technological breakthroughs of the post-World War II era, from the invention of the computer to the discovery of the DNA code, the energy machine metaphor could no longer accommodate the vastly expanded scope of scientific knowledge. Another dimension of description was needed in an age of radar, computers, genetic codes, and communication networks.

The shift from the dominant Newtonian model of an energy-based mechanical universe to a cosmos in which information is a fundamental force turned out to be as important to physicists, molecular biologists, and computer scientists as it did to communications engineers. The idea has such wide-ranging effects because the mysteries of energy, the secrets of life, and the nature of communication are all tied into the notion of how complex codes are constructed from simple elements. If you look at the universe as a code (what Norbert Wiener, the co-inventor of the science of cybernetics, once called "a myriad of to-whom-it-may-concern messages") rather than as a machine, you'll see things you didn't see before you changed your paradigm.

The importance of information as a powerful unifying concept was emphasized by others a short time before Shannon showed exactly how it was done. In fact, for a few years before Shannon came along, MIT's legendary prodigy Norbert Wiener and other cyberneticians had been making a concerted effort to solve the same problem that Shannon ultimately solved.[18]

Wiener saw information as a way to link the behavior of sophisticated automata such as computers and radar-aiming devices with the behavior of biological control systems and communication and control structures in social systems. The cyberneticians were able to create an information-processing model that was able to explain something about the way biological systems work and something about the way information-processing machines work. Yet they failed to come up with a specific way of measuring information, and they failed to capture the relationship of information to other physical entities in the form of mathematical equations.

During World War II, Wiener was involved in several war-related research projects that led him to suspect the importance of information as a fundamental concept. One of his problems involved thinking of ways to eliminate noise in radar systems. The engineers wanted their colleagues in pure mathematics to find out if there was any mathematical way to distinguish the real signal of an approaching airplane from all the false signals that showed up as "blips" on radar operators' screens.

Wiener and his colleagues realized that an important part of the radar noise problem had to do with the ability to distinguish one specific message from all possible messages. This might sound esoteric and tangential if you are an electronic engineer simply trying to calibrate your equipment, but it leads directly to the crucial connection between probability and information. It was Shannon who first discovered this connection when he tried to find out if there was a reliable way of getting messages across a noisy channel.

Shannon sought a mathematical principle that would make it possible to encode messages in such a way that they would resist misinterpretation, even when they are sent through a medium in which a great many false messages are interspersed—what communication engineers call a noisy channel. Shannon discovered that it is indeed possible to communicate any message reliably, no matter how noisy the channel, provided that the message is properly encoded. This is a stunning discovery in the field of communication, because it shifts the burden of clear communications from the hardware, which will always be partially beyond human control, to the *software*, which is, in theory, controllable. The discovery also had profound significance outside the specialized domain of communication engineering because the equations Shannon used to define the basic unit of information are the same equations physicists use to describe the transfer of energy in the universe.[19]

Shannon was investigating something deeper than ways to clean up static from telephone lines, however; he was looking at the fundamental nature of messages and the way information can be distinguished from noninformation, which had everything to do with certainty and uncertainty in communication. A noisy channel can obscure the information in a message, rendering it meaningless; but some messages manage to get through clearly, even against a noisy background. Shannon wanted to isolate the factor that maintains order, and this led him to contemplate the idea of a fundamental unit of information. He realized that it all depends on how many possible messages there are. If the message is a letter of the alphabet, you have 26 possible messages. If the message is "one if by land, two if by sea," you have two possible messages. And two possible messages is as simple as communication gets, because if there is only one possible message, you would have zero uncertainty from the beginning and no need to guess.

In his paper on information theory, Shannon compared communication to a game of 20 questions (which only allows yes or no answers). Suppose you are trying to guess which letter of the alphabet a friend has in mind. You could ask whether the letter is in the first half of the alphabet. No matter whether the answer is yes or no, you will have narrowed the number of possible choices by one-half. If the answer is yes, then you would know that the target letter was between A and M. If it is no, the target letter is between N and Z. If you divide your choices in half once again and then again, you could finally arrive at a yes answer that would identify the letter.

Shannon pointed out that any letter in the English alphabet can be specified in no more than five guesses. If you were to guess a letter at random, your uncertainty would be high, since the target letter could be one of any 26 alternatives.

Shannon's guessing game is one way of getting at the nature of the *bit*—the fundamental measure of information. Each yes or no reduces the uncertainty of the person guessing by one-half, which means that each answer represents one bit. Uncertainty about the identity of the mystery letter can be reduced to zero with five bits of information. The coherence of messages transmitted across noisy channels, Shannon realized, had to do with how much uncertainty was reduced with each message unit. The greater the possible uncertainty, the more information a message must convey to resolve it. If I tell you who won a horse race, I give you more information than if I had told you who won a boxing match.

One advantage of using simple signals is that the code can be made very resistant to misinterpretation. Paul Revere might have made a severe mistake if he had ordered his compatriot to shout "the British are coming by land" or "the British are coming by sea," instead of displaying one lamp or two in the tower of the Old North Church. It's much easier to detect the difference between one light and two lights accurately than it is to differentiate the words "land" and "sea."

Yes-no decisions can be perfectly expressed by the on-off switches in nineteenth-century telegraphs and twenty-first century computers. Through a simple code, Morse was able to transmit any natural language message. By using programming languages, computer scientists are able to use computers to manipulate almost any information that can be expressed in a natural language. In fact, it has been suggested that the computer's universe is best described in terms of an extended game of 20 questions. We'll return to this topic when we focus more closely on the binary system.

The key to understanding the amazing flexibility of computers as information processors is realizing that all information is simply represented by a series of on-off switches (i.e., as a string of ones and zeros). Whether information is a number, an airline ticket reservation, a page of text, a drill press instruction, or even part of the computer's own program, it is represented in exactly the same way. The dual role of programming languages allows us, the users, as well as the computer to interpret these binary strings in the proper manner.

Programming languages are the bridge between humans and computers and the remainder of this book explains how these bridges came to be built, the materials of which they are made, the principles by which they are constructed, and how they work as thought tools that both enhance our ability to think and enable us to communicate our thoughts to the computer.

2

Formal Language
and Formal Thought

The design of the following treatise is to investigate the fundamental laws of those operations of the mind by which reasoning is performed; to give expression to them in the symbolical language of a Calculus, and upon this foundation to establish the science of Logic and construct its method . . . and, finally, to collect from the various elements of truth brought to view in the course of these inquiries some probable intimations concerning the nature and constitution of the human mind.[1]

THE QUEST FOR A CALCULUS
OF THOUGHT

Ideas evolve in the strangest ways. Some of the greatest inventions were never planned; they simply happened. Other world-shaping discoveries started out as attempts to solve one kind of problem and ended up, hundreds of years after the quest began, to answer totally different questions. Consider the curious lineage of a notion that originated with Aristotle and ended up as the basis of all software—the idea that it is possible to create or discover a calculus of thought, a symbolic equivalent of human reasoning.

For at least 20 centuries, various lunatics, mystics, and mathematical mavericks have attempted to construct a formalized method of thought that could guarantee the proper functioning of human reasoning. Now that we know how the search ended—not with the discovery of an infallible system for thinking, but with the basis of computation—it is easier to see this once-obscure crusade as a natural extension of the evolution of thought tools.

It is impossible to specify who invented spoken language, and "the Phoenicians" is the closest anybody can come to naming the inventors of alphabetic writing. But the name of at least one critically important innovator in the history of human thought is well known: Aristotle developed the most important formal tool for expanding the power of thinking since the invention of writing.

Ancient historical records reveal that many cultures and individuals used the principles of logical reasoning; for example, the Golenischev papyrus from approximately 2000 B.C. demonstrates the sophisticated reasoning of Egyptian mathematicians. But it was not until the time of Aristotle (384–322 B.C.) that those principles became the object of study. It is one thing to think in a new way; it is quite another to know enough about what you are doing to teach it to somebody else.

In a remarkable series of works collectively known as *The Organon*, Aristotle set forth an agenda for the study of logic that would last throughout the Renaissance. The essence of this work, and the reason that Aristotle was the first true *logician* rather than a mathematician or rhetorician, is Aristotle's focus on the primacy of form over meaning.

The science of logic is concerned with the "goodness" of the connections between propositions rather than the "goodness" of the propositions themselves. And these connections, what we today call patterns of inference, are a function of the form of the argument instead of the meaning of the individual propositions. The abstraction of speech made it possible to argue about trees, even when there were no trees around at which to point. The abstraction of writing made it possible to argue about trees with people who weren't around to hear you talking. And the abstraction of logic made it possible to talk about the soundness or fallibility of your arguments about trees without paying any attention to trees or symbols for trees.

Aristotle's work concerned a form of argument known as the *syllogism*—an argument with two subject-predicate *premises* that share a common term. He was able to demonstrate that the validity of syllogisms could be determined independently of their content simply by studying their form. This can be demonstrated by inspecting the two examples that follow:

| ALL COMPUTERS ARE MACHINES | ALL COMPUTERS ARE THINKERS |
ALL MACHINES ARE INANIMATE	ALL THINKERS ARE ANIMATE
ALL COMPUTERS ARE INANIMATE	ALL COMPUTERS ARE ANIMATE

Clearly, both arguments are valid: *If* the premises are true, *then* the conclusion must be true. In fact, only the conclusion on the left is true. This is because the syllogism on the left consists of only true premises, whereas the one on the right has at least one false premise (which one you think is false should be a good clue to your beliefs about artificial intelligence). These word equations might seem simplistic, but complex chains of argument can be constructed from these elementary links. For 2000 years, the study of logic was the study of such syllogistic reasoning.

Although Aristotle is best known for the syllogism, he also made a second, immensely important contribution to the study of logic. By applying formal language to the study of logic, the first logician also became the first symbolic logician. Aristotle realized that all the propositions that could be used in a syllogism could be represented by one of four forms:

ALL S IS P	ALL MEN ARE MORTAL
NO S IS P	NO MEN ARE MORTAL
SOME S IS P	SOME MEN ARE MORTAL
SOME IS NOT-P	SOME MEN ARE NOT MORTAL

The representation of each form by a *schematic*—the distillation of a proposition into its logically important parts (e.g., key words such as *all*, *some*, and *not*) was the first step toward developing a *formal language*—an artificially created symbol system that precisely defines all its constituent elements. Aristotle went a step further on the pyramid of abstractions by labeling the four categorical propositions A, E, I, and O, and representing their logical relationships by means of his famed diagram of the square of opposition (see Figure 2.1).

In a flash of genius and a simple diagram, Aristotle not only clarified the role of *formal thought*—to represent relationships between propositions and discover all the conclusions implied by prem-

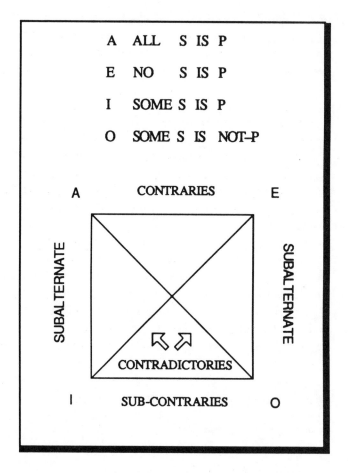

Figure 2.1 Diagram of the Square of Opposition

ises—he also provided the beginnings of a system, a formal language, for carrying out that task.

With the creation of the syllogism and the elaboration of a systematic science of logic, Aristotle demonstrated that at least one aspect of human reasoning was susceptible to formal analysis and could form the basis of a new system of abstractions. The greatest thinkers for centuries thereafter would use Aristotle's invention to expand the domain of philosophical knowledge. It would take almost 2000 years before they reached the limits of what could be accomplished with syllogistic logic.[2]

About a millennium after Aristotle, a Moslem mathematician in ninth-century Baghdad wrote the first textbook on algebra, a formal system based on a different but related kind of abstraction. The system would bear the name of that textbook, *Kitar al-jabr w'al-mgabala*, which means restoration and reduction, long after its origins were forgotten in Europe. Both algebra and logic amplified the thinking power of mathematicians and philosophers, but these two formal systems weren't the end of the quest for a general calculus of thought. They were only the beginning.

Algebra was a mysterious invention in the eyes of European thinkers. For hundreds of years it was used by the few specialists who dabbled or labored in the field of mathematics. But nobody knew where the system, or its strange name, had originated. Finally, in the nineteenth century, it was discovered that the system had been created 1000 years earlier by the author of the Arabic text.[3]

Algebra was an ingenious way of operating upon both mathematical and real-world problems by assigning values to variables in equations that then could be solved by taking a number of well-defined steps according to a set of rules. One of algebra's most powerful tools, and one that is also a fundamental part of all programming languages, is an operation in which a token symbolizes the value of an unknown quantity in an equation. For example, by using rules of restoration and reduction, such as factoring out equations by multiplying both sides of the equation by the same quantity, the equation can be manipulated to reveal the value of the unknown variable. In the high-school version of algebra, X is the name most often associated with this kind of variable, and the process of discovering the value of X is called solving for the unknown.

The name of the author of that Arabic text was *al-Khowarazmi*, which was the origin for the word *algorithm*. It is another mathematical term that is intimately related to computer languages and whose origins also had been forgotten in the West for over 1000 years. Centuries of failed attempts to formalize thought and create a kind of metalogic were to pass before algebra and algorithms were to reenter the quest for a calculus of thought.

Centuries of work by Greek Stoics and Catholic Scholastics expanded and explored but failed to change Aristotelian logic. Then, one day in the year 1274, the long stagnant domain of logic erupted in a bizarre manifestation when a Spanish mystic experienced a vision atop a mountain on the island of Majorca. The Spanish mystic proposed that syllogistic logic could be performed by a machine. He was absolutely convinced that it was possible to automate Aristotle's ancient system because he had seen a logic machine with his own eyes that day on Mt. Randa and had apprehended a method of using it, a "Great Art" whereby the mechanical manipulation of symbols could demonstrate the existence of God to mathematically minded heathen.

The mystic's name was Ramon Lull (a k a Raymond Lully), and his *Ars Magna* was an early, albeit ineffective, example of a logic machine. Lull traveled throughout North Africa, attempting to use his system to convert the Moslem intelligentsia to Christianity. Fortunately for future scholars, Lull wrote extensively about his logic system before he was martyred for his evangelical efforts. By modern standards, Lull's system isn't very interesting because you can't build a computer based on Lullian logic. But his idea captured the imaginations of other people through the centuries, one of whom eventually succeeded in creating a mechanical kind of logic.

Lull might have been one of the first, but he was surely not the last, to be attracted to the concept of a mechanized calculus of thought. Metaphysicians have long envied the physicists, with their equations and measuring devices. Philosophers and theologians had often yearned for some rigorous method—even a machine—that could infallibly demonstrate which of their beliefs were true.

Among the features of Lull's system was a code that used letters to symbolize words and phrases of syllogisms in order to reduce entire arguments to arithmetic-like equations. A kind of theological shorthand was created with these elementary symbols, and then the symbols were combined with each other according to a system of rules. The mechanical device that demonstrated Lull's rule system consisted of triangles, squares, and other geometric figures inscribed with coded symbols, made of pasteboard or wood, that rotated in relation to one another to produce new permutations of logical argument with each spin of the wheel (see Figure 2.2). Lull had produced a kind of super square of opposition.[4]

Lull's system was kept alive by a small cult that lasted centuries, although it eventually became fashionable to debunk Lullism, as his arcane system came to be called. But old ideas sometimes come back into fashion, and this one had already proved itself to be tenacious. In the middle of the seventeenth century, when Newton's equations of motion and gravitation put the fundamental laws of the

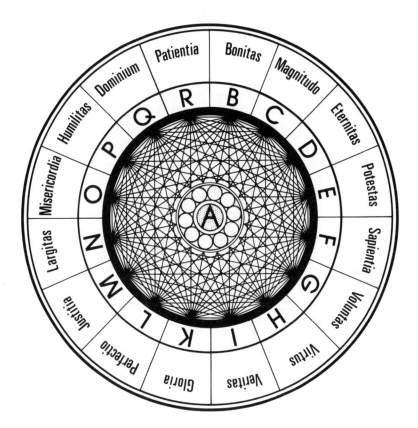

Figure 2.2 Lull's Machine

universe within reach of human thought, the idea of creating a theoretical foundation for a reasoning machine experienced a resurgence
of interest. And prominent metaphysicians once again began to long
for means of establishing their abstruse discipline in the rigorous
methods of mathematics and concrete syllogisms of logic.

By the seventeenth century, Lullists were fringe players on the
stage of Western civilization, but the next historical figure who is
known to have experimented with a calculus of thought was none
other than Gottfried Wilhelm von Leibniz, a scientist, philosopher,
and mathematician of staggering achievement and an enthusiast for
some of the ideas of Ramon Lull. Leibniz was the first modern
thinker to recognize that if logic could only be expressed algebrai-
cally, in terms of simple tokens and rules for combining tokens into

meaningful statements, many problems outside the realm of mathematics might become, in theory, as soluble as mathematics problems.

At the age of 19, Leibniz wrote his *Dissertio de arte combinatoria*, in which he first stated his firm belief in the possibility of developing a method that could not only perform logical operations in a mechanical manner, but which, if properly applied, could revolutionize the way people think and communicate. The great twentieth-century mathematician Bertrand Russell noted that Leibniz hoped to find a way of generalizing the techniques of mathematics to every domain of knowledge:

> Nevertheless he cherished through his life the hope of discovering a kind of generalized mathematics, which he called *Characteristica Universalis*, by means of which thinking could be replaced by calculation. "If we had it," he says, "we should be able to reason in metaphysics and morals in much the same way as in geometry and analysis. If controversies were to arise there would be no more need of disputation between two philosophers than between two accountants. For it would suffice to take their pencils in their hands, to sit down to their slates, and to say to each other (with a friend as witness if they liked): Let us calculate."[5]

Of course, not even computers have (yet) been able to live up to Leibniz's hopes of inanimate "philosophers' helpers." But as the artificial intelligence researchers of the past three decades will attest, it is not easy to leap from a method of mechanizing logic to a machine that is capable of thinking. The seductive idea that led from Aristotle to al-Khowarazmi to Lull to Leibniz and beyond, and that is still ardently pursued by artificial intelligence researchers, is the conviction that there exists some linkage, as yet unexplained, between the symbol-manipulating nature of thought, the symbol-manipulating nature of language, and the symbol-manipulating nature of mathematics.

In 1832, almost 600 years after Lull's mountaintop inspiration and 1000 years after al-Khowarazmi, a poor, self-taught, 17-year-old logician in England was also struck by a vision of a new kind of truth that he alone could bring to the world. The Englishman, whose name was George Boole, was walking across a moor when an entire system of knowledge came upon him in an instant. It was a vision that changed Boole's life, and led to drastic changes in the course of civilization.

Unlike all the theories and prophecies that preceded his, Boole's scheme actually succeeded in creating the long-sought algebra of logic. The primary difference between the Spanish mystic's vision and the revelation of the English logician is that we can, in fact, build a computer based on Boolean logic. Boole articulated a formal system in which logical propositions could be represented and manipulated like algebraic symbols, yielding all the possible conclusions based on those propositions. Boole's system didn't put an end to metaphysical conflict by providing a universal, ultimately certain tool for divining truth, as Lull and Leibniz had hoped, but Boolean logic did become an indispensable tool for computer builders when another group of thinkers on a different kind of intellectual quest stumbled upon the foundations of computation.

George Boole believed that his vision of symbolic logic was not just a mathematical landmark, but was an insight into the nature of the human mind. He was convinced that all the processes of human reasoning could be reduced to an algebra or other formal system, modeled after two valued (true/false, 1/0) logics.

Although Boole didn't find what he believed he had found (the ultimate key to the nature of thought), it has since become apparent that what Boole did find was most useful. Whereas machines that think for themselves might be difficult if not impossible to create, it turned out to be possible to build machines, using Boolean logic, that could amplify the power of human thinking by performing certain tedious operations such as calculations (but not limited to operations on numbers) at high speeds.

BOOLEAN ALGEBRA AND THE MECHANIZATION OF LOGIC

Boole developed his algebra not in the elementary way found in computer texts but from a deep and lengthy study of thought processes and natural language. "There exist, indeed," he wrote, "certain general principles founded in the very nature of language, by which the use of symbols, which are but the elements of scientific language, is determined."[6]

Boole didn't exactly put the psychologists out of business when he published *An Investigation of the Laws of Thought on which are*

Founded the Mathematical Theories of Logic and Probabilities in 1854, but he did furnish the conceptual basis for a language humans could use to communicate with machines, and he set the stage for the invention of the ultimate logic machines a century later.[7] Boole may not have found the key to the mysteries of thought, but he did find a link between the rules of pure mathematics and the way humans reason.

Boole's link between mind and mathematics will lead us to the place where computer languages meet computer components—the bottom level in the hierarchy of abstractions that constitutes a human-computer communication system. Before we can do that, however, we have to understand something about the way Boole connected Aristotle's system of abstractions with that of al-Khowarazmi.

For millennia, the syllogisms of logic had been the most rigorous forms in which thought-like processes could be encoded. Indeed, "logical" had become a synonym for any kind of reasoning that seemed to make sense. Algebra, Boole demonstrated, furnished rules of operation by which syllogisms and other inference patterns could be manipulated in new ways; he showed that algebra, with a slight modification, could be used as a grammar to govern the production of messages via the syllogistic alphabet. That meant that the formal rules of logic could be augmented to expand their scope vastly.

The secret of connecting logic and algebra, Boole believed, lay in restricting the range of the symbols to two and only two values. With two values, only one token is necessary: Either the token is there, which represents one value, or the token is absent, which represents the other value by default. You can't get any simpler than that. Boole saw a way of reducing logic to a kind of mathematics restricted to two quantities, which he designated 0 and 1, and which stood for "nothing" and "the Universe," or "everything." By manipulating variables according to algebraic rules, Boole was able to show how logical syllogisms could be solved by a kind of calculation.

Algebra, which was 1000 years old by the time Boole got his hands on it, had been significantly enhanced by some of Boole's intellectual contemporaries. Boole was one of a school of British logicians who saw that the linguistic properties of algebra as a formal system were equally as or more important than its numerical applications. Just as Aristotle created the abstraction of logic by focusing attention on the form of syllogisms rather than the meaning of their propositions, the British algebraists abstracted algebra by looking closely at its rules of operation.

Boole and other British logicians of his time made a significant step in the history of mathematics by investigating the operations and symbols of algebra apart from their numerical values. Heretofore, algebra had been used exclusively to provide numerical values for the unknowns in equations. But the *system* of algebra, strictly speaking, dealt in symbolic tokens of which numbers are only one possible kind. Boole and the other British algebraists perceived that the symbols of operation ($+$, $-$, etc.) could be separated from those that represent quantity and be treated as objects of calculation.

This separation might seem to be a rather esoteric point, but it is the core abstraction of symbolic logic. For centuries, mathematicians and logicians insisted that the tokens of algebra "represented numbers." Boole abstracted the rules of algebra, whereby he showed that they formed a consistent system themselves that didn't have to apply to numbers at all, and applied them to a simplified, two-value system of tokens instead of a decimal number system.

By applying the rules of operation he abstracted from algebra to the manipulation of logical syllogisms, Boole accomplished three things: First, he was able to use symbols to represent thoughts heretofore represented only by natural language; second, he was able to systematize the expression and evaluation of compound thoughts through the use of the device he called "truth tables"; third, he was able to use algebraic rules of symbol manipulation to test the truth of logical inferences.

Just as algebra deals with variable symbols that have no fixed meaning, such as x, y, and z, and are understood to represent numbers, Boolean algebra deals with variable (he called them "elective") symbols, such as a, b, and c that are understood to represent any meaning one decides to attribute to them. They can stand for classes or sets of objects, such as the class of all inanimate things or the set of all machines.

These elective symbols are combined with one another according to only three operations, designated $+$ (union), $\times$ (intersection), and $-$ (negation). Compound symbols that result from applying these operations to elective symbols are also considered valid symbols: $a + b$ and $a - b$ are understood to be valid symbols just like a and b. Just as in algebra, there is an identity operation, designated by the $=$ symbol. The rules governing the way these operations combine symbols are also simple, familiar-looking equations, such as $a + b = b + a$, and $a \times b = b \times a$, and $a \times (b + c) = a \times b + a \times c$.

Boole's definition of the operation × makes it functionally identical to the operation of *intersection* between two sets. If a = the set of all featherless animals and b = the set of all bipeds, then $a \times b$ = the set of all featherless bipeds. If c = the set of all computer programmers, then $a \times b \times c$ = the set of all featherless biped computer programmers. Boole called these successive restrictions of intersecting sets "acts of election," and stated that anything could be specified (reduced to a class consisting of only one object) by successive acts of election.

Boole's operation designated + specifies the act of *union*, that is, the operation of joining together two disparate sets into an inclusive set. If a = the set of all adult humans and b = the set of all human children, then $a + b$ = the set of all humans of any age. The *negation* operation, designated by − , indicates a reversal of the union process, a separation of elements rather than an aggregation. If $a + b = c$ in the above example, then $c - a$ = the set of all humans with the exception of the set of all children, which would mean that $c - a = b$. This inverse operation, when applied to the value 1 (which stands for everything) yields the useful operation for "everything except . . . ." For example, $1 - a$ in the above example would represent the set of everything except the set of adult humans.

As one example of how algebraic operations could apply to logical elements, Boole used an example in which a = all horned things and b = all sheep and showed that the statement $1 - a$ would mean all things that are not horned and $(1 - a) \times (1 - b)$ would mean all things that are neither horned nor sheep. By this manner, Boole showed how such elementary symbols could be used to reduce logical propositions to the form of equations that could be solved according to ordinary algebraic rules. Boole then demonstrated the generality of his system by showing how it could be used to derive any true conclusion logically contained in any given set of propositions.

Having established the absolute rigor and reliability of his system, Boole, apparently not immune from the same fervor that gripped Lull and Leibniz, turned his system to the solution of ancient logical–metaphysical conundrums. One historian wrote:

> Boole applied algebraic symbols to typical logical arguments such as "Absolute evil is either moral evil, or it is, if not moral evil, a consequence of moral evil." He also analyzed more positive theological proofs, such as "Unchangeable and independent Being must be

self-existent." The symbolic method was able to pull out many more deductions than were possible in the verbal reasoning.[8]

Boole's analysis of moral and theological arguments had an infinitesimal impact, if any, on the history of Western civilization. But the system he created from such simple elements as 0 and 1 made all the difference in the world. Because the two values of Boolean algebra can also symbolize true and false, Boole's algebraic notation is able to capture one of the essential components of both logic and computer languages—the if-then construction.

In syllogistic logic, we are concerned about the consequences of assuming the truth of certain premises; for example, if A is true and if B is also true, then C is true. The if-then construction is a perfect mathematical translation of syllogistic logic and a good way to code logical instructions for machines because the consequences of every situation are unambiguously specified: Boolean algebra makes it possible to encode all the possible inferences in terms of tables—the kind that even a machine could decode. If we consider the number of inference situations that are possible with two or three propositions, it is easy to create simple listings such as these:

If A is false then B is true.
If A is true then B is false.

or:

If A is true and B is true, then C is true.
If A is true and B is false, then C is false.
If A is false and B is true, then C is false.
If A is false and B is false, then C is false.

or:

If A is true and B is true, then C is true.
If A is true and B is false, then C is true.
If A is false and B is true, then C is true.
If A is false and B is false, then C is false.

We also could write sets of statements that would be exactly equivalent to the phrases listed above in a kind of Boolean shorthand known as *truth tables*, where 0 represents false and 1 represents true. Truth tables for the above examples are as follows:

A	B
0	1
1	0

A	B	C
1	1	1
1	0	0
0	1	0
0	0	0

A	B	C
1	1	1
1	0	1
0	1	1
0	0	0

You read these truth tables just as you read a page, scanning across the rows from left to right. The entry in the farthest right-hand column of each row is the result, that is, the value of the output derived by performing the specified operation on the input(s). Note that in the first truth table the value of each entry is always the opposite of the value of the result: If A, then not B; if B, then not A. You could, in a properly Boolean abstract manner, condense the entire table to a single symbol for the concept *not*, because the value of each term is *not* the value of the other.

In a similar manner, the second table shows that C is true if and only if both A and B are true; in all cases where either A or B or both are false, then C is false. You could condense the second table to a single symbol for the concept *and*. Applying the same rule to the third table, in which C is true in all cases in which either A or B or both are true, you could condense it to the concept *or*.

As simple as a truth table might seem, it is a supremely useful tool for software architects because they bridge the all-important gap between formal systems such as logic and physical machinery such as digital computers. In Chapter 3, we will see how electronic equivalents of truth tables constitute the basic logical elements of all digital computers and how the memory elements of digital computers, the elementary operations of processors, and the entire vocabulary of every computer language can be built up in successive layers of abstractions, starting with nothing but a set of switches that represent the logical functions *and* and *not*.

But computation isn't simply a matter of connecting the right nots with the proper ands. So far we have some data structures and some rules, but we have no instructions on how to proceed. We don't know how to encode instructions so that a mechanical equivalent of a collection of nots and ands can carry out the instructions. We aren't sure how a machine can be said to carry out instructions. We don't even have a clear definition of instructions. In fact, the clear definition of instructions is the only element we need to build a computing system from Boolean logic elements.

The modern notion of algorithm, together with mechanical or electrical instantiations of Boolean logic operations, were the two elements needed to create the first computer. Just as the history of the calculus of thought started out with syllogisms and ended up with truth tables, the history of logic machines also started out in the age of Greek science, originating with formal systems such as geometry and mathematics and culminating in 1937 with the creation of a purely theoretical device known as a Turing machine. The Turing machine was created because a group of mathematicians desperately needed a precise definition of what "instructions" really meant.

Within a decade of Turing's discovery, these two age-old quests (one emanating from the psychology of everyday human reasoning, the other from the search for a methodology of mathematical reasoning) culminated in the invention of digital computing devices.

THE QUEST FOR A
LOGIC MACHINE

> Thus, be it understood, to demonstrate a theorem, it is neither necessary nor even advantageous to know what it means. The geometer might be replaced by the "logic piano" imagined by Stanley Jevons; or, if you choose, a machine might be imagined where the assumptions were put in at one end, while the theorems came out at the other, like the legendary Chicago machine where the pigs go in alive and come out transformed into hams and sausages. No more than these machines need the mathematician know what he does.[9]

For the Greeks, the very idea of a logic machine would have been inconceivable. Not only did machines have to be made of material substance, they could only operate on material goods. Yet the methodology of Greek mathematics, as assembled and rigorously expressed by Euclid in his *Elements* (circa 300 B.C.), is the driving force behind our modern-day logic machines—computers and the programs that instruct them. If you want to understand the origins of modern computer languages, you have to go back at least 2000 years in Western history, or at least recall part of your own high-school education.

In the field of science in which today's "great" discovery often quickly becomes tomorrow's obsolete dogma, Euclid's exposition of a *formal system*—a method of proof that begins with a few propositions (axioms) believed to be "obviously" true and a few "self-evident" rules for manipulating the axioms, and attempts to demonstrate the truth of new propositions (theorems) by deriving them from the axioms—has withstood the test of time.[10]

Although the quest for a calculus of thought and the quest for a logic machine often used similar concepts (e.g., formal language as a tool for guiding formal thought), they differed markedly in their ultimate goal. The former had a strong psychological emphasis—Boole, for example, actually was searching for the rules the mind used in reasoning—whereas those searching for a logic machine were solely after a method of producing new knowledge. These latter logicians did not pretend that the mind functioned as a formal system, only that by using formal systems (much as an artisan employs a lathe) the mind was able to generate new truths about the world.

It was only when the two parallel tracks merged after more than 2000 years of independent evolution that it became possible to understand the key concepts underlying computer operation: proof, formal language, algorithm, and ultimately, the theory of computation. The invention of the general-purpose machine came about when methods derived from the search for a calculus of thought were applied to the solution of vexing paradoxes found in the foundations of formal systems.

More than two millennia of thinkers did not pursue this abstract puzzle-solving effort simply because of the technical challenge. It was nothing less than the noble idea of *truth*—methods for defining it, establishing it, discovering it, deriving it, generating it, and especially *proving* it—that started the idea in motion and kept it progressing toward its surprising conclusion for over 23 centuries.

It was the notion of proof that chiefly concerned Euclid: How could anyone ever be certain of the truth of a proposition? It was well known that our senses could play tricks on us, and the Sophists with their sleight-of-hand rhetoric had given the Greeks a reason to doubt the propositions of rhetoric. Even natural language was suspect because of antinomies such as the simple liar's paradox: the statement, "I am lying." In an attempt to avoid such pitfalls, Euclid and the other Greek mathematicians developed the idea of a formal system. Ironically, the liar's paradox ended up playing a central role in the end of the search for certainty in formal systems, more than 2000 years later.

In answer to the question, How could anyone ever be certain of the truth of a proposition?, Euclid had a simple answer: First, begin your reasoning only with propositions (axioms) that you know to be true, and, second, assert new propositions by using only rules of inference that you know to be truth preserving. By following these two rules, you can be certain that the end results of your reasoning will be true. Such reasoning is called a proof because it consists of a sequence of propositions such that each one is either an axiom or derived from an axiom. Exactly how this works can be seen in a simple, elegant proof directly from Euclid:

Proposition 19

To Prove: In any triangle, the greater angle is subtended by the greater side.

ABC is a triangle with angle ABC greater than angle BCA (see Figure 2.3). I will demonstrate that side AC must be greater than side AB:

1. If AC is not greater than AB it must be less or equal [application of the basic law of quantity].
2. AC cannot be equal to AB for if it were, angle ABC would also have to equal angle ACB [by Proposition 5, in an isosceles triangle the angles at the base are equal] and by stipulation they are not equal.
3. AC cannot be less than AB for if it were, angle ABC would have to be less than angle ACB [by Proposition 18, in any triangle, the greater side subtends the greater angle] and by stipulation ABC is greater than ACB.
4. Therefore, since AB ≠ AC and since AC is not less than AB, AC must be greater than AB. Q.E.D.

The strength and beauty of formal systems lie in their ability to rule out the extraneous and to focus on their own, precisely defined universe. In Euclid's case, the world was geometry, and beginning with 23 definitions (e.g., An acute angle is an angle less than a right angle), five postulates (e.g., All right angles are equal to each other), and five common notions (e.g., The whole is greater than the part) he was able to prove more than 400 theorems, many of them quite surprising and nonintuitive (e.g., the Pythagorean theorem, which states

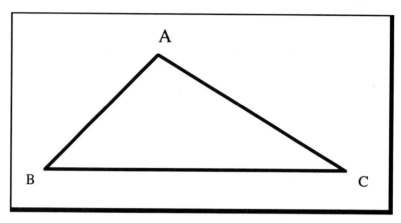

Figure 2.3 Triangle with Vertices Labeled A, B, C

that in a triangle, the square of the hypotenuse is equal to the sum of the squares of the other two sides).

Euclid's *Elements* were such an impressive demonstration of the power of formal systems that the methodology became the procedure to follow for all subsequent work in mathematics. A little less than 2000 years later, Isaac Newton was able to extend the method of the formal system into the realm of natural science. In his extraordinary three-book masterpiece, *Philosophiae Naturalis Principia Mathematica*, Newton began with three simple axioms, or laws of motion:

1. Every body continues in its state of rest, or of uniform motion in a right line, unless it is compelled to change that state by forces impressed upon it.
2. The change of motion is proportional to the motive force impressed; and is made in the direction of the right line in which that force is impressed.
3. To every action there is always opposed an equal reaction: or, the mutual actions of two bodies upon each other are always equal, and directed to contrary parts.[11]

By applying the methods of Euclid's formal system to the questions formerly reserved for natural philosophy, Newton was able to derive the very rules by which our universe is governed.

In a stroke of genius, Newton showed how a formal system like Euclid's was actually capable of explaining our physical universe. In the words of Jacob Bronowski:

As a system of the world, of course, it was sensational from the moment it was published. It is a marvelous description of the world subsumed under a single set of laws. But much more, it is also a landmark in scientific method. We think of the presentation of science as a series of propositions, one after the other, as deriving from the mathematics of Euclid. And so it does. But it is not until Newton turned this into a physical system, by changing mathematics from a static to a dynamic account, that modern scientific method really begins to be rigorous.[12]

Beginning with the work of Newton, the formal system became much more than simply a proof procedure for mathematicians. It had become one of the major means humans use to describe and explain our universe. With Newton showing the way, eighteenth-century thinkers applied formal systems to prove theorems in every discipline from philosophy to physiology. To those thinkers, it must have appeared as if the Age of Reason had indeed provided them with a logic machine. All someone had to do to generate new truths was stipulate a few plausible axioms and follow a rigorous method of proof. The golden age of knowledge seemed to be at hand.

Unfortunately, the other hand held a bombshell that would explode 150 years after Newton's classic work. In 1840 an obscure Russian mathematician, Nicholas Lobachevski, published his *Geometrical Researches on the Theory of Parallels*. This work began with the startling claim:

> In geometry I find certain imperfections which I hold to be the reason why this science, apart from translation into analytics, can as yet make no advance from that state in which it has come to us from Euclid. As belonging to these imperfections, I consider . . . the momentous gap in the theory of parallels, to fill which all efforts of mathematicians have been so far in vain.[13]

Lobachevski was about to demonstrate, following the same formal method that was used by Euclid, that Euclid's theorems were not the only ones that could be derived.

The crux of the dispute lay in Euclid's postulate 5, which states: "In a plane and through a given point, there is only one parallel line to a given line." Lobachevski simply denied this and replaced it with his own postulate: "In a plane and through a given point, there exists an infinite number of parallel lines for a given line." He then used

Euclid's rigorous method of proof to produce a totally consistent non-Euclidean geometry.

A few years later, Bernhard Riemann changed the parallel postulate once again to read: "In a plane and through a given point, there exist no parallel lines for a given line." He, too, produced a totally consistent non-Euclidean geometry. (In fact, Albert Einstein used the Riemannian geometry when he developed his theory of relativity that refined Newtonian mechanics, but that's another story.) Which of the three geometries was "correct"? How could that be decided? The methodology of the formal system that was originally developed to answer the question, How could anyone ever be certain of the truth of a proposition? was now itself the producer of doubt.

It was the solution to this crisis that began the merging of the calculus of thought with the logic machine. Quite clearly, the cause of the crisis wasn't the way in which the theorems were generated in the formal system. After all, Euclid, Lobachevski, and Riemann had all used the same methodology. Rather, the cause of the crisis was the status of the axioms: It seemed as if propositions that were "obviously" true, weren't. Once again, natural language had shown its ability to trick us, and so the logicians and mathematicians in the mid-nineteenth century began to develop formal languages that they hoped would have none of the ambiguity of natural language.[14]

Chief among those logicians was George Boole. As we've already seen, Boole was after "the fundamental laws of those operations of the mind by which reasoning is performed." Fortunately for the disciples of formal systems, his method involved the search for "certain general principles founded in the very nature of language, by which the use of *symbols*, which are but the elements of scientific language, is determined." (emphasis added) The system Boole developed used three types of symbols:

Proposition I:

All the operations of Language, as an instrument of reasoning, may be conducted by a system of signs composed of the following elements, viz.:

1st. Literal symbols, as x, y, & c, representing things as subjects of our conceptions.

2nd. Signs of operation, as $+$, $-$, $\times$, standing for those operations of the mind by which the conceptions of things are combined or resolved so as to form new conceptions involving the same elements.

3rd. The sign of identity, $=$.

And these symbols of Logic are in their use subject to definite laws, partly agreeing with and partly differing from the laws of the corresponding symbols in the science of Algebra.[15]

By replacing natural language classes (e.g., the set of all computers) with letters (e.g., C) and natural language connectives (e.g., and, or, not) with symbols (e.g., $\times$, $+$, $-$), Boole was able to generate a purely symbolic logic. Finally, by following the laws of algebra, he was able to determine the validity of an inference simply by treating his symbols as if they were numbers. For example, the Aristotelian syllogism discussed earlier in this chapter would be symbolized by Boole as follows:

ALL COMPUTERS ARE MACHINES	$C \times -M = 0$	(The class of things that are both computers and nonmachines has no members.)
ALL MACHINES ARE INANIMATE	$M \times -A = 0$	
ALL COMPUTERS ARE INANIMATE	$C \times -A = 0$	

Reaching the conclusion was simply a matter of letting the two middle terms (M and $-$M) cancel out.

Boole's symbolic logic had two important consequences. First, it was the final realization of Aristotle's goal to replace meaning with form, that is, to replace *truth* with the concept of *provability*. The validity of the syllogism now clearly had nothing to do with the meaning of its constituent terms. In Poincare's words, "to demonstrate a theorem, it is neither necessary nor advantageous to know what it means." All that was important was balancing the two sides of an equation.

Second, Boole's symbolic logic was one of the earliest demonstrations of the truly general nature of symbolic operation. If letters could be treated as numbers, then the same general principles of symbol manipulation might be applicable to many different classes of symbols. What Boole had demonstrated was that a symbol is merely a carrier of information and that the rules for manipulating symbols had a general character. One hundred years later that insight would be central in developing the computer—the general-purpose machine.

Boole's symbolic language was suggestive to the mathematicians of his day, but it still remained to be seen if it could be incorporated into the proof procedure of formal systems. It took about 50 years to add the necessary refinements to Boole's work, and in 1895 Guiseppe Peano published his *Formulaire de Mathematiques* with the aim of "making public the known propositions on various mathematical subjects. These propositions are expressed by formulas in a notation of mathematical logic as explained in the Introduction to the *Formulaire*."[16]

Peano began with five axioms (e.g., Every number has a successor, a ε No. ⊃ .a + ε No. [if a belongs to the class of numbers, then the successor of a belongs to the class of numbers]) and went on to deduce the laws of arithmetic formally. Peano not only had incorporated a formal language into a formal system, but also he had used the formal language to demonstrate that mathematics could be considered a branch of logic. This lesson would not be lost on the computer designers a half-century later.

In 1910, Bertrand Russell and Alfred North Whitehead published the first book of their monumental, three-volume *Principia Mathematica* (titled in obvious homage to Newton), which stands today as the classic example of a formal system.[17] The *Principia* was much more than an extension of Peano's work. It supplied an inclusive system of symbolic notation so that every statement of that subset of mathematics known as arithmetic could be expressed in a formal language, and it made explicit the rules of formal proof that could be used to demonstrate mathematical truths. Russell and Whitehead had taken the formal system methodology of Euclid and refined it until it was a smoothly running, totally formalized, logic machine; they succeeded in their goal of stating mathematics in terms of logic, which meant they succeeded in fitting formal thought together with formal language.

Unlike Euclid's formal system, which contained only two elements (i.e., axioms and rules of inference), the *Principia*, as well as other modern formal systems, contains five elements:

1. Vocabulary
   a. Nonlogical signs—p, q, r
   b. Logical signs—~, v, ., ⊃
   c. Punctuation—( ) (for grouping)
2. Formation Rules—rules to define what will constitute a well-formed formula in the formal system
   a. p, q, r are well formed
   b. if p is well formed, so is ~p
   c. if p and q are well formed, so are p v q, p ⊃q, and p . q
3. Axioms
   a. (p v p) ⊃ p principle of tautology
   b. q ⊃ (p v q) principle of addition
   c. (p v q) ⊃ (q v p) principle of permutation
   d. p v (q v r) ⊃ q v (p v r) principle of association
   e. (q ⊃ r) ⊃ [(p v q) ⊃ (p v r)] principle of summation
4. Transformation Rules (or Rules of Inference)
   a. Rule of Substitution—If a sentence of the system is logically true, then any nonlogical sign may be uniformally substituted without changing the truth value (e.g., Since p ⊃ (p v q) is true, so is r ⊃ (r v p).
   b. Rule of Detachment—If S is a logically true sentence and S ⊃ S' is logically true, then we may conclude that S' is logically true.
5. Interpretation

The previous four elements comprise a formal system's *syntactic* component. They are simply rules for expressing and manipulating marks on paper or electronic pulses in a computer. The interpretation is the *semantic* component that assigns natural language meanings to the formal symbols. In the case of the *Principia*, p, q, and r stand for natural language sentences and ~ stands for not, while v represents or, . represents and, and ⊃ represents if-then. By separating syntax from semantics, proof from meaning, Russell and Whitehead had provided a key insight into how to build a truly general logic machine: Create a hierarchy of abstractions with the syntax near the bottom and the semantics near the top.

With the establishment of the *Principia*'s formal system, it became possible to give a rigorous demonstration of the theory behind the syllogism:

Let p stand for "It's a computer."
Let q stand for "It's a machine."
Let r stand for "It's inanimate."
The premise "All computers are machines" is expressed $p \supset q$.
The premise "All machines are inanimate" is expressed $q \supset r$.
The conclusion "All computers are inanimate" is expressed $p \supset r$.

In order to prove that this form of the syllogism is valid, you must demonstrate that $(p \supset q) \supset ((q \supset r) \supset (p \supset r))$ is a theorem in the system:

  To Prove: $(p \supset q) \supset ((q \supset r) \supset (p \supset r))$
1. Axiom e: $(q \supset r) \supset ((p \lor q) \supset (p \lor r))$
2. By the rule of substitution, substitute $\sim p$ for p
   $(q \supset r) \supset ((\sim p \lor q) \supset (\sim p \lor r))$
3. By definition $p \supset q$ is equivalent to $\sim p \lor q$,
   $(q \supset r) \supset ((p \supset q) \supset (p \supset r))$
4. Axiom d: $(p \lor (q \lor r)) \supset (q \lor (p \lor r))$
5. By the rule of substitution, substitute $\sim p$ for p, $\sim q$ for q
   $(\sim p \lor (\sim q \lor r)) \supset (\sim q \lor (\sim p \lor r))$
6. By definition $p \supset q$ is equivalent to $\sim p \lor q$,
   $(p \supset (q \supset r)) \supset (q \supset (p \supset r))$
7. Apply the rule of substitution, $q \supset r$ for p, $p \supset q$ for q, and $p \supset r$ for r
   $((q \supset r) \supset ((p \supset q) \supset (p \supset r))) \supset ((p \supset q) \supset ((q \supset r) \supset (p \supset r)))$
8. Using lines 3 and 7, apply the rule of detachment
   $(p \supset q) \supset ((q \supset r) \supset (p \supset r))$ Q.E.D.

The work of Russell and Whitehead seemed to cap Euclid's search for a perfect system of formal thought. The ambiguities of natural language were banished from the system, and the chain of logic was impeccable. The logic machine seemed so powerful that even before the *Principia*, the great mathematician David Hilbert could suppose:

> Every definite mathematical problem must necessarily be susceptible of an exact settlement either in the form of an actual answer to the question asked, or by the proof of the impossibility of its solution and therewith the necessary failure of all attempts . . . one of the

things that attracts us most when we apply ourselves to a mathematical problem is that precisely within us we always hear the call: here is the problem, search for the solution; you can find it by pure thought, for in mathematics there is nothing that cannot be known.[18]

Yet, within three decades natural language would once again creep into the domain of the formal system. This time, however, it could not be expunged and in so proving that fact, a brilliant group of mathematicians not only demonstrated the limits of our logical abilities, they also invented the computer.

METALOGIC, PARADOX, AND THE THEORY OF COMPUTABILITY

The goal of my theory is to establish once and for all the certitude of mathematical methods . . . The present state of affairs where we run up against the paradoxes is intolerable. Just think, the definitions and deductive methods which everyone learns, teaches and uses in mathematics, the paragon of truth and certitude, lead to absurdities! If mathematical thinking is defective, where are we to find truth and certitude?[19]

Russell and Whitehead's *Principia* ended the long search for a logic machine, but the end of one quest gave immediate rise to another—this one designed to validate the machinery of logical reasoning. Just as any engineer would submit a new technology (e.g., a new microprocessor) to a series of trials or an empirical scientist would submit a new theory (e.g., that all languages share a universal grammar) to a series of confirmatory tests, mathematicians in the early part of this century needed to examine the adequacy of the new logic machine. Because their only tools for performing the analysis were logic and mathematics, the name given to the new discipline was *metalogic*, the application of logic to other, lower-level logical problems.

This validation process took on a special sense of urgency because of what came to be known as the "foundation crisis" in mathematics. Since the time of Euclid, mathematicians had assumed that a formal system consisting of axioms and rules of inference could produce proofs of theorems, thereby furnishing a certain method for the production of knowledge. Yet, after 2000 years of service, that certain method would be called into question, first, for the part of mathematics that dealt with objects in the real world, and then, only 50 years after the first crack appeared, for the foundations of mathematical thinking itself.

When Descartes, Galileo, Newton, *et al.* applied mathematics to the study of nature, thus creating our dominant, modern thought tool—science—it seemed inevitable that all knowledge systems eventually would be reduced to a calculus that would apply the method of mathematical proof to natural phenomena as well as to the objects of thought. But the discovery of non-Euclidean geometry threw this assumption into doubt. After millennia of certainty about the mathematical system that describes one of our most primary experiences—spatial relationships—mathematicians had to face the fact that at least one of Euclid's "self-evident" axioms wasn't necessarily true. And if geometry was not as certain as had been believed, then the overall structure of mathematics might not be certain either, causing the certainty of scientific knowledge to be imperiled as well.

The mathematicians of the late nineteenth and early twentieth centuries weren't as concerned with the epistemological bases of science as they were with the certainty of their own formal system. If Euclid's method could harbor monstrous contradictions such as non-Euclidean geometries, nineteenth century mathematicians were faced with the repugnant possibility that all branches of mathematics were subject to contradictions, and thus the entire structure of human knowledge would be doomed to uncertainty.

Even before the *Principia* was begun, there were indications that the logic machine rested on shaky ground. A contemporary of Peano's, Gottlob Frege, had tried to link axioms such as Peano's with Boole's intuitive notion of sets in order to extend the logic machine into the realm of arithmetic. In particular, Frege proposed using a common sense notion called the *axiom of extensionality*, whereby two sets are equivalent if and only if they each contain the same objects. Although this axiom seemed "obviously" true, as had Euclid's parallel axiom, that old enemy, paradox, lay just around the corner.

The ink was barely dry on Frege's manuscript when Bertrand Russell made a discovery that irrevocably and completely halted the effort to base mathematical certainty on set theory. Frege, after a long and strenuous effort, was about to publish his work on the set theoretical foundations of arithmetic when he received a disturbing letter from Russell, which left him with no recourse but to publish a postscript to his treatise stating, "A scientist can hardly meet with anything more undesirable than to have the foundations give way just as the work is finished. In this position I was put by a letter from Mr. Bertrand Russell, as the work was nearly through the press."[20]

The letter of Russell's concerned a paradox he had uncovered at the foundation of set theory. *Russell's paradox*, as it came to be known, is a special variation of the ancient liar's paradox. Like that ancient antinomy, it was based on the idea of self-reference. Only this time it was applied to sets instead of natural language.

Russell's paradox showed that set theory contained a contradiction built into the notion of set membership. It seems obvious that certain sets may contain themselves as members. For example, the set of all sets that have more than three members clearly has more than three elements as members; therefore, the set is a member of itself. The set of all sentences about sets is also a member of itself.

Other sets, such as the set of all computers, are not members of themselves since only computers, and not sets, belong to it. Using these intuitive notions, Russell then defined a special Russell set, that is, the set of all sets that are not members of themselves. The rule of membership to this set was clear: A set x belongs to the Russell set R if and only if it does not belong to itself ($x \varepsilon R$ iff $x \notin x$).

Russell was now ready to ask his paradoxical question: Does the Russell set belong to itself ($R \varepsilon R$ iff $R \notin R$)? The answer couldn't be yes, because a set could only belong to the Russell set if it was not a member of itself. But neither could the answer be no, because if the Russell set did not belong, then, by definition, it must belong. Since all of the premises and rules of inference used to construct his paradox are perfectly legitimate rules of set theory, it appeared that set theory itself, the foundation of all attempts to construct mathematics from logic, contained a fatal contradiction.

Russell's own "solution" to this paradox, and the one that he incorporated into the *Principia*, was his *Theory of Types*. Language is hierarchical (a notion that would play an important role later in the development of computer languages): At level 0 we operate with the domain of objects (computers); at level 1 we operate with the domain of sets (classes of computers); at level 2 we operate with the domain of sets of sets (the set containing all sets). By providing rules that forbid certain operations across types, Russell was able to block his paradox.

But even he, eventually, felt that this *ad hoc* theory had ultimately failed to solve the foundation crisis and validate the logic machine:

> I wanted certainty in the kind of way in which people wanted religious faith. I thought that certainty is more likely to be found in mathematics than elsewhere. But I discovered that many mathematical demonstrations, which my teachers expected me to accept, were full of fallacies, and that, if certainty were indeed discoverable in mathematics, it would be in a new field of mathematics, with more solid foundations than those that had hitherto been thought secure. But as the work proceeded, I was continually reminded of the fable about the elephant and the tortoise. Having constructed an elephant upon which the mathematical world could rest, I found the elephant tottering, and proceeded to construct a tortoise to keep the elephant from falling. But the tortoise was no more secure than the elephant, and after some twenty years of very arduous toil, I came to the conclusion that there was nothing more that I could do in the way of making mathematical knowledge indubitable.[21]

Russell and Frege were known as logicists because they believed that logic was the foundation of mathematics. Another school of mathematicians who hoped to solve the foundation crisis were known as formalists. Their role in the investigation of the roots of computation was critical, since it was the formalist program that brought the search for certainty to its astonishing conclusion. It did this by proving that all attempts to build an indubitable foundation for formal systems were, in fact, doomed to failure.

The great mathematician David Hilbert was the chief spokesman for the formalist school and the architect of its program—the view that mathematics could only be established with certainty by treating it as a set of rules and tokens that do not depend on anything but their own self-consistency. The formalists intended to put an end to the foundation crisis by accomplishing three subgoals: First, they intended to use formal language and rules of inference in order to represent each theorem of formal mathematics so that each proof could be tested by a set of mechanically checkable steps. Second, Hilbert created a new theory, known as *metamathematics*, which used the combinatorial properties of this formal language. The goal was to investigate methods of transforming one mathematical formula into another by sheer symbol manipulation. Finally, Hilbert called on formalist mathematicians to cap the system by proving that a contradiction could not be derived from it. Hilbert took Aristotle's doctrine of form over meaning to its logical limit. According to Hilbert's formalism, not only could mathematical form replace mathematical meaning, but there was no mathematical meaning apart from form.

The formalist stipulation that their system must consist of "mechanically checkable" steps is a key in our investigation of computer languages, for it was that precise phrase that later linked metamathematics to computation. The notion of being mechanically checkable originated as a way of reducing the distressingly general concept of certainty or indubitability to more specific and easily understood concepts and ended up giving rise to the modern computer.

Although the formalists rejected the logicist approach to the foundation crisis—the idea that all mathematics was reducible to logic and set theory—they intended to use Russell and Whitehead's system as a tool for attaining their own goals. While Russell and Whitehead did not succeed in their attempts to help Frege reconstruct set theory, they had a brilliant success with their *Principia*, the first full-scale attempt to reduce all of mathematics to a logical system. Here, in a real sense, was a version of the long-sought logic machine.

Hilbert proposed that certainty could be achieved if mathematics, as it was logically represented in *Principia*, could be shown to have two clearly defined properties. Formal language and formal thought could replace natural language and natural thought as the premiere truth-generating system if and only if Russell and Whitehead's logic machine had these two specific properties: First, it had to be possible to give a proof for every true sentence. This property was called *completeness*. Second, for any sentence in the formal language, it had to be possible to determine if that sentence was a theorem, that is, if it was the last line of a proof. This property was called *decidability*. Unless the logic machine could be shown to be complete, there would always be truths that would lie outside its domain; unless it was decidable, we could never know if it was generating all possible truths.

Like the logicists before them, the formalists met with promising successes at the beginning of their enterprise. Their initial investigations into these two properties seemed to confirm Hilbert's statement that "in mathematics there is nothing that cannot be known." It looked as if *Principia*, and hence the whole of mathematics, would be proven to be both complete and decidable. In 1921 Emil Post published a proof demonstrating that *sentential logic*—a fragment of the logic machine in which symbols stand for whole sentences and the only logical symbols represent the connectives not, and, or, and if-then (this is similar to the subset of *Principia* described earlier in this chapter)—was complete.[22]

Post was also able to demonstrate a decision procedure for the theorems of sentential logic; this was a completely automatic method that could be applied to any sentence of the system and that would indicate, after a finite number of steps, whether or not the sentence was provable. Hilbert's idea of a mechanically checkable set of steps had been refined to a completely automatic method.

Although Post's proofs were impressive, they only applied to a small portion of the entire logic machine. This is because sentential logic can only represent complete sentences as *whole* units and cannot represent the logical relationships *within* a sentence. For example, Aristotle's square of opposition demonstrates that if "All men are mortal" is true, then "Some men are mortal" must also be true. Yet, sentential logic cannot prove this simple truth because it cannot express the relationship between the quantifying words "All" and "Some." Sentential logic only studies the logical connections between sentences, not the logical information contained within sentences. This means, of course, that its ability to convey natural language expressions is quite limited.

Accommodating the logical information within a sentence requires the introduction of variables (a key concept in programming languages) and predicates [i.e., properties (is tall) that could be attributed to the variables]. This newer, more powerful logic is known as the *predicate calculus* and it represents a much more substantial portion of the logic machine. In this system, "All men are mortal" is expressed as $(\forall x)(Mx \supset mx)$ (For all x, if x is a man then x is mortal.); and "Some men are mortal" is expressed as $(\exists x)(Mx \, \& \, mx)$ (For some x, x is a man and x is mortal.). Using this notation, it is trivial to prove the relationships portrayed in the square of opposition. Once again, the generation of new linguistic tools enabled us to think in newer, more powerful ways. Because the predicate calculus begins to approach natural language as a system for expressing our thoughts, Kurt Gödel's 1930 demonstration[23] that the predicate calculus was complete seemed to signal that it was only a matter of time before the entire logic machine would be shown to be complete.[24]

As it turned out, that time would never come. Within a year, Gödel published another paper, "On Formally Undecidable Propositions of *Principia Mathematica* and Related Systems," that demolished Hilbert's vision, altered the way we look at formal systems and directly stimulated the theoretical work that led to the theory of computability.[25] This formal system was just slightly more general than the predicate calculus (e.g., it contained relational as well as attributable predicates), and Gödel was able to demonstrate that it was incomplete, in other words, that it contained true propositions that could not be proven within the system. Thus, the goal of building a formal system that could generate and prove *all* laws of science or mathematics was shown to be unattainable.

Gödel's paper was as surprising and remarkable for its method as its result. Although the paper was long and complicated, the key logical insight was very simple: Gödel developed a method for producing a formula "G" that simply represented a mathematical way of saying "I am not provable." In effect, "G" was a version of the Russell set applied to any system as complex as *Principia*'s. If proven, "G" would be false, and the formal system of mathematics would be shown to be inconsistent. If unproven, "G" would be true, but arithmetic would be incomplete. Either way, Gödel had demonstrated that far from all truths, not even mathematical truth was reducible to provability. The line of evolving thought tools that had begun with Aristotle had reached its end. Form would never totally replace meaning.

The objective of ridding formal languages of the self-referent properties of natural language that gave rise to antinomies such as the liar's paradox, the Russell set, and "G" had ultimately failed. Not only did formal systems generate their own paradoxes, but the very goal of equating truth with provability was doomed to fail as well. It was this ultimate irony that Gödel demonstrated: Because formal systems can express the notion of provable sentence, but not true sentence, within themselves, it follows that all such formal systems must be incomplete. The 2000-year-old quest for an infallible calculus of thought had contained the seed of its own destruction all along. It just took 20 centuries of thinkers to bring it to fruition.[26]

That seed, of course, was the fact that the notion of provability could be expressed within a formal language. This idea was possible because the concept of proof had remained as simple and intuitive as it had been for Euclid: Start with true statements and proceed to other true statements using rules of inference that are known to be truth preserving. Yet, it was that intuitive notion of proof that led to paradox. The mathematicians in the years immediately following

Gödel therefore set out to obtain a deeper understanding of the concept of proof—to understand exactly what it meant to say that a list of sentences in a given formal language was a proof.

Surprisingly, the key they rediscovered to formalizing the concept of proof was the thousand-plus-year-old notion of the algorithm:

> There are several other words that almost, but not quite, capture the concept that is needed: procedure, recipe, process, routine, method, rigmarole. Like these things an algorithm is a set of rules or directions for getting a specific output from a specific input. The distinguishing feature of an algorithm is that all vagueness must be eliminated: the rules must describe operations that are so simple and well defined that they can be executed by a machine. Furthermore, an algorithm must always terminate after a finite number of steps.[27]

An *algorithm* is simply an effective procedure for answering a given question about a formal system such as the number system; for example: Is 13 a prime number? An effective procedure is a means of generating the answer to a question like the one given within a finite number of mechanical steps. But this is exactly the same description that applies to the logic machine: a means to produce a finite number of sentences using only mechanical means in order to demonstrate that p is a theorem of F. It turned out, then, that the quest for the logic machine was really a quest for an algorithm that would answer the question, Is this sentence provable within a given formal system? Two thousand years of intellectual searching hinged on giving an adequate explanation of the concept of the algorithm.

Many competing analyses were offered, but the clearest, most intuitive account was given by the British mathematician Alan Turing.[28] He suggested that algorithms were *computable functions* and then designed an idealized computer to demonstrate exactly what he meant by computable. Although actual working computer hardware would not be developed for almost 10 years, Turing's explanation of his hypothetical machine is still used to describe the workings of a virtual computer. As Figure 2.4 illustrates, the hardware of a Turing machine consisted of an infinite tape segmented into a series of squares and a scanning head that could inspect only one square at a time. Each square could contain only a 1 or a 0 (this, of course, is analogous to the binary-coded machine language in today's computers).

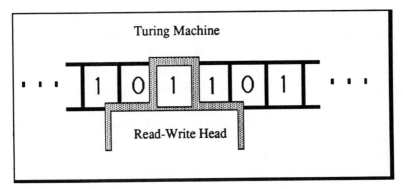

Figure 2.4 Tape and Read/Write Head of Turing Machine

The specification for the completely automatic procedure required by Hilbert's formalism—the programming language of the Turing machine—was the set of rules Turing used to describe how the machine operated. (It is easy to see, given the minimal nature of Turing's hardware, that the computer really *is* the program.) In particular, the machine could only perform five actions:

1. Write the symbol 1
2. Write the symbol 0
3. Move one square right
4. Move one square left
5. Stop

The language that instructed the machine which action to take consisted of three elements:

1. The numbers 0-n used to represent the state of the machine. (It would, of course, be possible to use only the numbers 0 and 1 and represent all states in binary code.)
2. The numbers 0 and 1 used to represent the data on the tape.
3. The letters L and R used to instruct the head to move one cell to the left or to the right.

The syntax of the Turing programming language consisted of only one rule which described how the three elements would be combined: A well-formed Turing statement is a 5-tuple of the form (state, contents of cell read, write instruction, move instruction, new state). For example, (5,1,0,R,9) is a Turing instruction that tells the machine that if it is in state 5 and reading a 1, it is to write a 0, move one cell to the right, and enter state 9. A table of instructions such as this make up a Turing program.

If all this seems needlessly abstract, it is well to remember that Turing was after a completely concrete, mechanistic computing procedure. Sometimes abstraction is the best way to rule out any extraneous information. Whether the computing agent was a human or a machine, Turing was seeking a set of instructions that could only be followed in one way and that would always yield the same results.

The following doubling program is an example of a Turing machine in operation. Beginning with two 1's on the tape, it proceeds to duplicate them, separating the pairs by a lone 0. The 23 steps in the program seem a long way to go to prove that $2 \times 2 = 4$, but Turing was not concerned with efficiency, only with demonstrating that an algorithm existed that would get the job done.

011000	1,1,1,R,1
011000	1,0,0,R,2
011000	2,0,1,L,3
011010	3,0,0,L,3
011010	3,1,1,L,4
011010	4,1,1,R,5
011010	5,1,0,R,6
010010	6,0,0,R,6
010010	6,1,1,R,7
010010	7,0,1,L,8
010011	8,1,1,L,8
010011	8,0,0,L,3
010011	3,0,0,L,3
010011	3,1,1,L,4
010011	4,0,0,R,9
010011	9,1,1,R,10
010011	10,0,1,R,10
011011	10,0,1,R,10
011111	10,1,1,L,11
011111	11,1,0,R,12
011011	12,1,1,R,12
011011	12,1,1,R,12
011011_	12,0,0,L,0 (STOP)

Because the first two items in the 5-tuple (i.e., machine state and cell contents) always determine the actions that the machine is to perform, it is possible to provide a table that generalizes the doubling program for any input as long as the machine always begin in state 1 and starts by scanning the rightmost 1 of the series (if you are ambitious, you may want to use this table to generate the 12 steps needed to double 1):

Machine State	Symbol Scanned	
	0	1
1	0R2	1R1
2	1L3	1L2
3	0L3	1L4
4	0R9	1R5
5	—	0R6
6	0R6	1R7
7	1L8	1R7
8	0L3	1L8
9	—	1R10
10	1R10	1L11
11	—	0R12
12	0L0	1R12

By producing a specific Turing machine to solve a given problem, Turing demonstrated that the problem was computable and, hence, an algorithm existed to solve the problem. But Turing was not totally satisfied with his creation of job-specific machines. He was really after a *universal* Turing machine, one that could solve any computable problem. He was able to invent just such a machine by devising a coding scheme that allowed the program of any particular Turing machine, along with its data, to become the input for the universal machine. Just imagine that the 23 steps in the doubling program were first put into a binary code and that the program was then followed by the input, 11. The universal machine would read the coded program and perform the exact same operation on the inputted data as the original doubling machine.

Turing's realization of the universal machine was triply profound: First, it demonstrated that there is no important difference between programs and data—a key concept for the operation of modern computers. Second, it led directly to the notion of the all-purpose machine—a computer capable of solving an infinity of different types of problems. Third, it gave a formal description to the logic machine—Euclid and all his successors were really in search of a universal Turing machine.

With his invention of the universal Turing machine, Turing had all the machinery he needed to tackle the issue of decidability. He had shown that the concept of proof was reducible to the notion of an algorithm, that an algorithm was really a computable function, and that an algorithm was expressible as a Turing machine. Hilbert had supposed that "every definite mathematical problem must necessarily be susceptible of an exact settlement." But this would only be the case if the universal Turing machine had a decidability program, that is, a program that could be used to tell us if a specific Turing machine (like the doubling machine) would come to a halt (i.e., the program would stop the tape with the correct answer). By demonstrating that there was no such program, Turing explicitly proved that problems existed for which there was no algorithmic solution; in other words, the logic machine was undecidable. Contrary to Hilbert's fondest dreams, definite mathematical problems existed for which there was no hope of exact settlement.

Like Gödel's incompleteness result, Turing's proof involves excruciating detail. But the heart of the proof is a straightforward application of the paradox of self-reference:

1. Suppose there is a decidability program called DECIDE. The Turing machine running the program accepts as input another program (P) (since Turing has shown that there is no intrinsic difference between data and programs) and its data (d). DECIDE outputs Halt if P(d) stops and outputs Run-on if P(d) fails to stop.
2. Now, we can run DECIDE again, this time using it to check on the status of a self-referent program. By self-referent, we simply mean a program whose data is the program itself. Once again, DECIDE will output Halt if P(P) stops and will output Run-on if P(P) fails to stop.
3. Next, we modify the output of DECIDE and call the modified program DECIDE1. Its input is still a self-referent program. As output, DECIDE1 fails to output Halt if P(P) halts, and it does output Halt if P(P) fails to halt.
4. Finally, Turing carried self-reference one step further by letting the input to DECIDE1 be the DECIDE1 program itself. This results in a total contradiction: DECIDE1 fails to halt if

DECIDE1 halts, and DECIDE1 outputs Halt if DECIDE1 fails to halt.

Since the only assumption made in this chain of reasoning that leads to a contradiction is the supposition that a decidability program exists, there can be no such program. The universal Turing Machine, and hence the logic machine, is not decidable.[29] Turing's results received almost instantaneous corroboration by the American Alonzo Church. Instead of using Turing's machines to describe algorithms, Church developed his own notational system called the lambda calculus. Although it had none of the intuitive charm of the Turing approach, Church was also able to prove that the logic machine was undecidable.

Once again, the key to a great mathematical discovery had been a version of the liar's paradox. Russell had used it to produce the Russell set in order to demonstrate that set theory cannot serve as the foundation for mathematics. Gödel had used it with the concept of provability to demonstrate that the logic machine constructed by Russell and Whitehead was incomplete—there are truths that are not provable. Turing had used it with the concept of computability to demonstrate that the logic machine was undecidable—there are truths we cannot know through the use of algorithms. Yet the ultimate paradox was that their works only gave strength to the ideas of formal thought and formal language. Bobby Burns' words were never truer:

> For thence—a paradox
> which comforts while it mocks
> shall life succeed in that
> it seems to fail:[30]

For in setting the limits of the logic machine, these men had given birth to the theory of computability and the modern computer—a machine with well-defined limits but unlimited promise for future problem solving.

3

Computer Language and Hierarchies of Abstractions

The hierarchical principle we have applied here to the organization of an operating system is one that has proved to be one of great utility throughout the natural sciences. After all, structures and events in the natural world span many orders of magnitude in space and time and cannot be grasped all at once: it is not possible to comprehend the evolution of a galaxy by plotting the trajectories of its constituent atoms. Of all man-made objects computer systems have the greatest disparity between the smallest and the largest components. The designers of operating systems have begun to cope with that vast range of scales by creating a hierarchy of abstractions.[1]

BUILDING CATHEDRALS OUT OF BRICKS

A single keystroke command to the operating system of a computer can cause more than 10 million individual changes of state to occur in that computer's logic gates. The program known as the operating system is designed so that the same 10 million events occur in the same order every time the same command is given. Designers of large-scale computer software systems, who must synchronize such staggeringly complex collections of events, can be forgiven for comparing the creation of software to the evolution of galaxies.

The job of building the most elaborate structures out of the simplest materials is the software architect's blessing and curse. A "vast range of scales" is indeed one of the primary sources of the power of computation—and one of the main causes of headaches for program-

71

mers. *Complexity* is the name for the distance between the single keystroke and the 10 million interrelated microelectronic events it engenders. How that complexity is managed, and how it eventually results in programs that can order airplane tickets, play chess, or edit documents, is the story told in this chapter.

Programming languages exist in the form they do today because human beings can't hold 10 million things in mind at the same time. Thus, software designers and system programmers must transform complexity from an obstacle into a tool. Just as we can use a lever to amplify the power of our arms, computer programmers use a kind of conceptual lever to pile up those tiny but numerous events into human-comprehensible patterns. The gap between human thought and electronic events is bridged by a hierarchy of interlocking *virtual* machines of varying degrees of internal complexity. Computer languages are the formal systems—the tool-making tools—that make this possible.

All software, no matter what language it is written in or for what purpose, must have a connection with the native language of the computing machine that runs that software. The programmability of every computing machine derives from the basic vocabulary of commands that are built into its arrangement of logic gates, which are nothing more than tiny two-state switches. The way logic gates are linked to one another in each computer's central processor defines that computer's machine language.

The first level of logical machine is the basic machine language vocabulary that is actually wired into the hardware: Every computer has an *instruction set* which is a built-in code that enables the hardware to take instructions from programmers. This instruction set is the logical machine that transforms the physical elements into a true computer. It is a specification of how the physical elements of the computer can be combined into a kind of logical code.

This logical-machine-within-the-physical-machine that constitutes the machine-language instruction set is a specialized but indispensable kind of computer language—a language for telling a computer how to imitate other machines. It is, however, only the first step of a dizzying hierarchy of logical machines that imitate physical machines. Assembly language, the next higher level, constitutes the first level of abstraction where ease of use on the part of the human programmer becomes important: Programmers can write programs in the easier-to-read assembly language, which are automatically translated into the language of the instruction set by the special program written in the machine's instruction set, known as an *assembler*.

Higher-level languages such as BASIC and FORTRAN are the next level up, bootstrapped onto the instruction set via the special translator programs known as *interpreters* or *compilers*. Computer languages such as BASIC and Pascal are logical machines built from the instruction set's logical machine within the computer and are themselves used to turn general-purpose computers into business machines, artistic media, scientific tools, educational aids, or games. Computer languages are tools for dividing complexities into mind-sized chunks. Computer programs—the individual compositions written in a computer language and executed via an assembler, interpreter, or compiler—are even higher levels of a virtual machine.

One of the paradoxical restrictions on what the system of virtual machines can do is the constraint that complicated instructions must be written with the simplest possible alphabet. The fundamental code for all programming, no matter which brand of computer or high-level language is used, consists of only two kinds of electronic impulses: dot and dash, 0 and 1, on and off—call them what you will. The reason computation can be done by machines is this mechanical simplicity of the tokens. Although the overwhelming majority of programmers seek a more comprehensible notation to write their compositions, their programs eventually must be translated into monotonous strings of 1s and 0s. The usefulness of higher-level languages lies in the way lower levels of logical machine perform the translation *invisibly*, without cluttering up the human programmer's limited attention space.

If you plan to build a cathedral out of bricks, a symphony out of notes, or a word processor out of microcode, you need a strategy for organizing very complex patterns into mind-sized modules. A strategy that appears to work in thinking, as well as in architecture, musical composition, and computer programming, is the process of *building abstractions*, that is, arranging fundamental elements into symbolic structures, thereby compressing chunks of information into the form of building blocks for the next highest levels of abstractions.

Although abstraction building might sound like some esoteric intellectual skill best left to mathematicians, its guiding principles are familiar to every one of you reading this book. In order to read this paragraph, for example, you have to recognize patterns of individual letters, understand the definitions of words, connect words into sentences, and follow the flow of thoughts represented by sentences through sequences of paragraphs. While you are trying to understand the meaning of these words and sentences and paragraphs, your brain is processing billions of fundamental information transactions every second.

People have a knack for making lower-level cognitive skills automatic as soon as the skill has been consciously mastered: Once you learn to read, you no longer need to be aware of every letter, or even every word. Eventually you read a sentence instead of decoding a string of letters. Artificial intelligence researchers who try to program computers to perform similar tasks can testify that the process of reading is as tricky and complicated as it sounds. But every literate person learns how to do it—usually in childhood, always beginning with the ABCs.

Complex abstractions such as written languages are constructed from more fundamental abstractions, and each higher level of abstraction conveys more information than its lower-level constituent parts. At each level of written natural languages—letter, word, and sentence—the possible universe of combinations grows larger, the rules for combining elements grows more sophisticated, and the information-carrying power of the system increases. Programming languages, not entirely accidentally, are constructed in a similar way.

Written natural language is encoded hierarchically, and that is how we learn it: After we memorized the alphabet, we learned word and sentence recognition, then the rules of grammar and composition. As soon as we learned to recognize the letters, we no longer had to think about them; the abstraction became automatic, freeing us to think about the next higher level. In much the same way, machine code makes rewiring the machine automatic, and assembly language makes reading and writing machine code automatic.

The ability of higher levels to make use of lower-level operations without explicitly directing their details is the source of great power, if it can be organized efficiently. But such a hierarchy is more than a rank ordering of elements. At every shift in level, there must be a qualitative as well as quantitative shift in the power of the system. In natural language, there is a threshold somewhere between words and sentences where the skill of literacy shifts from a code-breaking routine to a meaning-making task. Eventually fluency is achieved, and we no longer consciously read the words; rather, we read the contents of books—the flow of meanings created by the sequences of symbols.

Thus, a hierarchy of abstractions from alphabet to book transforms a code made of combinations of simple symbols into a medium for communicating knowledge.

The computer programmer uses software machines such as interpreters and compilers to help create abstractions (known as *algorithms* and *data structures*) in the computer's electronic code. The programmer doesn't want to deal with all the fine-level changes of state in logic gates; thus, the software machine takes care of those low-level tasks while the programmer deals with higher-level abstractions. The people who use the program don't care about the features of the software that concern the programmer. To them, the program is the machine that enables them to deal with higher-level abstractions such as profit-and-loss statements, filing systems, graphic designs, and games.

Before higher-level abstractions can be created, their foundation must be established. The building blocks must be fabricated and put into place before any buildings can be constructed. In the case of digital computers, the fundamental building blocks are as fundamental as it is possible to get in the realm of information. In the rest of this chapter, we are going to climb the hierarchy of abstractions that constitutes every computer system as illustrated in Figure 3.1, beginning with the binary level.

THE BINARY BASIS
AND THE UNIVERSAL GAME
OF TWENTY QUESTIONS

Neither is it a small matter these Cypher characters have, and may performe: For by this Art a way is opened whereby a man may expresse and signifie the intentions of his minde, at any distance of place, by objects which may be presented to the eye, and accommodated to the eare; provided those objects be capable of a twofold difference onely; as by Bells, by Trumpets, by Lights and Torches, by the report of Muskets, and any instruments of like nature.[2]

Sir Francis Bacon, author of the passage quoted above, was a colorful and influential figure in Elizabethan politics, as well as one of the people who created the foundations of modern science—a kind of James Bond, Isaac Newton, and Henry Kissinger rolled into one.

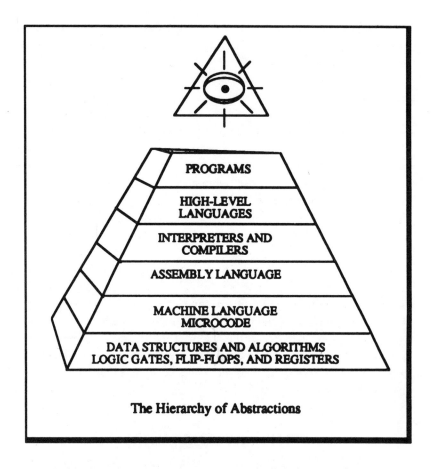

Figure 3.1 Pyramid of Abstractions

He described a binary coding scheme, the first written description in the Western world of a binary code, as part of a cipher he invented for encoding secret diplomatic messages. Despite the primitive state of Elizabethan technology, Bacon was astute enough to foresee that his code could act as a powerful extension of the human "minde."

Bacon noticed something that was so obvious, so seemingly trivial, that previous thinkers throughout the centuries had missed it: It was that a "twofold difference" makes it very easy to represent, encode, and communicate complex information by means of simple signals ("by Bells, by Trumpets . . . and any instruments of like nature"). In fact, anything you can communicate with words can be communicated by means of an alphabet consisting of just two symbols. A two-symbol alphabet is an idea of deceptive simplicity, but it is intimately connected with several of the most powerful ideas of our time, including the formal definitions of information, communication, and computation.

The incredible powers of 2 have been known in the West since Bacon. They have been known in the East even longer. A few decades after Bacon, Leibniz came across a translation of the *I Ching*, a 5000-year-old Chinese book of wisdom and divination that included an ordered sequence of binary numerals. The real power of a binary-coded perspective didn't emerge, however, until the twentieth century, when two young men, working on entirely different problems, created the theoretical bases for computation and information theory.

In 1937, 24-year-old Alan Turing described a kind of universal algorithm machine that could perform an astonishingly wide range of calculations using only two kinds of tokens. In the same year, a 22-year-old MIT graduate student by the name of Claude Shannon discovered that the behavior of electrical switching circuits could be rigorously described by the formulas of the two-state symbolic logic invented a century earlier by George Boole. When Boolean algebra was applied to the technology of Shannon's day, it became possible to build universal Turing machines (better known today as digital computers) out of electrical elements.

Before computers were invented, there was no obvious connection among the binary system, Boolean algebra, metamathematics, information, and switching circuits; but as soon as those separate ideas collided, it became possible, in theory, to build a computer. Put Boole's and Turing's discoveries together with Shannon's and you have all the conceptual tools needed to build computers or communications technology. During World War II, teams of military-funded technologists did just that.

The central paradox of computation—the question of how sophisticated software can be created out of strings of 0s and 1s—is a variation on an old and surprisingly general problem that can be stated in several different ways, in terms that appear to apply to unrelated questions: What is the most efficient way to organize complexity? How can you keep track of a billion units of anything and make sure you can find each unit as quickly as possible? How do you move many things from one point to one of many other points by the shortest route?

You don't need skill in mathematics or training in logic to answer these questions. All you need to do is look around you, because the solutions to all the foregoing problems can be described in terms of a shape that is as familiar as the silhouette of a tree against the sky: One characteristic that doesn't vary much from one tree to another is the way smaller parts of the tree, the larger and smaller branches and twigs, reflect the shape of the entire tree; a programmer would recognize the tree as a "recursive structure." This shape is the reason trees look treelike, and the concept furnishes a crucial clue to resolving the central paradox.

The natural world of trees and rivers and arteries and the artificial worlds of mathematics and logic and computer memories are filled with branching things. A tree of the botanical variety is shaped the way it is because branching is the most efficient way to distribute moisture to a hundred thousand leaves. The tree shape is familiar even to people who live near floodplains instead of forests because trees are not the only phenomena to adopt this form for reasons of efficiency. Indeed, branching structures seem to be one of the fundamental shapes in the universe.

Examine an aerial photograph of a river delta next to an X-ray arteriogram of a human lung and you'll see that branches aren't limited to forests. This similarity of form in very different natural systems is no accident. Rivers branch when they run into their own sedimentary deposits because an arboreal shape is the most efficient way to distribute the river's flow when the main channel suddenly becomes shallow. Pulmonary arteries branch because that enables the lungs to distribute oxygen to the blood rapidly.

And tree-shaped data structures are essential parts of all computer software systems at both the lowest and the highest levels because trees are such an efficient way to store and retrieve large amounts of ordered information. Trees also reflect the shape of binary codes, and that puts them very close to the heart of computation. A tree in which each node branches into exactly two more branches is the direct visual analog of a binary code, because you can get from the trunk to any one of the leaves by making either one of two decisions at each branch (e.g., take either the left branch or the right branch at each successive node, starting from the trunk and ending at the specified leaf).

If you were compulsive enough, you could assign a unique address to each leaf on a tree by specifying the binary decisions that a bug would have to make to travel directly from the trunk to that leaf. You could, for example, specify the leaf on the first right branch after the first left branching of the right fork of the main trunk and call it right-left-right (or, for brevity, r-l-r, or, for that matter, 010 or 101). Figure 3.2 illustrates another tree-bug-leaf code.

This scheme might be helpful to people in cities, as well as to bugs on trees: For example, we can apply the same analogy to the problem of explaining how to find a certain location in a city to a newcomer who can count but can't read street signs: "Take your first right, go two blocks, turn left for one block, and so on."

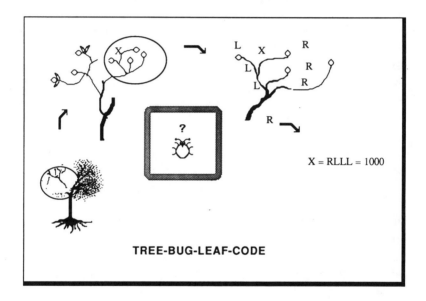

TREE-BUG-LEAF-CODE

X = RLLL = 1000

Figure 3.2 Tree-Leaf-Bug Code

When you begin attaching instructions to a binary-branching structure, as in the case of the instruction-literate bug or the illiterate traveler, you actually are describing the basis of computer software, the fundamental alphabet and grammar of every computer language. Binary code is the bottom-most abstraction in the software hierarchy: the "on and the off of it" is where the computing machine meets the abstractions of language.

There are several reasons why a binary code is an ideal medium for bridging human and machine languages. First, binary codes consist of the simplest, least ambiguous components possible—a big advantage when a code has to be simple enough to enable humans to communicate with machines. Ambiguity is anathema to machines and communication schemes. When you instruct a machine to perform a task, you have to be painstakingly explicit about exactly what you want the machine to do and how you want it done. Stop for a moment and try to think of how you would instruct a machine to unlock a door with a key, for example. It is up to you to describe *exactly* those things that must be done with the key from the virtually infinite list of all the things that could be done.

Eliminating ambiguity in instructions to machines is a matter of specifying what you want to do or say. When you have to break all your messages into finer and finer detail, it is only natural to wonder where it is going to end, which leads to the notion of a *fundamental unit of information.* It turns out that a binary code is as fundamental as it is possible to get and still convey information. The binary signal is also as unambiguous as it is possible to get, since each signal is either one thing or it is the other, and there is never any question that it might be anything but one of those two things.

By limiting the number of choices of symbols to two, it is possible to reduce the informational content of each token to the most fundamental unit of information. And only one token is needed (along with the *absence* of that token) to represent both symbols. The number 1 or a switch that is set in the on position is as simple as a token can get; the number 0 or a switch in the off position, far from representing nothing, signifies the absence of the other token. As anthropologist and cybernetics pioneer Gregory Bateson put it, "Information is any difference that makes a difference."[3]

The turn left or turn right instruction on a verbal map or a tree-shaped data structure, the on or off state of an electronic switch, the 0 or 1, or dot or dash of Morse code that means a difference exists, a signal has been sent, or a datum has been stored or retrieved is the famous *bit*, the humble brick out of which cybernetic cathedrals are built. Although the word *bit* originated as an acronym for binary digit, you would be correct if you thought of it as a kind of fundamental particle of information in the same way that an atom is a fundamental particle of matter.

A second reason that binary codes are ideal tools for building computing machinery is that the tokens are so simple, unambiguous, and unvaried that binary-based electronic computer components can be constructed from very tiny switches, all alike, that are connected to one another in circuits. Since each switch can be turned either on or off, and only on or off, the setting of each switch, like the leaves on a two-branching tree, can be uniquely specified by a binary code.

If you can come up with a code that associates fixed meanings with different patterns of on and off switches, you have the makings of an information processor. If your information processor can imitate a universal Turing machine, you have a digital computer. The difference between a machine that spews random electronic numbers and a machine that orders airline reservations is the set of rules you build into the machine to govern the way it manipulates tokens. It is literally a matter of how you arrange for the switches to be turned on and off.

The computer itself exists in these patterns of settings, not in the nature of the switches: Any device that can switch back and forth between two states will do. In *Computer Power and Human Reason*, computer scientist Joseph Weizenbaum talks about a computer that consists of a roll of toilet paper and two kinds of pebbles.[4] In present technology, electrons flowing through silicon chips activate the switches that convey the patterns of binary signals. In the future, photons passing through optical circuitry will serve the same purpose. The important point is that although the switching technology changes, the fundamental switching code doesn't—and the switching code is binary.

Another advantage of the binary code is that it provides a mathematical tool that enables computer designers to build logic-based machines out of networks of switches. This useful mathematical instrument is Boolean algebra, a formal system that uses only two symbols. Switching circuits that communicate the right kind of binary-coded signals have the capability of solving problems in propositional logic (another name for Boole's algebra), which is the reason computing machines have the capacity to make if-then decisions, as well as to perform calculations. Indeed, the unique power of computation, and of computer languages, comes in part from the way that the decision-making and calculating capabilities are created from combinations of basic Boolean logic components.

Boolean algebra is more than a handy tool for building logic circuits; because of its binary basis, propositional logic is important at a very deep theoretical level. For example, the way in which decimal numerals are converted to binary numerals is an exact translation of the guessing game Claude Shannon suggested as a means of representing the alphabet in the form of a binary code. The point of the game is that numbers, like everything else, can be reduced to a game of 20 questions. In fact, we all play a similar game unconsciously when we read decimal numbers.

In our base 10 numbering system, we understand that each digit of a number, read from right to left, is multiplied by a progressively higher power of 10; reading a number is equivalent to asking questions such as these: "How many 1s are in the first place? How many 10s are in the second place? How many 100s are in the third place? and so on. A binary numbering system multiplies each digit of a number, also read from right to left, by a progressively higher power of 2, which is equivalent to asking these questions: How many 1s are in the first place? How many 2s are in the second place? How many 4s are in the third place? and so on.

Suppose you want to specify the number 58. The encoding algorithm—the set of steps you use to convert 58 to its decimal equivalent—is the good old 20 questions procedure: Start with the rightmost digit of your binary number and ask yourself, Are there any 1s? In this case, the answer is no (58 is even), so the first digit is 0. The next question is, Are there any 2s? The answer is yes, so the second digit of your binary equivalent is 1. The questioning continues with progressively higher powers of 2: Are there any 4s? 8s? 16s? 32s? Finally, we see that 58 is represented in the binary system as 111010 ($32*1 + 16*1 + 8*1 + 4*0 + 2*1 + 1*0$). It takes six binary digits (bits) of information to represent the decimal number 58.

Binary numbers are easily added, subtracted, divided, and multiplied, which comes in handy for the number-crunching parts of computation. But it was the relationship between binary-coded systems and the algebra of logic that made the first electronic computers possible. The man who discovered this connection was the same Claude Shannon who later, in 1948, invented information theory at the age of 33.

In 1937, at 22, Shannon published his famous master's thesis in which he explained his discovery that the formalism best able to describe the behavior of relay and switching circuits was the propositional calculus of symbolic logic. His historic paper on the topic, "A Symbolic Analysis of Relay and Switching Circuits," was published in December 1938.[5] Shannon's hypothesis describes a system that is, in essence, very simple.

Consider an electrical circuit in which a battery sends a stream of electrons through a wire to a light bulb, where the resistance of the wire to the flow of electrons causes the filament to glow and emit light. Now suppose you were to cut one of the wires and install a switch, creating a kind of mechanical gate that regulates the flow of electricity. When the switch is closed, the circuit is intact and electrons flow: The light is on. When the switch is open, the circuit is broken and electrons do not flow: the light is off. Schematically, this type of circuit with one switch would look like Figure 3.3.

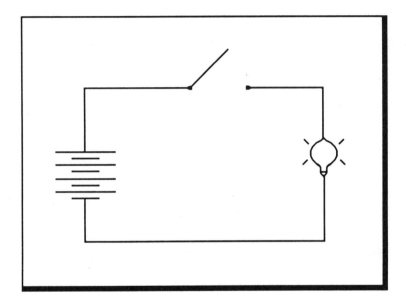

Figure 3.3 Schematic of Circuit with One Switch

Now consider a circuit that is broken by two switches in a row—what electricians call a series circuit. A circuit with two switches in series is schematically shown in Figure 3.4.

The light bulb is bright only when both switches are closed (or on) and is dark when either one of the switches is open (or off). You could say that the light is on only when one switch *and* the other switch are on. With two switches—call them A and B—and two possible states for the switches—call them on and off—you could summarize all the possible states of the circuit in a table as follows:

When Switch A Is	and	Switch B Is	Then Bulb Is
on		on	on
on		off	off
off		on	off
off		off	off

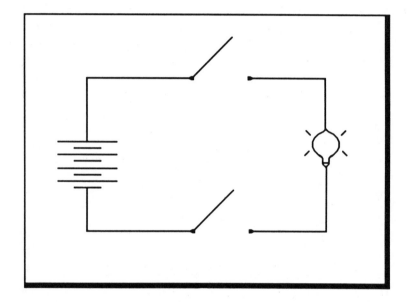

Figure 3.4 Schematic of Circuit with Two Switches in Series

Now consider another kind of circuit with two switches; this time, the switches are wired in parallel, which means that there are actually two alternative paths for electrons to flow between the battery and the bulb. The light bulb will go on when either switch A *or* switch B is on, which means that the bulb is on whenever one switch or the other is off, but not if both are off. Figure 3.5 is a schematic of a circuit with two switches in parallel.

The final, important, primitive circuit contains only one switch between the battery and the bulb; but in this case, the main switch is itself controlled by another switch that we'll call the control switch. When the control switch is on, a small circuit turns the main switch

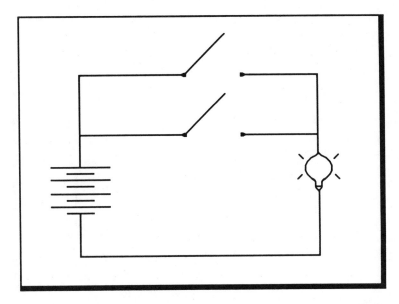

Figure 3.5 Schematic of Circuit with Two Switches in Parallel

off. When the control switch is off, the main switch goes back on. You could describe this kind of circuit, called an inverter circuit, by saying the bulb is on when the control switch is *not* on. It is shown schematically in Figure 3.6.

Claude Shannon found the Boolean connection when he became interested in ways to describe the behavior of relays and switching networks mathematically. A relay is a variation on the inverter circuit in which a small switch controls a main switch. In a relay, the smaller circuit activates an electromagnet that controls a switch for a larger circuit. A switching network is not too different from having several of the simple series and parallel switching circuits described above all connected into a greater entity.

Large collections of relays were objects of study in the 1930s because they were used at that time to automate communication technology. The old-fashioned human-operated switchboards that had controlled the routing of telephone communications were replaced by networks of relays that automatically opened and closed communication pathways. As these collections of switches grew more complex, electrical engineers needed a way to describe and predict the behavior of these circuits systematically.

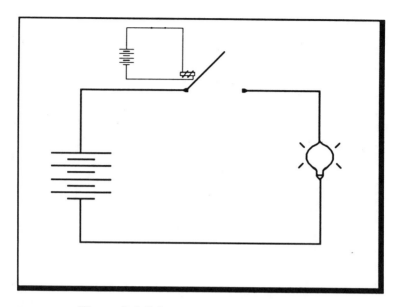

Figure 3.6 Schematic of Inverter Circuit

Shannon noted what you have undoubtedly deduced by now—
that the tables used to describe the different possible states of these
simple circuits are identical to the truth tables George Boole used
as the basis for his algebra of logic. As shown in the following table, it is possible to write sets of statements that would be exactly
equivalent to the behavior of the circuits described above in a
Boolean shorthand, where 0 represents false (or off) and 1 represents true (or on).

NOT [B = −A]   AND [C = (A and B)]   OR [C = (A or B)]

A	B		A	B	C		A	B	C
0	1		1	1	1		1	1	1
1	0		1	0	0		1	0	1
			0	1	0		0	1	1
			0	0	0		0	0	0

The symbols underneath the tables are used to signify the basic logic elements of electronic switching circuits. They are known, appropriately, as *NOT*, *AND*, and *OR* gates. The symbols stand for the abstract operations specified by the truth tables described above. Because of Shannon's discovery, it is possible to use the same symbols to represent simple circuit elements that also behave according to those truth tables. The Boolean formalism made a certain kind of electrical information system equivalent to a certain kind of logical calculus.

The entities described by these symbols—*logic gates*—are the abstractions by which linguistic atoms can be manipulated by machinery. Groups of these logical atoms can be combined to form the most primitive molecules of any computer, that is, *memories*, *adders*, and *control logic*. Just as Boole used combinations of elementary algebraic equations to represent progressively more complex syllogisms, engineers use combinations of logic gates to build higher-level logic structures.

The mysteries of today's solid-state logic are essentially no more complex or mysterious than the simple switches described above; the miraculous powers of integrated circuitry derive from the huge numbers of simple, two-state switches that the wizards of Silicon Valley are able to fit on tiny chips. But their basic components are nothing more complicated than logic gates combined in various ways by directing the output signal of one gate to the input signal of another.

The power of a language is not a direct derivation of the physical tokens that represent its alphabet or the medium that transmits the tokens, just as the power of computation is not a direct function of the electronic impulses or the computer circuit. The code constructed from those grooves on clay, marks on paper, or patterns of electronic switches in a computer, when interpreted by humans, effects no physical change, but it is capable of transmitting information and knowledge.

GATES, REGISTERS, AND ADDERS—TRANSFORMING HARDWARE INTO SOFTWARE

By a complex system I mean one made up of a large number of parts that interact in a nonsimple way. In such systems the whole is more than the sum of its parts, not in an ultimate, metaphysical sense but in the important pragmatic sense that, given the properties of the parts and the laws of their interaction, it is not a trivial matter to infer the properties of the whole. In the face of complexity an in principle reductionist may be at the same time a pragmatic holist.[6]

Boolean logic makes it possible for machines to perform complex tasks by manipulating very simple tokens using very simple rules. Although digital computers are based on Boolean logic and modeled after universal Turing machines, these are theoretical, logical devices, not tangible machines made of metal or silicon. How are the operations of the logical machine translated into physical events in the computer? The most fundamental question to ask about the logical architecture of a computer is, Where are the bits? In other words, How does a computer store information? What kind of "memory" can a machine have? How can sets of switches "remember" information?

In today's computers, each switch has been reduced to a microscopic semiconductive zone on a silicon chip, which responds either to a low-voltage-signal input (designated 0) or a high-voltage-signal input (1) and outputs either a low voltage or a high voltage. Linking switches together so that the output signals of one or more switches furnish input to other switches creates logical pathways. The specific ways in which switches can be linked plays an important role in computer building. As demonstrated in the previous section, it is possible to create electronic AND, NOT, and OR gates by connecting small groups of these microswitches into series and parallel circuits.

We now have all the fundamental elements we need to build a computer: It is possible to create every other logical structure (and from those build every data structure) used by computers starting with only AND, OR, and NOT gates. The computer's ability to do everything from word processing to moon landings is embodied in just these three operations.

Logic gates and pathways can transform input bits into output bits, but they have to be interconnected in a specific way in order to *store* information as well as move it from place to place. In this case, and on every higher level of abstraction, the solution lies in the way elementary structures are combined into higher-level units. The three logic components created thus far can be combined into a simple circuit known as a *flip-flop* circuit, the basic memory element of every computer—the place where bits are kept (see Figure 3.7). This particular combination of gates has the useful property of retaining stored information.

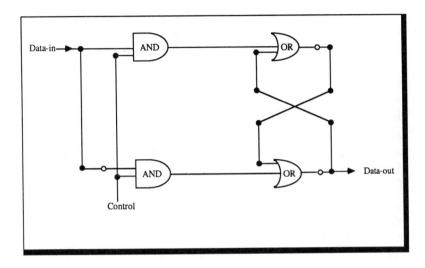

Figure 3.7 Flip-Flop Circuit

Each flip-flop circuit has two inputs, called the *control* and *data-in* inputs, and one output, called *data-out* output. When the control input is turned on (set equal to 1), then data-out is the same as data-in: The circuit simply acts as an open conduit, channeling data-in through to data-out. The real usefulness of flip-flop circuits, however, occurs when the control input is turned off (set equal to 0). When this is done, data-out is prevented from changing, no matter how often the data-in input changes: The circuit now acts as a conduit that is closed to new signals. Until the control input changes again, resetting the circuit, the output will always reflect the last data-in input before the control was set to 0.

The flip-flop circuit, therefore, can store exactly 1 bit of information. You can't do much with a single bit, so information is packaged into a series of progressively larger chunks. The smallest chunk is 8 bits, called a *byte*. A byte contains enough information to represent a single alphabetic character or any number up to 127 (64 + 32 + 16 + 8 + 4 + 2 + 1). After the byte, the next largest chunk of information is a less well-known unit called a *word*. This measure varies from computer to computer—different microprocessors use different word sizes. One flip-flop circuit is needed to store each one of the bits in a word, so a word-size of 16 bits (2 bytes) would require

16 flip-flop circuits. The set of flip-flop circuits used to handle a word-sized chunk of information is called a *register*.

A register is both a high-level hardware component and a low-level software component—a pattern of bits in a particular location. And what those patterns of bits mean is up to a programmer, not a machine. These bits can represent instructions or data; also, whereas the register is a specific configuration of physical switches, the symbolic nature of the bits it contains means that software structures can be built out of registers and their contents. A data structure, such as a sequence of numbers, is a programmer's abstraction, constructed out of the contents of registers. The specific configuration of hardware switches that make up the register is no longer the focus of attention, just as the letters of an alphabet cease to be the focus of attention when a writer combines them into words and orders the words into sentences.

Because they hold information that is used frequently, the registers in the computer's central processor are constructed from the fastest switching technology, which makes them relatively expensive. These fast elements are needed to be stored to control the operations of the computer. In addition, the data the computer operates upon and the programs it uses to transform that data require some kind of memory storage device. The memory components of a computer extend beyond ultrafast processing elements used in the central processor into the realm of larger, slightly slower memory elements—the computer's *RAM* or *main memory* (not to be confused with *mass memory*, such as a tape or disk in which information is stored until needed by main memory).

In the main memory, there are word-sized groupings of flip-flop circuits called *memory-cells*. (These cells are logically equivalent to registers, but they are made from a slower, less expensive hardware technology). At this point, a crucial transition occurs, because memory cells are the highest level of the hardware hierarchy (Figure 3.8) with which we need to be concerned. From now on, all our descriptions of the computer, all the succeeding layers of abstraction, will refer to software structures rather than physical components.

The physical components that make up the memory cells, like the logic gates, are organized as arrays of microscopic components on a silicon chip. Their *logical* organization, however, is what turns the storage cells into a memory device. Each memory cell is identified by a unique number known as its *address*. The address identifies the

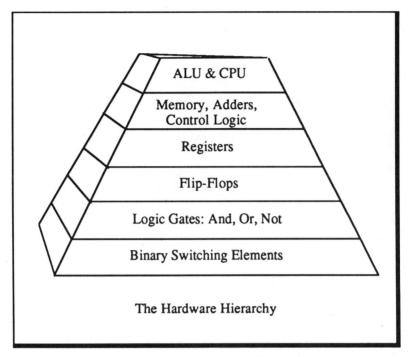

ALU & CPU

Memory, Adders,
Control Logic

Registers

Flip-Flops

Logic Gates: And, Or, Not

Binary Switching Elements

The Hardware Hierarchy

Figure 3.8 The Hardware Hierarchy

location of one word of stored information. In order to store information in the main memory, the memory must be presented with an
address and a word of binary data to store at that address. To retrieve
information, a programmer (or program) submits an address to the
main memory, which will retrieve the word of binary data stored at
that address.

The logical arrangement of memory cells is like a miniaturized
array of mail slots, such as the kind used in old-fashioned post offices. Each mail slot has a unique address. The address of each slot
never changes. There is nothing to prevent several slots from containing identical contents, and there is nothing to prevent the contents of
each slot from changing frequently or not at all.

Our mail slot analogy will be useful again because the idea of
memory as a logical location where information is stored is a good
way to visualize the relationship between a variable and its value.
But we must ascend several levels of the software abstraction hierarchy before we can talk about values and variables. At this point all

we have is a device that can store bits in registers and find them again and is capable of performing AND, OR, and NOT operations.

The hypothetical machine we've constructed is hardly a computer. At this point, it can't even calculate. The next level of abstraction involves building an *adder*, a logical device capable of adding numbers. Once again, we use a truth table to guide the logical design. In this case, a binary addition table can furnish hints about performing arithmetic with logical operations. An addition table, like a multiplication table or a logical truth table, is a system for displaying the results of combinations of elementary operations. An addition table for the decimal number system looks like this:

0 + 0 = 0, carry 0
0 + 1 = 1, carry 0
0 + 2 = 2, carry 0

    .

    .

    .

4 + 5 = 9, carry 0
4 + 6 = 0, carry 1
4 + 7 = 1, carry 1

A binary addition table would look like this:

0 + 0 = 0, carry 0
0 + 1 = 1, carry 0
1 + 0 = 1, carry 0
1 + 1 = 0, carry 1

We can build a simple adding machine by translating the numerical operations into the logical operations of the gates. First, notice that a carry is necessary only when both input digits are 1. Since this is the exact condition in which an AND gate outputs 1, we can use AND gates to compute carrys. Second, notice that the sum of two digits equals 1 only when one digit is 1 and the other is 0. Using the vocabulary of logic gates, we can describe the condition as follows: (first digit AND NOT second digit) OR (second digit AND NOT first digit).

By combining these two operations, we have the computer component known as a *half-adder*, which is a device that can add two input digits and output one sum digit and one carry digit. The half-adder circuit is reproduced schematically in Figure 3.9.

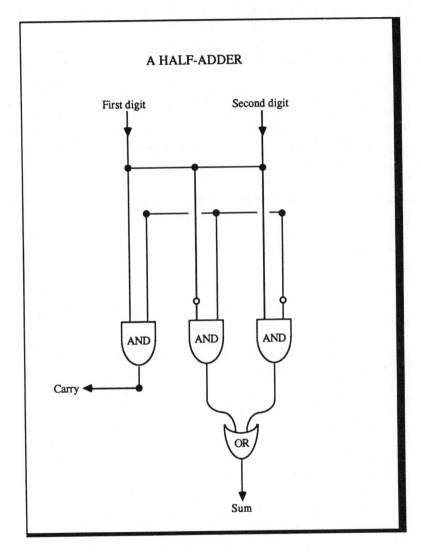

Figure 3.9 Half-Adder

Half-adders are concatenated to create multidigit adders. By other, similar stratagems, it is possible to use gates, registers, and cells to perform all the mathematical operations needed to carry out sophisticated calculations.

Thus far we have constructed a fairly complicated (if hypothetical) arrangement of machines for storing or retrieving information and performing logical or mathematical operations on the information. But these devices are useless if they are unable to communicate with one another in a systematic manner. Before all these operations can be coordinated, information must be channeled into and out of cells and gates. For every bit stored in memory, for every microinstruction that executes a program, electrons must flow (or cease flowing) through a physical channel on a silicon chip. This informational highway, known as a *data bus*, interconnects the essential components of a computer.

Every level of complexity brings with it a new level of challenges. When you interconnect a large number of memory, logic, and arithmetic devices by means of a data bus, you face a monumental traffic problem: Anyone who has ever navigated a car on a freeway knows that collisions are bound to occur when enough vehicles move rapidly through a network of pathways. Thus, two additional components are needed to make sure that the internal messages of computing devices don't crash into one another—a *clock* and *control logic*.

One way to keep millions of bits of data from crashing into one another is to regulate their flow by means of a schedule that is synchronized to regular timing pulses emitted by a computer's clock. Because all programs must be broken into microinstructions that are executed one at a time, the speed of a computer's clock determines how fast that computer can process information. Clock speeds are now measured in millions of instructions per second.

The control logic component uses the clock pulses to synchronize the activities of the computer's components and regulate the flow of data and instructions. We have already seen one example of control logic in the flip-flop circuit, where a control signal is used to store a bit of information and to reset the circuit. Each flip-flop circuit, each adder, and virtually every other fundamental component of the computer has at least one data input and one control input, both of which are regulated by the control logic.

All the arithmetic and logic operations described thus far are performed by subunits of a component known as the *arithmetic and logic unit*, or ALU. The ALU, together with the control logic unit, make up the essential core of every computer known as the *central processing unit*, or CPU.

Besides performing calculations, the ALU can determine whether one number is equal to, less than, or greater than another number and whether one alphabetic character is the same as another. The results of such comparisons can be used by the control logic to determine which instruction to execute next. This built-in ability of computers to change their own course of operations on the basis of comparisons like these is a source of enormous computational power and one of the factors (along with programmability and the ability to store information) that distinguishes a true computer from a mere calculator.

The control unit *fetches* instructions from the main memory, one instruction at a time, according a schedule regulated by clock pulses and then decodes the instructions and sends the proper control signals to the ALU or I/O devices (input/output devices such as keyboard or video screen). Thus, all the operations of the computer are funneled into a two-part cycle: In the first part of the cycle, an instruction is fetched; and in the second part, it is executed. Just as the binary code is the fundamental linguistic unit of all data structures, the fetch-execute cycle is the fundamental unit of all the software operations that are ultimately executed by some computer's CPU.

This rigid template for executing binary-coded instructions one at a time according to clock cycles is the logical blueprint for the way all digital computers operate. The scheme was set forth in the 1940s by the creators of the first computers. In "Preliminary Discussion of the Logical Design of an Electronic Computing Instrument," an historic 1946 report to the U.S. Army (the first and still dominant supporter of computer research), von Neumann and his coauthors stressed that all electronic digital computers should be divided into the five components just described (CPU, main memory, I/O, bus, and secondary memory), that all data and all instructions should be binary coded, that the instructions should be executed serially, according to a clock-regulated fetch-execute cycle, and that both data and instructions should be stored in the main memory.[7] This logical plan is known as the *von Neumann architecture*, after the mathematician John von Neumann, one of ENIAC's creators. The von Neumann architecture is a description of an efficient, electronic version of a universal Turing machine.

The specification that instructions should be stored in the main memory was a great breakthrough into the software age. When the operators of the first electronic digital computer, ENIAC, wanted the machine to do different calculations, they had to reset a plugboard, one

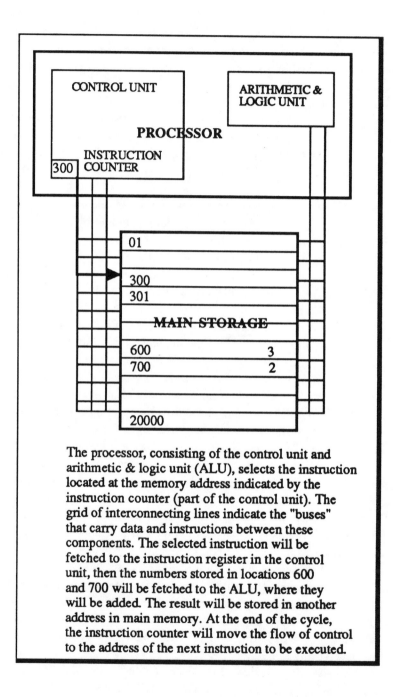

The processor, consisting of the control unit and arithmetic & logic unit (ALU), selects the instruction located at the memory address indicated by the instruction counter (part of the control unit). The grid of interconnecting lines indicate the "buses" that carry data and instructions between these components. The selected instruction will be fetched to the instruction register in the control unit, then the numbers stored in locations 600 and 700 will be fetched to the ALU, where they will be added. The result will be stored in another address in main memory. At the end of the cycle, the instruction counter will move the flow of control to the address of the next instruction to be executed.

Figure 3.10 Diagram of Computer with Five Main Components

switch at a time. Although the first computers could calculate thousands of times faster than humans, the laborious procedure of changing the machine's circuits in order to run different programs severely limited the computer's versatility. The solution to this problem, the *stored program*, made computation not only possible, but practical.[8]

The principle of the stored program enabled the first computer programmers, by changing the bits stored in the computer's memory instead of rearranging its circuitry, to change the function of the software Turing machine that was imitated by the hardware computer. To transform the programming process from that of physically rearranging circuit elements to that of the more efficient process of rearranging the contents of the machine's memory cells, the control system of the arithmetic and logic unit must contain hard-wired circuits that represent the simplest units of instruction in the program. Programmers create their own "words" (high-level commands), "sentences" (subroutines and procedures), and "compositions" (programs); only their "alphabet" (primitive instructions) need be built into the machine itself. This alphabet takes the form of electronically stored truth tables that unambiguously link every elementary software instruction with a unique set of hardware operations.

When the binary switches have been organized into logic gates and gates have been combined into registers, memory cells, and adders, the components have been linked by a bus, regulated by control logic, and synchronized by clock pulses, and the instructions have been stored in main memory along with data, the device has reached the threshold of computation. With the addition of software, the device becomes a computer (see Figure 3.10)—and all the machines we build from now on will be *virtual* machines.

FROM THE FUNDAMENTAL PARTICLES OF MICROCODE TO THE COSMOS OF THE OPERATING SYSTEM

When a computer program is running, it can be viewed on a number of levels. On each level, the description is given in the language of computer science, which makes all the descriptions similar in some ways to each other—yet there are extremely important differences between the views one gets on the different levels. At the lowest level, the description can be so complicated that it is like the dot-description of a television picture. For some purposes, however, this is by far the most important view. At the highest level, the description is greatly *chunked*, and takes on a completely different feel, despite the fact that many of the same concepts appear on the lowest and highest levels. The chunks on the high-level description are like the chess expert's chunks, and like the chunked description of the image on the screen: they summarize in capsule form a number of things which on lower levels are seen as separate.[9]

During World War II, the U.S. Army commissioned the invention of the first electronic digital computer, ENIAC, because human calculators were unable to keep up with the demand for the ballistic calculations artillerymen needed to aim their weapons. Along with every long-range gun that was manufactured, a set of firing tables had to be calculated to help artillerymen aim their weapons. The production of new kinds of artillery meant that more and more people had to work with hand calculators to produce firing tables. If the weapons came along any faster, or became more sophisticated, as they were bound to do, the calculations would overwhelm the people assigned to perform them.[10]

ENIAC worked remarkably well at the task it was designed to do. The most complex ballistic calculations could be accomplished over 1000 times faster than had been possible with the best kind of mechanical calculator. But the mathematicians' amazement with their new tool soon turned into frustration. Nuclear weapons and other postwar technologies were requiring calculations far more complex than ballistics equations. It seemed that just as soon as one advance in high-speed calculation was achieved, a physicist or mathematician would find an even more difficult problem to solve.

The first obstacle to overcome in meeting this demand for ever faster, ever more flexibly programmable computers was the tedious process of rewiring the computer's control system to run different kinds of calculations. The first stored-program computers solved this problem, but the need for faster, more easily programmable computers didn't go away. Indeed, even today the kinds of tasks programmers would like to accomplish still seem to be just slightly beyond the capabilities of the newest computer technology. But after the first stored-program computers started operating, electrical engineers were no longer the only people working on faster, more flexible computers. The programmers began to build their own labor-saving machines—software machines.

Today, programmers work with high-level computer languages that are supported by several levels of these software machines, each one built upon the foundation created by a lower-level machine, from the microcode that controls the flow of bits between registers to the interpreter that allows programmers to work with algorithms instead of registers. The remainder of this chapter ascends from the lowest level of these software machines, at the point at which hardware and software machines meet (microcode), rises through the levels of machine language and assembly language, and goes to the upper levels of compilers, interpreters, and operating systems.

The control systems of the first von Neumann computers (the hard-wired control logic) used combinations of specially connected registers and gates to represent the instructions of the computer's machine language. That is, the way electronic impulses (i.e., bits of data) were routed as they traveled among different registers, counters, and memory cells was determined by the processor's physical circuitry. Every time the ALU of such a computer received an instruction, the control logic supplied the correct control signals during the right clock cycles in order to perform the specified operation upon the specified data. To execute the program specified by the sequence of instructions, logic gates opened and closed along signal pathways, storing, retrieving, adding, multiplying, and comparing inputs in the right order at the right time. The plan governing which gates were supposed to open or shut in order to accomplish each instruction was determined by which hard-wired circuit was activated.

A British computer pioneer, Maurice Wilkes, set out in 1949 to discover a more flexible method than hard-wired control logic. If, as von Neumann et al. demonstrated, it wasn't necessary to hard-wire the programs, Wilkes pointed out that it wasn't necessary to hard-wire the control logic that executed the programs either. He realized that the electrical connections in the control logic component could be represented by data rather than hardware pathways; that is, control instructions could be designated by an address in the computer's memory instead of a circuit. The instructions stored at the specified memory address (the contents of which could be changed, unlike wired-in control circuits, which could not be changed without changing the hardware) would then take over the regulation of control signals.

With microcode, the sequence of pathways a signal must follow in order to accomplish an instruction is controlled by a program stored in the special microcode memory unit built into the processor.

MICROCODE

Wilkes called his scheme *microprogramming*. Each memory address that designates the combination of control signals to be activated during each clock cycle is known as a *microinstruction*. The microinstructions transfer bits between high-speed registers and main memory, between different registers, and between registers and processors such as adders. Combinations of microinstructions are known as *microprograms*.[11]

Substituting software for hardware (coded instructions for actual hard-wired circuits) had two immediate advantages: First, this substitution made it much easier to build the control system and to modify the control system while it was being designed. Second, it meant that the computer's control system could be completely changed at a later date (what engineers call *retrofitting*) simply by altering the contents of the microprogram memory cells. In this way, the same hardware could be "software engineered" to serve many different functions.

Unfortunately, the hardware technology needed to implement Wilkes' ideas (solid-state electronics rather than vacuum tubes) did not become available for about 15 years. Fortunately, engineers at IBM remembered the idea and introduced microprogrammed computers in the 1960s. When microprocessors were developed in the early 1970s, microprogrammed ALUs became the standard way of creating the fundamental language for each new microprocessor.

These modern computers store their microprograms on a single chip's *instruction set* in a special read-only memory (i.e., a section of permanently encoded, nonerasable memory cells) within the CPU. Although the microcode is not hard wired in such systems, the software in read-only systems can't be changed by programmers after the computer leaves the factory. This ambiguous state between virtual machine and physical machine—unalterable software—is called *firmware*. A further advance in substituting software for hardware is the current generation of microprogrammable computers. In these machines, programmers can actually change the machine language by manipulating the microcoded control logic.

Since today's computer manufacturers do not expect their clients to do any microprogramming, all computers are provided with a built-in *machine-language interpreter*, a microprogram that defines the primitive operations of the computer. Each machine-language instruction (which may consist of several microinstructions) is translated by the microcode interpreter (permanently stored in the control logic component) into a pattern of control signals (also a microprogram), which in turn regulates the flow of bits through data paths. The computer defined by the microcoded machine-language interpreter is a Turing machine that supports an increasingly powerful hierarchy of virtual computers, each one created by a lower-level translator program. The machine-language microinterpreter is the bottommost translator program of the software pyramid and the highest level that communicates directly with hardware.

But ordinary computer users and even the most sophisticated programmers use computer languages at least two levels higher than microcode when they communicate with computers. The lowest level any programmer wants to look is the level of machine language—and you have to be a hardcore computer fanatic, even for a programmer, to enjoy staring at strings of 0s and 1s for very long.

MACHINE LANGUAGE

The lowest levels of the hierarchy of abstractions—gates, flip-flops, registers, adders, control logic, microcode—are interpreted solely by the machine. Machine language is the first level at which humans (on rare occasions) are called upon to read and write the code. Machine language instructions in human-readable form are designated by strings of 1s and 0s; the machine-readable equivalent consists of electronic on and off signals in place of 0s and 1s.

Each machine-language instruction specifies an operation to be performed on the contents of a specific cell. The leftmost 4 bits of each machine language instruction, known as the instruction's *operation code*, or *opcode*, identifies the operation to be performed. The rightmost 12 bits specify the address of a cell in main memory, known as the *operand*. This linkage of an operation and an address is reflected, in different ways, all the way up to high-level language programming.

The machine-language LOAD operation (known to the machine by a designation such as 0001) copies a value from an address in the main memory into one of the short-term registers, known as the *accumulator*. The reverse operation, STORE, copies the contents of the accumulator to a main memory cell specified by the rightmost 12 bits, the operand. ADD, SUBTRACT, MULTIPLY, and DIVIDE perform arithmetic operations upon both the value in the accumulator and the contents of the memory cell specified by the operand (e.g., Add the number stored in memory cell X to the value currently stored in the accumulator.)

Machine-language programming involves a herculean amount of loading numbers into the accumulator and storing the contents of the accumulator in memory cells. For example, just to add two numbers, the first number must be loaded into the accumulator, then the second number must be added to the value stored in the accumulator, and the resulting value must be stored in yet another specified memory cell.

The machine-language operations that deal with *transfer of control* bring in the rich world of logical possibilities and make the computer something more powerful than an automatic arithmetician. The JUMP operation causes the host computer to abandon temporarily its built-in pattern of fetching and executing instructions in serial order. JUMP tells the machine language interpreter to jump out of sequence to perform the operation specified by the contents of another memory cell.

JUMPSUB will transfer the control of operations to a subroutine stored in a specified block of memory cells. Every time a program calls for the extraction of a square root, for example, the program can jump to the square root subroutine stored in main memory instead of having to insert all the steps of the square root procedure into the program every time it is needed. RETURN is the machine-language instruction for returning to the previous sequence of instructions after executing a subroutine.

Most machine languages include about a hundred such operations in their instruction set, but an ultrasimplified machine language that used only the operations discussed thus far could accomplish a great many sophisticated computing tasks—and cause a great deal of painstaking labor on the part of any programmer condemned to create programs in raw machine code. To programmers, creating a program of any complexity in machine language is like trying to build Notre Dame from alphabet blocks.

ASSEMBLY LANGUAGE

Because machine-language instructions must specify all the suboperations needed to perform every procedure in precise, step-by-step detail, programmers quickly tire of trying to write their programs in this code. The fact that humans find it difficult to read long strings of 0s and 1s—a perfectly ordinary feat for any computer—makes machine language even more difficult to use as a programming language. For this reason, a more human-readable form of machine language known as *assembly language* is as close as most programmers ever get to the bottom of the software hierarchy.

Every assembly language instruction is equivalent to a specific machine-language instruction, but is easier for programmers to read. A translator program called an *assembler* converts the programmer's assembly language program into machine language. Assembly language is not a high-level language like BASIC because every assembly language is so closely linked to the machine language of a specific processor. For example, when microcomputer enthusiasts speak about assembly language for Apple's Macintosh, they are actually referring to 68000 assembly language, based on the machine code interpreter for Motorola's 68000 microprocessor chip, which serves as the Macintosh's CPU.

Aside from its overall increased readability, the foremost difference between assembly and machine languages is the way memory cells are specified. In machine language, memory cells are specified by their 12-bit address—the operands of machine-language instructions. Assembly language allows the programmer to choose a name for a block of memory cells. To do this, the programmer sets up a temporary instruction table within the program, substituting simple names like A and B for the more cumbersome addresses like 000000000010. This kind of symbolic condensation of complicated instructions into more easily manipulable chunks is an early, low-level case of abstraction building.

The binary opcodes of machine language become the more natural-language-like *mnemonics* of assembly language. An assembly-language version of the machine-language instruction for loading the accumulator would be LDA B instead of 0001000000000001. A short machine-language program for adding two numbers would look something like this:

```
LDA  B
ADD  C
STA  D
```

LDA B copies the value of the memory cell (or block of cells) named B to the accumulator; ADD C adds the value contained in the memory cells named C to the value in the accumulator; and STA D stores the contents of the accumulator in memory location D.

The strength of assembly language is the speed with which the code is executed by the machine. Higher-level languages require more sophisticated and complicated translator programs to transform the programmer's code into the machine's language, which slows down the process of executing programs. Because the assembly-language programmer can write commands that directly control the machine's registers, the machine can execute the program at higher speeds. During the video game craze, the best game programmers wrote in assembly language in order to produce fast-moving, high-resolution graphics.

The assembler that turns a programmer's assembly language into machine-readable code is not considered a higher-level translator like an interpreter or a compiler because the syntax of assembly language is rigidly limited in order to make this translation easier. A higher-level translator must *parse* programs in order to determine how to translate the commands into sequences of machine instructions. An assembler simply substitutes machine code for assembly mnemonics and addresses, with no high-level parsing.

Assembler programs also identify abstract names with specific memory addresses (a process known as *syntactic analysis*) by creating a temporary symbol table in the computer's memory, then entering the names and corresponding memory addresses into the symbol table as they occur in the program. The process of converting assembly language terms into machine code (a procedure known as *lexical analysis*) is also simple: Since each assembly language mnemonic specifies one machine language instruction, a "dictionary" written into the program automatically translates mnemonics into the appropriate machine language instructions.

COMPILERS AND INTERPRETERS

Neither assembly nor machine language is suitable for composing complex algorithms or writing programs that can be executed by more than one kind of machine. When computers were first developed, all programs had to be written in raw machine code, which limited programming to those rare individuals capable of obsessive and meticulous attention to abstract detail. During the 1950s, computer hardware grew much more powerful than it had been when programming was first developed, and it became obvious that programmers had reached the limits of their ability to program computations by means of machine language. The tool set for software engineers was too primitive to make use of the computational power of the new hardware. Some pioneering programmers began to propose the creation of complex programs that could automate some of the lower-level details of programming—a higher-level computer language built from machine language.

The kind of program required to create an interpreter or compiler for a higher-level language was exactly the kind of complex programming task that tested the limits of machine language. Indeed, when the idea of high-level languages was first proposed in the early 1950s, there was debate about whether high-level translator programs could ever create programming code as efficiently as a human programmer.

The creation of high-level languages was a challenge to the talents and vision of the software pioneers. The first *compilers*, or high-level translation programs, were pioneered by the legendary Captain (now Commodore) Grace Hopper on the first UNIVAC, and were taken to a new level by the IBM FORTRAN team led by John Backus.

In order to create a high-level language capable of building powerful abstractions, a compiler for that language must be capable of performing far more difficult syntactic and lexical analysis than that accomplished by assemblers. An equally formidable challenge to the compiler designer is the need for a complex, up-to-date, accurate referencing of the computer's memory resources, an activity known as *memory management.* Each time a stack is created or an address is assigned a name, or a subroutine is called, the proper memory cells must be allocated. The compiler must not only translate high-level commands into machine-executable code, but it must participate in regulating the allocation of the machine's memory resources. (In this task, the compiler works in tandem with another, even more complex program, the machine's operating system.)

Compilers accept as input *source code* from compiled languages such as FORTRAN and COBOL and convert it to *object code* output that closely resembles the machine language or assembly language of the object computer. Programmer-created source code is processed by the compiler; then the entire object-code program is executable by the computer.

Compilers showed that high-level translation programs could dramatically boost programmers' abilities to create complex programs. The bootstrapping that had already begun by using machine-language programs to create a higher-level language was bound to continue. Could other translation programs be possible? If we consider a compiler similar to a person who translates from one language to another by painstakingly looking up words in a dictionary, what about having a program that does what a human interpreter does—perform translations while the conversation is actually going on?

The *interpreter*, the second kind of translator program, made programming languages more accessible to expert and novice programmers alike. Whereas compiled languages cannot run a program until the entire program has been translated into machine language, interpreted commands can be translated as they are submitted, one command at a time, which means the programmer can interact directly with the translator.

Both compilers and interpreters contain mechanisms for communicating *error messages* to the programmer to indicate why a certain program or part of a program is in error. Interpreters must produce an intermediate form of their source code, which must be processed again into machine code before the instruction can be executed. Compiled programs generally execute at greater speed than interpreted programs because they do not require that extra step to get to machine code, whereas interpreted programs are easier to debug because the programmer doesn't have to wait until the entire program is compiled to discover that a single command was incorrect.

OPERATING SYSTEMS

Strictly speaking, translator programs are not the first level directly above machine language, because all translator programs above the microcode level are executed by the virtual machine known as the *operating system*, the computer's master control program. The operating system is a program, implemented in machine language and executed by the microprogrammed virtual computer, that coordinates all the components of the hardware-software system into a programmable computer.

Just as all computers are provided with a built-in machine-language interpreter by the manufacturer, all computers of any degree of complexity are provided with *system software*, either by the hardware manufacturer or by a third-party programmer who works closely with the hardware manufacturer's specifications. The operating system, which might consist of hundreds of thousands of lines of code, takes care of everything from keystrokes to memory management—all the behind-the-scenes processes needed for a human to communicate with a computer and for a computer to execute programs. You might say that an operating system regulates a computer system's operations the way control logic regulates the CPU's operations.

The part of the computer system in which the programmer or user interacts with the computer, known as the *human interface*, consists of a system of messages transported between people and a variety of input devices, output devices, and software. These human-machine communications are coordinated by the operating system, which enables the user to accomplish programming tasks directly without paying attention to the details of hardware operations or the computer's internal informational housekeeping tasks.

On the machine side of the interface, part of the system has to keep track of itself. Memory management, which is only partially addressed by translator programs, is one of the important hidden tasks accomplished by an operating system: A programmer creates variables and other abstractions when composing a program; the operating system keeps track of where those abstractions are stored in the computer's memory, or the details of how they are moved around the registers and memory cells.

The operating system also must provide a method for moving data in and out of main memory to a slower, high-storage capacity form of mass memory device, such as disk drives, on which applications programs are usually stored until needed. The office worker's word processor, the business manager's spreadsheet, and the programmer's interpreter are all stored on a storage medium such as a floppy disk. When someone wants to use one of these tools, part of the operating system loads the program into main memory. Similarly complex informational housekeeping tasks are involved in linking the CPU with a keyboard, video display, or printer.

The levels upon levels of events orchestrated by the operating system to implement even the simplest actions on the part of the computer user are the basis for the statement made at the beginning of this chapter about a single keystroke that can cause 10 million distinct events. The operating system implements the hierarchy of abstractions in order to tame the complexity inherent in such a huge scale of operations. Each successive level of computer language is created out of lower-level elements, using lower-level tools, an example of the procedure known as *bootstrapping* that is used to create leverage against complexity at every level of the software hierarchy.

Bootstrapping takes abstraction a step further by making it self-propagating. The first level of bootstrapping is accomplished by a part of the very small store of read-only memory (ROM) in the CPU, known, appropriately, as a *bootstrap program*. The bootstrap program is the answer to the paradox created by the need for an operating system: If the computer is so complicated that it needs a special program just to oversee its internal operations—including operations for accepting input—then how do you get that special program into the computer in the first place? The bootstrap ROM holds a short machine-language instruction that is automatically triggered when the computer is turned on. The ROM initiates a command to the hardware to read a certain sector of the disk memory into main memory, thus loading a program that loads the entire operating system: The system turns itself on by its own bootstraps.

Once the operating system is loaded and signals to the user that the computer is ready to receive commands, a special "listener" subroutine monitors the input circuits coming from the keyboard and other input devices. The listener program reads each letter from the keyboard buffer; when the user pushes the RETURN key, it loads the disk directory and searches for a program with the same name. If one of the programs listed is a LISP interpreter and the user is a LISP-literate programmer, for example, then the bootstrapping process can be carried a step further by invoking the interpreter program. The programmer will type a name such as LISP.COM; then the operating system will determine whether there is room in main memory to load the interpreter, will transfer the program from disk to main memory, and will signal the programmer when the program is loaded.

Upon seeing the interpreter's ready signal, the programmer can write and execute LISP programs, courtesy of an interpreter loaded on top of an operating system written in machine language that is interpreted by the CPU's microcoded machine-language interpreter that directs the changes of state in Boolean logic gates etched onto a microprocessor chip—a hierarchy of abstractions, most of which are invisible to the person using the computer.

Just as the development of natural language has had a profound effect on natural thought, the evolution of computer language has dramatically increased the capabilities of computer "thought" (that is, the computer's ability to process information, not the artificial intelligence meaning of computer "thought" as a simulation of human higher reasoning processes). As we ascend each level of the hierarchy of abstractions, we discover new uses for the computer; and as we begin to better understand the ways computers manipulate information, we discover methods for improving computer language. Today, computer language and computer thought are as inseparable as natural language and natural thought. How we use that relationship to instruct computers to help us do our work is the topic of the next chapter.

4

Computer Thought—
From Languages to Programs

Data structures and algorithms are the materials out of which programs are constructed. Furthermore, the computer itself consists of nothing other than data structures and algorithms. The built-in data structures are the registers and memory words where binary values are stored; the hard-wired algorithms are the fixed rules, embodied in electronic logic circuits, by which stored data are interpreted as instructions to be executed. Thus at the most fundamental level a computer can work with only one kind of data, namely individual bits, or binary digits, and it can act on the data according to only one set of algorithms, those defined of the instruction set of the central processing unit.[1]

ALGORITHMS: POWER TOOLS
FOR THE MIND

A computer program, according to the above definition, is nothing more than a set of instructions for changing some initial data (input) into different data (output). The input data is presented to the computer by the programmer in the form of abstractions known as *data structures*. The rules for changing input data into output data are presented to the computer by the programmer in the form of abstractions known as *algorithms*. Using programming languages to write programs that contain only these two elements, we can instruct a computer to order an airline ticket, process text, generate a lifelike landscape image, clarify an image of a distant galaxy, or find the largest known prime number.

One clue to the central paradox of how computers can do so much when they appear to do so little is that the computer programmer is really a computer designer. Computer languages enable people to create new machines simply by writing new sets of instructions. Contrast the programmability of a computer with the effort needed to reconstruct an oil boiler to use coal, or try to imagine what it would be like to reengineer a calculator into a typewriter. With a computer, all we need to do to change the machine's function is to write a program.

In this chapter we ascend above the layers of logic gates and microcode to investigate the higher level tools and materials of computer programming—algorithms and data structures—and the thought tools we use to manipulate them. Yet these abstractions are more than elements of computer programs. They are also tools for solving problems. And that is what the entire hierarchy of abstractions is for—to build a lever for extending the power of human thought.

Algorithm is a word that only a few people know, but it is the name for something that everybody uses. An algorithm is a kind of mental machine. Many such mental machines exist, and many more are invented every day, each one suited to a particular task—from extracting a square root to weaving a blanket to cooking soup. An algorithm is really just a refinement, and in many ways a simplification, of a notion we all know well—the process of giving instructions.

As instruction-processing agents, people know both how to recognize instructions and how to act on them. Computers are also instruction-processing agents (in fact, they are little else), but they only recognize completely explicit, totally unambiguous, perfectly communicated instructions that are expressed as strings of 1s and 0s, and they can only carry out instructions that can be implemented by the operations hard wired into the CPU of the machine. These rather restrictive requirements, along with the limits imposed by the theory of computability, mean that computer instructions must take a special form; this form is the algorithm as programmers know it.

Algorithms are distinguished primarily from the larger set of all instructions, recipes, directions, and formulas by a need for precision. Just as any thought that can be expressed in a programming language can be expressed in a natural language but not vice versa, any algorithm that can be expressed in a programming language can be expressed in a natural language, but not all natural language instructions can be expressed in a programming language (i.e., as algorithms). An algorithm is a set of rules that provides a sequence of operations that meet the following four requirements:

1. The algorithm must be comprised of a set of instructions of finite size.
2. There must be an instruction-processing agent that can follow the instructions and carry out the computations.
3. There must be facilities for making, storing, and retrieving steps in the computation.
4. For any given input, computation must proceed in a discrete, stepwise fashion.

Not surprisingly, these four requirements are a perfect match for the capabilities of the modern computer: The first requirement corresponds with the computer's program, the second with the CPU, the third with the computer's memory, and the fourth with the computer's digital design (i.e., the strings of discrete bits, processed in serial order).

A fifth requirement speaks to the type of instructions in the first specification above: They must be unambiguous. Instructions such as turn left at the *large* building and cast on *about* 45 stitches are ambiguous because of the imprecision conveyed by the words "large" and "about." They are adequate instructions for human instruction processors but not for computers, which require algorithms that can only be acted on in one way.

The theory of algorithms is a growing specialty in mathematics, and although it is easy to become bogged down in all the intricacies, the concept of the algorithm in programming can be stated and understood easily: An algorithm is a sequence of instructions that can be executed by a computer; computer programs are a means of representing algorithms in terms that both humans and computers can understand.

Suppose you wanted to teach a child or a computer how to determine if the number 13 was prime (only divisible without a remainder by itself and 1). You don't have to teach your instruction-processing agent about the general concept of prime numbers; you just have to come up with a definable recipe that can be followed to determine, without fail, whether a number is prime. How would you go about it?

The simplest, although not the most efficient, method would be to divide 13 by 2, then by 3, and keep increasing the divisor by 1 until you reached 13. If you find a number that divides 13 exactly, you know it is not prime; otherwise it is. Given this method, your instructions should look like something like this five-step algorithm:

1. Let N = 2.
2. If N = 13, print "13 is Prime" and stop.
3. Divide 13 by N.
4. If the answer is an integer, print "13 is not Prime" and stop.
5. If the answer is not an integer, increase N by 1 and go back to instruction 2.

Compare these instructions with the five criteria for algorithms to see if they meet them. Of course, even though they do, a computer couldn't operate on them. They must first be written in a programming language such as in the BASIC and Logo examples that follow:

BASIC

```
10 N = 2
20 IF N = 13 THEN PRINT "13 IS PRIME": GOTO 60
30 X = 13/N
40 IF X = INT(X) THEN PRINT "13 IS NOT PRIME":
   GOTO 60
50 IF X <> INT(X) THEN N=N+1: GOTO 20
60 STOP
```

Logo

```
to prime
  if :n = 13 [(pr "13\ is\ prime) stop]
  make "x 13/:n
  if :x = int(:x) [(pr "13\ is\ not\ prime) stop]
  if not (:x = int (:x)) [make "n :n + 1]
  prime
end
make "n 2
```

These programs, especially the second one, might look alien. Don't worry about having a complete grasp of the syntax of these languages; just see if you can find some of the ways that the parts of the natural language algorithm have been translated into parts of the programming language algorithms.

As we continue the discussion of algorithms, keep two points in mind: First, although our example deals with a mathematical problem, it is possible to construct algorithms for everything from making coffee to diapering babies. Of course, algorithms for computer use will usually involve only the manipulation of information, not the manipulation of physical objects (i.e., a coffee pot or a baby's bottom).

Second, the algorithm itself is independent of the language (natural or programming) that is used to express it. This means that we already have lots of real-world experience with the subtleties of designing algorithms that work. We only have to recognize this existing knowledge in order to be in a position to apply it to computer applications. The program design techniques discussed in the following section are the tools that allow us to construct algorithms for the wide array of problems that are now solvable by computer.[2]

SEQUENCE, SELECTION, AND ITERATION: DESIGN TOOLS FOR ALGORITHMS

The idea of control flowing or changing its locus did not become commonplace until the advent of computers. Here, the sequencing of instructions makes the notion of flow of control natural, and branch instructions make it equally natural to think of passing or sending control to some other place. When control-passing is combined with a...reminder of where the control came from, so that it can be returned later, *subroutines* are born. And since subroutines can be nested—that is, they can themselves send control to still lower subroutines, and so on, with the assurance that it will eventually find its way back—the notion of a *hierarchy* of control also emerges.[3]

Because every algorithm is a precisely ordered series of unambiguous instructions, a crucial factor to keep in mind when designing an algorithm is the order in which those instructions are to be processed. The most simple algorithms (called *sequential algorithms*) are just sequences of instructions that have the following four properties:

1. The steps are executed one at a time.
2. Each step is executed exactly once; there are no omissions or repetitions.
3. The order of execution is identical to the order to presentation.
4. Termination of the last step terminates the algorithm.

Clearly, the algorithm to determine if 13 is prime is not a sequential algorithm since it violates stipulations 2 and 3 above. Sequential algorithms are extremely inflexible because the order of execution is fixed and cannot be modified by circumstance. They are also extremely inefficient because every action must be explicitly stated; if a step is to be repeated five times, the instruction must be written five times. Programmers, who prefer abstractions like RE-PEAT FIVE TIMES, will not find much use for purely sequential algorithms. Humans, however, often use sequential instructions in tasks such as giving traffic directions, as in the following example:

1. Drive across Memorial Bridge.
2. Exit at Main Street.
3. Turn left at first stop light.
4. Go past three stop lights.
5. Turn left at fourth stop light.
6. Park in front of 100 Elm Street.

Yet, even for information processors with human skills, such an inflexible, sequential algorithm may prove difficult to follow. What happens if there are no vacant parking spaces in front of 100 Elm Street or if the Main Street exit is detoured? In order to handle contingencies, that is, to be able to direct the instruction flow based on circumstance, many algorithms include a type of step known as *selection*.

Selection is the fundamental method for diverting the flow of instructions from the constraints of sequential processing. It usually takes the form of an if-then construction:

If a stated condition applies,
    then proceed to step x,
    else proceed to step y. (The else clause is optional.)

The if-then construction can be used to build algorithms out of options between two alternatives. Many recipes conclude with a line such as "Bake for 1 hour in a 350 degree oven or until the top browns." In algorithm form, this instruction is telling us:

If the bread top is brown,
    then take it out of the oven,
    else continue baking at 350 degrees for the remainder of the hour.

In the traffic direction example, we might amend the last line so that the directions still work even if there is no parking at 100 Elm:

If there is parking at 100 Elm Street,
    then park there,
        else park at the nearest legal location.

Although simple selection only allows us to choose between two options (the then and else clauses), we can nest if-then clauses within if-then clauses to obtain as many decision points as we feel our algorithm needs. For example, our recipe example might be amended to account for the possibility that the bread top is still not brown but the bread has baked for 1 hour:

If the bread top is brown,
    then take it out of the oven,
        else if the bread has baked for 1 hour,
            then brush with butter
            and bake 5 minutes more.

Even though selection allows us to alter the flow of instructions, it does so only at a given point. After the if-then clause, instructions are again processed in sequence. In order to maintain a permanent diverting of instruction flow, it is also important to treat if-then clauses as switches that can direct the instruction flow onto a whole new track. For example, if we wanted to account for the possibility of the Main Street exit being closed in our traffic direction example, we would give directions that branched from exit at Main Street.

Such uses of selection are referred to as *branching of the instruction tree*. The if-then clause is a decision node that determines which branch of the tree the information processor is to follow. The computer, like the bug on the tree or the illiterate pedestrian in our discussion of binary codes, is the instruction-following agent that executes the series of binary decisions needed to arrive at the destination specified by the programmer.

In programming languages such as BASIC and FORTRAN, branches usually begin with GOTO or GOSUB statements (e.g., 20 IF N = 13 THEN PRINT "13 IS PRIME": GOTO 60). Today, the use of GOTO and GOSUB is discouraged since programs using these instructions are often difficult to understand, especially when they are large, complex programs. Newer languages such as Pascal and Logo use a more structured approach in relating program modules; the particulars of such structured programming are explored later in this and subsequent chapters.

Neither sequential nor selective algorithms really take advantage of the computer's major strength—high speed, error-free computation. In order to do this, as well as meet the instructional needs for an infinite variety of human tasks, we need to add a third type of algorithmic instruction—*repetition* or *iteration*. Algorithms with this type of instruction allow us to repeat certain steps an arbitrary number of times. Continuing our bread-baking example, a typical cookbook instruction might read, Knead bread until the dough is smooth and elastic. Putting this type of locution into an algorithmic instruction sequence yields the standard iteration construction:

> Repeat:
> >   knead
> until dough is smooth and elastic.

An occurrence of iteration in an algorithm is called a *loop*, and the part of the algorithm that is repeated (e.g., the kneading) is the *loop body*. The until clause is called the *terminating condition*; it specifies when the repeating will stop.

Iteration is extremely powerful because it allows a process of indeterminate duration to be described by an algorithm of finite length. Imagine how long recipes would have to be if each kneading stroke had to be specified. This power is obtained at a cost, since special attention must be paid to the terminating condition or it is possible to find yourself in an infinite loop. Pity the poor algorithmic baker who puts too much water in the dough, thereby creating a situation in which no amount of kneading will lead to a smooth, elastic dough.

One way out of this bind is to use *definite*, or *counted*, iteration. In such constructions, the number of repetitions is defined before the loop body so that we are always certain that termination will occur. Such instances of definite iteration take the form

> Repeat N times:
> >   Body of loop.

Cookbooks often prefer to give instructions in the form of definite iteration (e.g., knead vigorously for 50 strokes), and it is easy to see how this would look as an algorithm:

Repeat 50 times:
    knead vigorously.

Of course, *indefinite*, or *conditional* loops (i.e., those that terminate upon fulfillment of a condition) are much more powerful, and it is quite easy to see that conditional loops can always do the work of counted loops but not vice versa.

A final, important distinction in iteration regards the positioning of the termination condition. The repeat-until construction is a *posttested* loop because the until clause comes after the body of the loop. This means that the loop must always be executed at least once. Such loops are often called "fools rush in" loops because this construction can lead to the following type of problem: Suppose you wanted to construct an all-purpose mixing algorithm; that is, a little instruction you could put into the beginning of a cookbook that would instruct your readers how to go about mixing any list of ingredients. You might try this:

Put first ingredient into bowl.
Repeat:
    put next ingredient into bowl and mix
    until all ingredients are in bowl.

The problem is that this algorithm "crashes" when there is only one ingredient. The information processor gets to the loop body and looks for the next ingredient, but there isn't one. Therefore, the execution grinds to a halt. Of course, the termination clause is supposed to prevent this, but in cases in which the loop should never be entered, posttested termination conditions fail.

The solution is a *pretested* termination condition that has the general form

While condition is true, do:
    body of loop.

Using this construction, the mixing algorithm becomes the following:

Put first ingredient in bowl.
While there are still ingredients outside the bowl do:
    put next ingredient in bowl and mix.

Pretested loops are called "look before you leap" loops because they first test to see if the loop should be entered. In practice, both loops can be applied to the a wide variety of tasks, and most programming languages have control words that allow both types of construction.

Another important concept in the design of algorithms is illustrated by the difference between the BASIC and Logo programs presented earlier in this chapter. They are quite similar structurally, except that the BASIC program relies on GOTO statements to recycle through the program, whereas the Logo program repeats the name of the procedure (program)—prime, in our example—just before the end of it. Any algorithm that calls itself, that is, uses its own name within the procedure, is *recursive*. This means that the Logo algorithm proceeds sequentially, and if none of its stop conditions obtain, it reaches the word "prime" and starts all over again. Because recursive procedures are bookended by their name, they are sometimes referred to as a "snake swallowing its tail."

Suppose you had to build an algorithm for the number countdown of a space launch. Using iteration, the algorithm might look like this:

1. N = 10.
2. Repeat:
     Announce N, then N - 1
Until N = 0.

Using recursion, the algorithm would look like this:

N = 10
To Countdown N:
    If N = 0 Stop.
    Announce N.
    Countdown N-1.
End.

Recursive procedures, like unlimited iteration, can get trapped in an infinite loop unless they are carefully constructed. Therefore, it is important to make sure that a terminating condition is included. It is also true that anything that can be accomplished with iteration can be accomplished with recursion and vice versa. The programmer's choice of iteration or recursion is really a matter of convenience and efficiency in each particular case, not a matter of the technique's inherent limits.

Recursion is especially helpful in processing lists and text. For example, an algorithm to reverse the order of a character string is simply

```
To reverse string:
        If only one letter is in string,
                then output it;
                else output the last character in string.
        Reverse string.
End.
```

This would reverse the word LISP in the following way:

```
LISP LIS LI L
            P PS PSI PSIL
```

Think about how much more complicated the algorithm would have to be using iteration. Older languages like BASIC, FORTRAN, and COBOL are not recursive (e.g., they do not support the use of recursive procedures); languages such as LISP, Logo, FORTH, and Pascal are recursive.

An advantage of recursive programming is that the structure of the program mimics one of the most powerful thought tools humans use to solve problems—breaking them down into smaller, similar problems. LISP was specifically designed to take advantage of this ability to mimic human reasoning processes, since its purpose was to facilitate artificial intelligence research.

Quite remarkably, mathematicians have proven that if it is possible to construct an algorithm for describing a particular process, then that algorithm can be designed using only sequence, selection, and iteration. In the next section, we'll explore the reasons why these three constructs are so powerful and try to find the limits of algorithmic problem solving.[4]

COMPUTABILITY, COMPLEXITY, AND CORRECTNESS: ADEQUACY CONDITIONS FOR ALGORITHMS

Can a Turing machine do *anything* useful? Several example programs might be given to convince you that it can at least be programmed to do some simple things like addition and subtraction. However, the argument that we really wish to make is a lot stronger: a Turing machine can do *everything* useful (in the realm of computations)! That is, we would like to show that every computation can be expressed as a program for a Turing machine, and thus the language used for programming a Turing machine is a universal language . . . .

The formal statement of this idea is known as *Church's thesis* (after the mathematician A. Church): any computable function can be computed by a Turing machine.[5]

Because the instruction processor we call the computer only responds to one type of instructions—algorithms—it is important to know just how adequate algorithms are for giving problem-solving instructions. In particular, we need to know the answers to three questions:

1. Is there any problem a computer could not solve because no algorithm could possibly exist describing the instruction set to solve it?
2. Even if an algorithm exists, are there any problems a computer could not solve because it would require an infeasible amount of computer resources?
3. Finally, how can we ever be sure that a particular algorithm really provides the instructions to solve the problem we designed it for?

In the world of the mathematician, the first question concerns *computability*, the second *complexity*, and the third *correctness*. Computability has at least a 2000-year-old history, and its genesis is based on a simple, common-sensical notion: If we can adequately specify a problem, then we should be able to produce an algorithm to solve it, or at least provide a proof that no such algorithm could exist. Yet, the shocking and surprising work of Kurt Gödel and Alan Turing demonstrated that, no matter how common-sensical it might seem, this idea was false: There are problems for which no algorithmic solutions exist.

In the 15 years that preceded the advent of the modern computer, mathematicians turned their efforts toward determining just how far-ranging these noncomputable problems were. Some of their most interesting results include the following:

- All reasonable definitions of the algorithm concept are equivalent (the Church-Turing thesis). This idea is important because it means that we can never expect to prove a proposition such as Gödel's "G" simply by changing what we mean by algorithm.
- Any algorithm that can be implemented on one computer can be implemented on any other computer, and any program that can be written in one programming language can be written in any other programming language. This is called the *universality of algorithms*, and it means that, theoretically at least, all computers and programming languages are equivalent, that is, they can all perform the same tasks.
- There is a large class of noncomputable problems. Among these are determining whether an arbitrary program will enter into an infinite loop or whether it will stop (the halting problem), whether two programs will actually perform the same tasks (the equivalence problem), and whether an arbitrary program performs a given task as specified by a given algorithm (Rice's theorem).

The results regarding noncomputability must be put into proper context. We know that computers perform many useful tasks, so it is clear that there are thousands, millions—an unpredictably large number of problems—that admit of algorithmic solution. And even though there is no algorithm that solves the halting problem in every case, some individual cases of the halting problem are easy to solve (e.g., we know that the program to determine if 13 is prime will stop). Noncomputability is a spur to the programmer, as well as a constraint upon programs, because the existence of noncomputable problems highlights the need for creative problem-solving strategies—the kind that human minds are still best at providing.[6]

If the study of computability is of theoretical interest (remember, most of its major findings about the limits of computation were discovered before the advent of computers), the study of complexity (with most of the results coming in the last 15 years) is of practical interest. Complexity theorists ask a simple question: Given that a problem is computable, that an algorithm exists, is it a feasible problem to solve? Then, they proceed to produce the most mindboggling, complex equations in order to attempt to solve it. Yet, like Gödel's insight, complexity theory is not itself so complex that you need anything beyond elementary school mathematics to understand its conceptual foundation.

In the computer world, resources are measured in how long it will take a computer to solve a given problem (e.g., The computer can determine if 13 is prime in a very short period, but what if we want to determine if $2^{10657} - 1$ is prime?) and memory (i.e., How much storage space is required by the algorithm and the need to save intermediary calculations?). Furthermore, these two resources must interact with the actual instructions and data that are input to solve a particular problem, so the feasibility of a problem is dependent on the size of that input as well as the resources needed.

The key result in complexity theory is this: The execution time of some algorithms grows exponentially (e.g., it grows according to the formula 2^N), whereas the execution time of other algorithms is polynomial (e.g., it grows according to the formula N^2). Exponential algorithms are infeasible for all but the smallest data sets because their run time rapidly exceeds the possible limits of any possible computer (e.g., an exponential algorithm that solves a problem in 2^N microseconds would take 10^{14} centuries for an input of merely 100). Polynomial algorithms tend to be feasible (e.g., an algorithm that solves a problem in N^2 microseconds would take .01 seconds for an input of 100 and only 1.7 seconds for an input of 10,000).

Once such a distinction is made, it becomes important to develop a test to determine which algorithms are exponential and which are polynomial. Unfortunately, no such test exists. Like the law, complexity theory is developed on a case basis. An example of a known exponential algorithm involves trying to determine the winning strategy in chess. It is sometimes said that a computer could be unbeatable in chess simply by programming it to follow the consequences for each piece of every possible move and then choose the best move. The first person to note that such a strategy grows exponentially, and soon becomes infeasible by even the fastest computers, was Claude Shannon, the same man who created information theory and discovered the connection between Boolean logic and switching networks.[7] Computers play very good chess because computer programmers have developed algorithms that do not rely on this infeasible approach. (The best known polynomial algorithms are the ones we use every day for addition, multiplication, subtraction, and division.)

The young theory of complexity also has a large pool of problems in limbo—problems for which no one has found a polynomial algorithm but also for which no one has proven that such an algorithm doesn't exist. Two of the most practical are the traveling salesman problem and the timetable problem. The former problem asks this question: Given a road map of N cities, is it possible for a salesperson to complete a round trip within a specified minimum time, visiting each city only once? The latter problem asks this: Given a list of subjects, the students enrolled in them, and the time slots available, is it possible to produce a list of schedules so that no student has a clash?

Of course, traveling salespeople and school registrars solve these kinds of problems every day, but we have to be careful about what we mean by "solve." Mathematicians are seeking a general solution, one that will always work no matter how large the route or number of students.

Individual salespeople and registrars need only worry about solving a specific problem of determinate size. Even though complexity theory seems to indicate that certain problems are infeasible, one of its most practical results has been to find polynomial algorithms that can approximately solve a given problem (e.g., schedule classes with so few clashes that they can be handled individually, or schedule a reasonably short trip or one that only needs a one city backtrack). There are also probabilistic algorithms that yield results within a specified tolerance for error (e.g., we may be able to guess if $2^{10657} - 1$ is prime quickly, but the output may have a 1 in 1 million chance of being incorrect).[8]

Ultimately, complexity theory is important because it reminds us that computers, no less than human instruction processors, also have real-world limits. Although they are capable of extremely fast, error-free computation, it does not mean that we can solve all computable problems simply by creating an algorithm and letting a computer grind away. Creative problem solving will always be needed.

For the most part, issues of computability and complexity will not concern people sitting in front of their home computers trying to write programs that will help compute taxes or run a statistical test on a collection of experimental data. What will concern them, as well as most professional programmers, is the question of correctness: How can one be certain that a program will perform the task for which it was designed? In order to answer this question, programmers usually rely on a testing process: First the program is run with some sample data input; then, if the results are consistently correct for a substantial number of test cases, the program is pronounced correct.

This testing procedure, however, really only determines that the program is correct for the domain of the test data. It is no guarantee that the program is error free for all possible data sets. In order to provide such a guarantee, the programmer must produce a proof that the algorithm actually solves the specified problem. (Once again, we see a tension between the two major modes of knowing—Bacon's empiricism and Descartes' formal approach.)

Because such proofs are usually more difficult to produce than the program, programs are generally tested and not proved. As a result, most programs have *bugs*, those annoying errors that crop up when they are least expected. This does not mean that tested programs are not useful; it only means that we can never be 100 percent certain that a tested program will work when presented with some never-before-seen data as input. And the probability of error increases with the complexity of the program, the amount of data, and the speed with which it is processed, which means that it is not yet possible to prove that the most complex programs (such as those that command and control the world's nuclear armament systems, for example) are bug free.

What then should we conclude about the adequacy of algorithms? Are they sufficiently flexible to allow us to use computers to solve a wide range of problems? Only someone who's been hiding in a cave since World War II could possibly answer no. In the past 40 years, computers have revolutionized every aspect of our lives, from business and communications to medicine and education. Yet, as Figure 4.1 illustrates, algorithms and computers can't even help us solve half of the problems we can dream up.

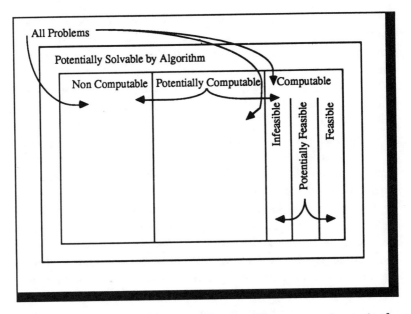

Figure 4.1 The arrows indicate that problems may migrate in the direction the arrow is pointing.

In particular, as mathematicians continue to work with these as yet unsolved problems, the potentially computable and potentially feasible categories should continue to shrink. Likewise, as work proceeds in artificial intelligence, the number of problems potentially solvable by algorithm should grow. Is the glass half-empty or half-full? Happily, in the case of the universe of problems, the glass is so large that, even though it is only half-full, we're going to need a long time to empty it.

INFORMATION IN SPACE: THE DATA STRUCTURE CONCEPT

A data structure is an essentially spatial concept; it can be reduced to a map of how information is organized in the computer's memory.[9]

Viewing the computer as an instruction processor helped us understand the role of algorithms in computer programs: They are the program's control structure; they tell the computer what to do and when to do it. But computers also process other types of information, and the most general description of a computer is as an information processor. In particular, the data in a computer program are what it processes, and *data structures*—groups of aggregated data—are the means to ensure the efficient transformation of that raw material into a finished product (more data in a new form). Data structures are simply data that have been organized to reflect the logical relationships between the individual elements.

Just as we use algorithms every day without recognizing them as such, as information processors we have been using data structures since long before the advent of computers. In fact, language itself would be impossible without such an idea. As an example of what might be called unstructured data, think about what it would be like if you wrote all the phone numbers in your personal directory on small slips of paper and threw them in a shoe box in random order, then wrote all the names in your personal directory on different pieces of paper and threw them in, as well. You would have stored all the data you would need to find out how to make a call to everyone in your directory, but the form in which you stored the data prevents you from retrieving it efficiently.

The solution is to structure the data for efficient retrieval by writing the name, telephone number, address, and other relevant information pertaining to each person on the same piece of paper. And that is the same data structure (known as a *record*) that a computer programmer might use to represent a telephone directory in a data base program.

In written natural language, alphabet letters are individual bits of data, and it is only by recognizing the data structure known as a *sequence*—a set of items that is ordered such that every item except one (the last) has a successor and every item except one (the first) has a predecessor—that we can string letters together to form words. Likewise, sentences are simply sequences whose individual data elements are words, and numbers are sequences whose data elements are digits.

The ideal computer program is one in which algorithm and data structure are perfectly matched in order to enhance efficient processing. In the case of sequences, which are especially useful when we need to process one datum after another, the general algorithm form might look like this:

Start at the beginning of the sequence.
    While end of sequence not reached do:
        process next item.

We've already seen how such an algorithm is used in our mixing ingredients example. Of course, not all applications call for a sequential data structure. For example, how would you represent a hierarchical grouping of data? One of the major problems for computer theorists has been to design programming languages that incorporate all the data structures needed for efficient operation.

Data structures are the Janus-like objects of computer programs. Unlike algorithms, which require complete specification by the programmer, data structures are only partially specified by the programmer. When the program is actually being executed by the computer (a phase known as *run time*), the programming language virtual computer may define new, intermediate data structures. In this way, data structures face both outward toward the programmer and inward toward the machine.

Data structures are aggregates of individual data elements, specified by four criteria:

1. *Number of components*: A data structure is of *fixed* size if its number of components remain invariant during its program lifetime. In this way, it is analogous to a constant whose value is also invariant. Examples of fixed-size data structures are the number of months in a year and the number of digits in your Social Security number. A data structure is of *variable* size if the number of its components can change during its program lifetime. This is analogous to a variable whose value can change. Examples of variable-sized data structures are the appointments in your monthly calendar and the number of people on the Social Security rolls.

   Fixed-size data structures are sometimes referred to as basic, *static* data structures while variable-sized data structures are referred to as derived, *dynamic* data structures.

2. *Component types*: A data structure is *homogeneous* if all its components are the same data type (e.g., months in a year,

digits in a Social Security number). A data structure is *hetero-geneous* if its components are of different types (e.g., different notations in a monthly calendar, different types of information on a Social Security card). When a data structure is heteroge-neous, it is often referred to as a *record* and the individual com-ponents as *fields*.

3. *Selection operator*: Aggregating individual data components into a data structure would be a meaningless exercise if there were no method for the orderly retrieval of the individual compo-nents. This retrieval is generally accomplished by a *selection operator*, that is, a specific way of naming and recalling the elements of the structure. For example, we frequently just list and number the elements of a data structure and retrieve them by the number corresponding to their place in the list (e.g., number the months 1 through 12 and retrieve September by calling number 9). More complex selection operators include subscripts (e.g., referring to a square on a chess board as E_4, meaning the intersection of column E and row 4). In this way, the 64 elements in the chess board data structure can be se-lected (e.g., C_{A1} through C_{H8}). It is also possible to select ele-ments by location (e.g., the topmost members of a family tree are the patriarch and matriarch) or by position (e.g., the first item in a list).

4. *Component organization*: The essence of a data structure is the method used to organize its individual elements. Of course, in the computer the data are just electrical blips on a flat chip. But it is helpful to conceptualize how data are stored by the use of metaphor and example. Some of the most common static data structures are the following:

a. *Array*—a sequence of fixed length in which each item is identified by its position. An example is a list of finishers in a race or items in a menu. Arrays are particularly useful when each individual data element needs its own address.

b. *Matrix*—a two-dimensional array composed of columns and rows in which each data element is identified by a two-number index [e.g., A (2,4), which means the element in data structure A whose address is the cell at the intersection of row 2 column 4]. One example of a matrix structure is the aforementioned chess notation. Matrices are valuable any time the data to be represented are in tabular form.

c. *Set*—a data structure containing an unordered collection of distinct components. Sets are useful when we're interested in the property of membership: Is Jones on the Social Security rolls? The program will output *true* if the element named Jones belongs to the set of Social Security recipients and *false* if it does not.

Some of the most important dynamic data structures are the following:

d. *Queue*—a sequence of variable length in which items are always added at one end and removed from the other end. Dynamically speaking, this means that data objects are removed in the same order in which they are added. For readers with a business background, you can think of a queue as the FIFO (first-in first-out) data structure. For everyone else, just think of getting in line at the bank. Queues are important when you want to handle data in the order in which they arrived.

e. *Stack*—a sequence of variable length in which items are added and removed at only one end of the sequence. Dynamically, this means that data elements are removed in the reverse order from which they are added. For readers with business training, this is the LIFO (last-in first-out) data structure. For everyone else, just think about driving your car into a long narrow lot with only one exit. When it comes times to leave, you'll have to wait for all the cars who entered after you to exit first. Another metaphor used to describe this data structure is that of a stack of cafeteria trays. Stacks play a crucial role in machine-language operations, as well as in the high-level programming language FORTH.

f. *List*—a linear data structure with a variable number of components of possibly different types (including other lists). Because lists may change in size as the result of insertions and deletions, individual elements cannot be easily specified simply by numbering them as in an array. Instead, selection is based on the relative position of a component in the list (e.g., first, third, next, last). Examples of lists include everything from your list of things to do today to the alphabetizing of a new dictionary. Lists are especially important in the LISP (an acronym for LISt Processing) and Logo programming languages.

g. *Trees*—a hierarchical data structure that is used to represent the logical relationships between different elements of the structure. In Chapter 1, we used a tree structure to depict the relationship between parts of a sentence; they reappeared in Chapter 3 as the key to understanding the binary code. In computer data structures, the same rules and terminology apply: The tree is composed of nodes (branching points) and branches (data addresses). The top of the tree is the root, and the lowest extremities are the leaves. All of the data on any one level are logically equivalent and are all logically subordinate to the data on the upper nodes.

One notable fact about trees is that every node in the tree is itself the root of a smaller tree. This means that a tree may be defined recursively as a node plus a set of (possibly

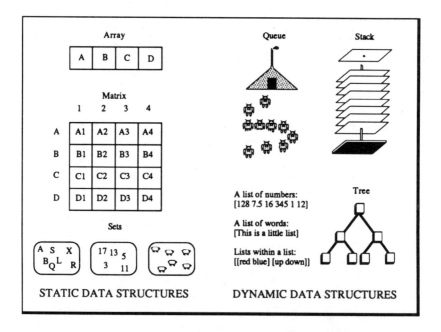

Figure 4.2 Schematic Representations of Data Structures

empty) branches, each leading to a tree. Because of this recursive property, trees are very useful data structures when dealing with recursive algorithms. Of course, we see them every day as company organization charts and process flow charts.[10]

Figure 4.2 shows a schematic representation of the static and dynamic structures we have described.

THE GRAND SYNTHESIS: ALGORITHMS + DATA STRUCTURES = PROGRAMS

The computer encourages a kind of playful trial and error, a manipulation of electronic possibilities, so that it becomes almost irresistible to view programming as the ultimate sort of game. It is after all Turing's game, governed by the rules of finite automata and the limitations of the electronic components. The programmer makes up further rules as he works, rules that define the permissible data structures and the manipulation of those structures. Each program is a game-within-a-game. Like a player moving pawns on a chessboard, the programmer maintains absolute, and therefore almost disinterested, control over his electronic resources.[11]

Just as all programming languages are essentially equivalent, it is also true that whatever can be done with one data structure can be done with another. In fact, it is usually possible to use one type of data structure to simulate another (e.g., Logo, which uses lists, can simulate an array by using a simple program to refer to the elements in the list by number rather than position). The issue is always convenience and efficiency rather than the absolute power of a given structure. In fact, as you'll see in the next chapter, most computer languages only support a few of the data structures directly; the rest are programmer-created abstractions.

By choosing data structures and algorithms appropriate to the problem, each programmer sets up a hierarchy of abstractions for each program. Indeed, the choice of data structure can strongly influence the choice of algorithm. The programs that we used to demonstrate the idea of an algorithm were so simple that the notion of a data structure was never needed. The following real-life examples of computer programs illustrate how algorithms and data structures are used in relation to one another to form programs.

Anyone who has ever had to alphabetize a long list of names understands the nature of drudgery—any task requiring the same mindless operation to be repeated *ad nauseum*. Fortunately for the sanity of human alphabetizers and the efficiency of companies such as banks and utilities that require the sorting of huge lists of data, alphabetizing is exactly the type of task at which computers excel. Simply provide the list of names and an alphabetizing program, press the button, and come back after a brief interval to find the list in order. Aside from an inhuman speed and resistance to error, computers alphabetize in much the same way as a human might.

There is, however, one significant difference. Numbers and letters are treated identically by a computer because all characters are translated into their ASCII code equivalent, which is a number. Alphabetizing for a computer is really the same as putting a list of numbers in ascending order (i.e., a computer would put A before B because the code for A is 65 and the code for B is 66). This is yet another reason why computers are so flexible: They need only handle numerical operations, but the software, through a process of translation, makes it appear as if they can do many different things (e.g., alphabetize).

Suppose you were asked to provide an algorithm that would sort a group of numbers into ascending order. The algorithm might look like this (this is probably the least efficient, but easiest to understand, approach):

1. Put the list of numbers into the computer.
2. Compare the first two numbers.
3. If the second is smaller than the first, exchange them.
4. Continue looking at adjacent pairs of numbers and following the instructions in step 3.
5. Whenever an exchange occurs, return to step 2.
6. When numbers are in order, print them.

Because you need a way to refer to the numbers in the group (e.g., compare the fourth and fifth number), an array seems like a viable data structure to use. The following BASIC program incorporates an array in the algorithm design:

```
10 DATA 7,4,5,3,10,2,4
20 N = 7
30 DIM X(N)
40 FOR I = 1 TO N: READ X(I): NEXT I
41 REM__THESE FOUR LINES PUT THE DATA INTO AN ARRAY
   SO THAT X1 = 7 ..... X7 = 4
50 FOR I = 1 TO N-1
60 IF X(I)>X(I+1) THEN SWAP X(I),X(I+1): GOTO 50
70 NEXT
71 REM__THESE THREE LINES DO THE ACTUAL SORTING.
   SWAP IS A BASIC FUNCTION THAT WILL REVERSE THE
   ORDER OF ITS TWO ARGUMENTS. THE FOR...NEXT LOOP
   IS BASIC'S METHOD OF ITERATION
80 FOR I = 1 TO N: PRINT X(I): NEXT
90 END
```

An alternative approach is to view the group of numbers as a list and to refer to the numbers by position (first, last, next to last, etc.). A programmer who saw the problem in this way might produce the following Logo program, which uses approximately the same algorithm but with a totally different data structure:

```
to sort :l
    op sort1 :l []
end

to sort1 :u :s
    if emptyp :u [op :s]
    op sort1 bf :u sort2 first :u :s
end

to sort2 :c :l
    if emptyp :l [op fput :c :l]
    if :c < first :l [op fput :c :l]
    op fput first :l sort2 :c bf :l
end
```

Logo is difficult for the uninitiated to follow because it doesn't use familiar-looking words and relies on the compact recursion process. But the process is easy to follow when it is explained in natural language: The sort procedure is used to accept the unsorted list (inputted as :l) and to print out (op) the sorted list that results from sort1. Sort1 uses the butfirst command (bf) to take the smallest element from the list that sort2 is working with and output it to sort. In this way, the list to be sorted keeps getting smaller. Sort2 does the actual sorting by comparing the first and second elements in the list.

Just as all programs use algorithms and data structures, all programmers use a few general, high-level tools to help develop and construct programs. These tools, which are similar to problem-solving strategies in other disciplines, are really techniques for systematically manipulating natural thought and language. As such, these methods and metaphors enable mechanical devices to extend and amplify human thought.

PROGRAMMING STYLE: METAPHORS AND METHODOLOGIES

In many creative activities the medium of execution is intractable. Lumber splits; paints smear; electrical circuits ring. These physical limitations of the medium constrain the ideas that may be expressed, and they also create unexpected difficulties in the implementation.

. . . .

Computer programming, however, creates with an exceedingly tractable medium. The programmer builds from pure thought-stuff: concepts and very flexible representations thereof. Because the medium is tractable, we expect few difficulties in implementation; hence our pervasive optimism. Because our ideas are faulty, we have bugs; hence our optimism is unjustified.[12]

The methodology of programming evolved from Turing machine instruction tables to high-level languages in less than 20 years. At every successive stage of this evolution, programmers found that the only way to exploit the increasing amount of computational power that the hardware engineers made available was to expand their ability to provide the computer with instructions. One solution to the problem of human-computer communication was to develop general methods for thinking about algorithms and data structures. When it came to the practical matter of using the power of computation, these methodologies proved to be as important as hardware and software.

Programming, or coding as it was then known, began in the late 1940s when a program was simply a long series of machine code instructions for a computation to be performed by a specific machine. The first few years of software design consisted of finding out what computers could do—which ultimately meant finding the limits of machine language. In the 1950s, the increasing power of computer hardware and the decreasing efficiency of writing large programs in machine language spurred the development of higher-level languages.

When FORTRAN and COBOL came along, the focus of attention moved from *whether* it was possible to write programs to *how* programs should be written. These languages provided a formalism for communicating algorithms, but they didn't show the programmer how to express any specific algorithms or how to control the flow of a series of algorithms. These early programmers were in the same positions as students who are learning to write compositions—they had a syntax and vocabulary but lacked the basic rules necessary to put it all together into a coherent message. Without an agreed-upon methodology for writing programs, the high-level languages were just formalisms.

One of the first and still one of the most powerful programming techniques was *flowcharting*. A flowchart is an abstraction of a program in action, a road map that makes it easier to follow the flow of instructions in a program. Flowcharts illustrate how sequences of operations specified by the algorithm lead to decision points that divert the flow of operations into two or more branching sequences, each of which can divide into further branches. A flowchart helps the programmer keep track of this complexity and after an algorithm is selected or invented, helps the programmer *plan* a program.

To compose a flowchart (or flow diagram, as they were originally named), programmers use rectangles, diamonds, parallelograms, circles, arrows, and other notations to show how a program is organized. Each shape indicates a different kind of operation: Diamonds represent decisions, rectangles represent functions, and other shapes represent various ways to input and output data. A flowchart is deciphered by starting at the top of the diagram and following the arrows down through the program until a STOP instruction is reached.

Branching algorithms produce treelike diagrams, and a branching procedure in which one of the branches leads back to the beginning of the original procedure is a perfect symbolic model of a loop. Many of these program design features are illustrated in the flow chart shown in Figure 4.3.

The flow diagram, like the concept of stored program computers, was invented by the same inspired group who were involved

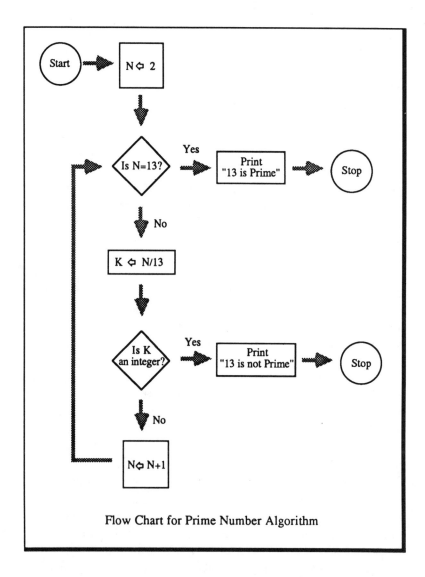

Flow Chart for Prime Number Algorithm

Figure 4.3 Small Flowcharts of Sequence, Branch, Loop

in the ENIAC project—John von Neumann, Herman H. Goldstine, and others. Just as the stored program made it possible to use computers for many different tasks, flow diagrams made it possible for programmers to approach their work methodically. In 1946, the people who had constructed the software architecture for the first electronic digital computers turned to the founding of a new intellectual discipline. As Goldstine recalled years later:

> In the spring of that year von Neumann and I evolved an exceedingly crude sort of geometrical drawing to indicate in rough fashion the iterative nature of an induction. At first this was intended as a sort of tentative aid to us in programming. Then that summer I became convinced that this type of *flow diagram*, as we named it, could be used as a logically complete and precise notation for expressing a mathematical problem and that indeed this was essential to the task of programming . . . Out of this was to grow not just a geometrical notation but a carefully thought out analysis of programming as a discipline.
>
> The purpose of the flow diagram is to give a picture of the motion of the control organ as it moves through the memory picking up and executing the instructions it finds there.[13]

The "picture of the motion of the control organ," an illustration of the process known as the "flow of control," enables people to visualize the way a computer would execute any algorithm. Such a means of visually modeling the activities of programs gave programmers a new language to use when communicating with one another. When a programmer wants to communicate algorithms to a computer, FORTRAN will suffice; but when programmers want to communicate with each other, flow diagrams are better. Flow diagrams also serve as creative aids for individual programmers, providing a kind of chalk board upon which they can test the effects of various approaches: How would it work if I tried it this way?

Like maps, flowcharts enable programmers to see the big picture. In fact, a flowchart is like an aerial view of a program. But this perspective is gained by sacrificing detail. Flowcharts may help systematize the way programs are organized after the programmer has a rough idea of the algorithm, but they aren't much good in the earliest stage of the creative process. What was needed was something to help programmers approach the preliminary design of complex software: A methodology was needed for describing what goes on *inside* the boxes of a flowchart.

Just such a methodology was proposed by Niklaus Wirth and published in a paper called "Program Development by Stepwise Refinement."[14] Wirth described a systematic approach to the creative side of programming—a way that large teams or lone programmers could tackle big programs. The idea is simple: Start out as simply as you want; write everything in a sequential list; next write a longer, more detailed list; then fill in the details as you take successive steps of refinement. In other words, break big problems into subproblems, and worry about the subproblems after you know what they are.

Everyone who learned to write outlines in fifth grade English class already knows the appropriate form for recording the process of stepwise refinement. Start with a one-item outline that states the problem; then write a series of successively more detailed outlines that break it down into subproblems and subsolutions. For example, an algorithm for instructing your household robot to make a bowl of breakfast cereal turns out to be a surprisingly complex project. The first step would be called "Make Cereal," and the first refinement would look like this:

Make Cereal
    (1) get ingredients
    (2) get a bowl
    (3) combine ingredients

The second refinement would look like this:

    (1) get ingredients
        (1.1) get milk
        (1.2) get cereal
    (2) get a bowl
        (2.1) look in cupboard
    (3) combine ingredients
        (3.1) pour cereal into bowl
        (3.2) pour milk into bowl

The third refinement would look like this:

(1) get ingredients
    (1.1) get milk
        (1.1.1) open refrigerator door
        (1.1.2) take milk out of refrigerator
        (1.1.3) close refrigerator door
    (1.2) get cereal
        (1.2.1) open pantry door
        (1.2.2) take cereal box out of pantry
        (1.2.3) close pantry door
(2) get a bowl
    (2.1) look in cupboard
        (2.1.1) open cupboard door
        (2.1.1) take bowl out of cupboard
        (2.1.2) close cupboard door
(3) combine ingredients
    (3.1) pour cereal into bowl
        (3.1.1) open cereal box
        (3.1.2) put bowl and milk on table
        (3.1.3) pour cereal into bowl
    (3.2) pour milk into bowl
        (3.2.1) open milk carton
        (3.2.2) pour milk into bowl

The process must be broken down into even finer steps because your robot doesn't know that it must lift the cereal box and position it directly over the bowl, then tip the box so the cereal can pour out. When enough refinements result in an adequately detailed list of instructions, the instructions must be translated into the robot's native language. This stage of the programming cycle is known as coding and requires a knowledge of the syntactic mechanisms provided by each language for translating algorithms into executable code.

Finally, you load the program and send your robot off to the kitchen, only to find that this program, like all programs, has a few bugs. Unless you insert an instruction to fill the bowl half-full of cereal and specify a test for determining how full the bowl is, your robot will empty the entire box into the bowl. Ditto the milk. You have to clean up the mess, insert the proper instructions into the sequence, and try the program again.

But this time the robot, having emptied the milk and cereal cartons, encounters a condition that wasn't foreseen by the original algorithm: It looks in the refrigerator, finds that there is no milk carton, and cannot proceed. So you have to either insert an instruction for the robot to inform you when an ingredient is missing so you can go to the store, or you have to add another, even more complicated module instructing the robot to go to the store and purchase ingredients. Welcome to the craft of programming, where most of the work consists of tracking down bugs. Imagine the headaches involved in debugging a lunar landing, a sort of the U.S. census data, a means of tracking air traffic, the operation of a nuclear power plant, and so on.

Successive refinement, also known as the *top-down approach*, does have its drawbacks. This is because it starts from the most general, top level of specification, the task, and proceeds by steps through the algorithm to the most specific, bottom levels of instructions, the programming language code. But because computers can only execute properly coded algorithms, there is no way to test parts of the program in action (and interaction) until the lowest levels have been specified. Still, successive refinement is an excellent tool for developing the intricacies of program design.

The final methodology is both a philosophy of programming and a response to the phenomenal success of computer designers. As computer power accelerated and programming tasks grew in complexity, it became clear that no single individual could be responsible for the software controlling moon rockets or submarine-launched missiles.

The 1960s brought monumentally complex software projects involved with weapon systems like the Polaris missiles and equally ambitious commercial software projects like IBM's Operating System 360. The organizational problems inherent in constructing large programs by using large teams of programmers made it necessary for managers of such projects to break the project down into relatively autonomous subprojects, each of which could be tackled by a smaller team.

The divide and conquer strategy isn't exactly a new chapter in the annals of human invention, but its application to software design had tremendous impact both at the level of large-scale planning and at the level of individual programmers accomplishing their tasks. The strategy of *decomposition* complements the programmer's other tool, abstraction, and it reflects the basic Turing strategy for using a simple machine to perform complex computations: If the big problem can't be solved directly, can it be divided into a number of smaller, more easily solvable problems?

The most influential trend in software design during the 1970s was a design philosophy known as *structured programming*, first advocated by the international team of O.J. Dahl, E.W. Dijkstra, and C.A.R. Hoare.[15] According to this method, all programs are supposed to be made up of small subroutines known as *modules*, which pass values to one another in such a way that a hierarchy of such modules can be constructed. The algorithms appropriate to the solution of each module are within reach of the individual programmer's ability; if all the modules work and the mechanism for passing information from module to module is sound, then the larger problem can be solved by linking together all the smaller solutions to the subproblems into a mainline program.

A development closely related to the structured programming movement was Niklaus Wirth's invention of the programming language Pascal. The need for a new programming language was a natural result of the structured programming philosophy because existing languages used certain constructions, particularly the eternally controversial GOTO operation, which offered the programmer tempting diversions from hierarchical, modular programs.

Natural languages had existed for thousands of years before Noam Chomsky got the bright idea that they all must share certain universal features. The genesis of computer languages evolved from the opposite direction. Much of the logical framework that supports computer languages was developed well before the very idea of a computer existed, and more modern notions such as algorithms and data structures were in place at the dawn of the computer age. How these conceptual tools are actualized (implemented) in the big seven modern programming languages, FORTRAN, COBOL, BASIC, LISP, Logo, Pascal, and FORTH, is the story told in the next chapter.

5

The Family of
Programming Languages

Programming languages and their dialects number at least several hundred, and possibly a few thousand. The natural languages of human communication may be more numerous still, but in some respects programming languages are more diverse. Each language has its own distinctive grammar and syntax, its own manner of expressing ideas. In principle most computational tasks could be accomplished with any of the languages, but the programs would look very different; moreover, writing a program for a given task would be easier with some languages than with others . . . .

. . . . .

The great diversity of programming languages makes it impossible to rank them on any single scale. There is no best programming language any more than there is a best natural language. "I speak Spanish to God, Italian to women, French to men, and German to my horse," said Charles V (presumably in French). A programming language too must be chosen according to the purpose intended.[1]

FROM PROGRAMMING CODE TO PROGRAMMING LANGUAGE— FORTRAN

FORTRAN did not really grow out of some brainstorm about the beauty of programming in mathematical notation; instead it began with the recognition of a basic problem of economics: programming and debugging costs already exceeded the cost of running a program, and as computers became faster and cheaper this imbalance would become more and more intolerable. This prosaic economic insight, plus experience with the drudgery of coding, plus an unusually lazy nature led to my continuing interest in making programming easier.[2]

Philosophers often say that the 2000-year-old history of Western philosophy consists of nothing more than footnotes to Plato. In a similar fashion, the 30-year history of high-level programming languages may be viewed as nothing more than footnotes to FORTRAN—FORmula TRANslator—the first widely used programming language. Almost every programming language idea is a refinement of FORTRAN (e.g., variable names of unlimited length instead of limiting them to six letters) or a reaction to a FORTRAN idea (e.g., eschewing the GOTO statement in favor of structured programming). How FORTRAN achieved this exalted status and how it maintains its position as the granddaddy of programming languages is a story that reveals as much about the business of computing as the logic of programming.

The earliest computers were developed during World War II to help the army plot trajectories for new weapons. Their names—ENIAC, MANIAC, MARK I—recall the sci-fi films of the early 1950s, and, looking back, they bear the same resemblance to today's high-speed, silicon-chipped marvels as *Star Wars* does to *It Came From Outer Space*. They were huge machines; ENIAC weighed more than 30 tons and was as big as a small house, and relatively slow; MARK I was only capable of three additions per second. But they were full-fledged, digital computers and, as such, were capable of emulating a myriad of different kinds of machines as their programs were changed. Unfortunately, ideas about programming (no one was using that word in the late 1940s to early 1950s) were even more primitive than the computers in need of programs.

With millions of personal computers in homes today, it is natural to consider transportability of a program as a desirable trait. All programmers want their software to run not just on the IBM, but on the Apple, the Commodore, the Tandy, and every other machine. But this transportability means that the program cannot be machine (i.e., hardware) specific; it must be written for a virtual machine that all the different computers on the market share. Of course, this virtual machine is the FORTRAN, or BASIC, or Pascal (or whatever language the program is written in) virtual machine. But neither transportability, nor the concept of virtual machine was much on the mind of those first military coders, as programmers were then called. Just the name "coder" gives you a clue as to the difference between the type of programs (codes) written then as opposed to now.

In the early days, there were only handful of computers, each of them unique, and the task at hand was simply to compute a given trajectory on a given machine, not to worry about how to make the same program run on different machines. (The shining exception to this shortsightedness is the brilliant work of Alan Turing.)

Because of the machine-specific nature of programming, all programming was done in machine code—the long strings of 1s and 0s that directly controlled the computer hardware. In machine code, all numbers are written in binary form (or complicated variations known as octal, a base-8 system, or hexadecimal, a base-16 system). Functions such as square roots or logarithms are not allowed, there are no exponents, variables are also represented as numerical strings, and logical concepts such as if-then and GOTO must be represented as a special sequence of 1s and 0s. Machine code was laborious to write, almost impossible to read, and very prone to programmer error. Just see how long it takes you to catch the difference between these two strings of machine code:

$$1110101000011000 \qquad 1110101100011000$$

In the words of John Backus, the manager of the FORTRAN project,

> It's really difficult for a programmer today, who wasn't involved then, to realize how ignorant we were then, and how primitive the ideas and tools were that we felt were really advanced and sophisticated stuff. In late 1953 computers were pretty crazy things. They had very primitive instructions and extremely bizarre input-output facilities . . . . So, overcoming the difficulties of these computers and cramming programs and data into little tiny stores made programming really a black art.[3]

Transportability aside, the twin desiderata of speed and efficiency were soon pressing those early programmers for improvements in productivity. As opposed to the MARK I's paltry three additions per second, the UNIVAC I was capable of 3000 additions per second. Thus, in the words of Grace Hopper (one of those early program-

mers and a seminal figure in the history of programming languages),
"It was chewing up programs awful fast. And the programmers had
not accelerated in an equal degree. It was perfectly clear that we
were going to have to produce programs faster."[4]

The first attempts at what was then called "automatic programming" were a series of interpreters built in the very early 1950s. All
these systems did was to provide improved input/output facilities and
allow the programmer to operate with floating-point (real) as well as
fixed-point (integer) numbers. (It is hard for us today to imagine what
an intractable problem this fixed-floating point problem was for early
programmers and designers.) But if they really weren't much of a
boon to the down in the pits programmer, if they didn't liberate the
programmer from the strings of 1s and 0s, they did provide a sharp
whack in the head to the programming theorists, for they were the
first systems to demonstrate the feasibility of the virtual machine. No
longer was the programmer tied to a particular piece of hardware. As
John Backus put it, "They just converted the peculiar host machine
into a different synthetic machine."[5]

Following quickly on the heels of these interpreters was a series
of compilers that made automatic programming more of a reality. The
most advanced of these was the WHIRLWIND system of J.H. Laning
and N. Zierler (1953). As the example below demonstrates, WHIRL-
WIND programs, although not yet embodying a programming language, were a far cry from a string of 1s and 0s:[6]

```
     v|N = <input>                      CP 3,
     i = 0,                             z = 999,
1    j = i+1,                           PRINT i,z.
     a|i = v|j,                         SP 4,
     i = j,                          3  PRINT i,y.
     e = i-10.5,                     4  i = i-1
     CP 1,                              e = -0.5-i,
     i = 10,                            CP 2,
2    y = F¹ (F¹¹  (a|i))+5(a|i)³        STOP
     e = y-400,
```

By the end of 1953, the groundwork was established for the
first true programming language. Yet, if the theoretical foundation
for a true programming language was in place, the programming
community displayed a great deal of skepticism about the possibil-

ity of true "automatic programming" in which programmers could concentrate on algorithms and data structures and computers could take over the task of turning human-readable programs into machine-readable code. In the first place, the early interpreters and compilers were quite cumbersome to use, often slowing the computer down by a factor of 5 or 10. It seemed that the efficiency gains in generating code were coming at the expense of executing that code.

Perhaps more importantly, the inflated claims of the gurus of automatic programming that their systems had almost human abilities to understand natural language and the needs of the user kept turning out to be nothing but hot air (in fact, such claims are still mostly hot air today). Once again, however, it was the market that finally decided the argument in favor of automatic programming. In the words of John Backus,

> In 1954 the cost of programmers associated with a computer center was usually at least as great as the cost of the computer itself. In addition, from one-quarter to one-half of the computer's time was spent debugging. Thus programming and debugging accounted for as much as three-quarters of the cost of operating a computer; and obviously, as computers got cheaper, this situation would get worse.[7]

In early 1954, IBM, which was fighting to gain supremacy in the still fledgling computer market, authorized Backus to begin work on an automatic programming project for its new 704 computer.

The goals of that project, which by November 1954 was called the IBM Mathematical FORmula TRANslating System (FORTRAN), were, according to its manager John Backus,

> To design a language which would make it possible for engineers and scientists to write programs themselves for the 704. We also wanted to eliminate a lot of the bookkeeping and detailed, repetitive planning which hand coding involved . . . . We certainly had no idea that languages almost identical to the one we were working on would be used for more than one IBM computer, not to mention those of other manufacturers. But we did expect our system to have a big impact, in the sense that it would make programming for the 704 very much faster, cheaper, more reliable. We also expected that, if we were successful in meeting our goals, other groups and manufacturers

would follow our example in reducing the cost of programming by providing similar systems with different but similar languages.[8]

The FORTRAN project was actually two intertwined projects: The goal of the first project was to produce a language; the second goal was to produce an efficient compiler for that language. In fact, according to Backus, it was the compiler problem that received most of the attention:

> It was our belief that if FORTRAN, during its first months, were to translate any reasonable "scientific" source program into an object program only half as fast as its hand coded counterpart, then acceptance of our system would be in serious danger. This belief caused us to regard the design of the translator [compiler] as the real challenge, not the simple task of designing the language . . . . To this day (1979) I believe that our emphasis on object program efficiency rather than on language design was basically correct. I believe that had we failed to produce efficient programs, the widespread use of languages like FORTRAN would have been seriously delayed.[9]

As it turned out, the compiler did need most of the attention. Although the FORTRAN language itself was basically fully described in the group's preliminary report (November 1954),[10] work on the compiler continued for another 3 years until FORTRAN was finally released to the general public in 1957. The following sample program from the first FORTRAN manual demonstrates many important features of the language:[11]

```
C      PROGRAM FOR FINDING THE LARGEST VALUE
     X            ATTAINED BY A SET OF NUMBERS

       BIGA = A(1)
       DO 20 I = 2,N
       IF (BIGA - A(I)) 10, 20, 20
 10    BIG(A) = A(I)
 20    CONTINUE
```

Perhaps the most important feature of the language is that it is algebraic. The notation borrowed from standard mathematical convention (e.g., arithmetic operators, the equal sign, subscripted variables) was chosen intentionally to be familiar to FORTRAN's scientist and engineer clientele. A second important feature is that, as opposed to later text-oriented languages that could be input from a terminal, FORTRAN is column oriented. It has this feature because it was designed to be input using the soon to be ubiquitous "do not bend, fold, or spindle" computer punch card. Use of the punch card mandated that each FORTRAN program line be broken into four zones:

1. Columns 1–5 are used to label statement lines with positive integers so that they may be referenced by other lines. Also, a C punched in column 1 indicates that the line is a comment and not to be included in program execution.
2. A punch mark in column 6 indicates that the line is a continuation of the previous line.
3. Columns 7–72 are used to punch the FORTRAN statement.
4. Columns 73–80 are ignored by the computer and may be used to denote card sequencing, a cheap source of insurance should a deck of 2000 cards be dumped.

A final feature is that key words like IF for selection and DO...CONTINUE for iteration have the look of a modern programming language. In fact, FORTRAN, although 30 years old, is a lot closer to today's programming languages than to the machine code that preceded it by only a few years.

Fortran underwent a few early revisions and was standardized by the American National Standards Institute (ANSI) in 1966 as FORTRAN IV. Eleven years later a new standard, FORTRAN 77, was approved, which accommodated some of the new philosophy of structured programming by adding improved character handling and the IF-THEN-ELSE control structure. Now 30 years old, FORTRAN is still going strong whereas other languages developed at the same time—PRINT, IT—are deader than Latin. What accounts for this impressive longevity?

First and foremost, FORTRAN program execution is extremely efficient. In fact, according to Terrence Pratt, an acknowledged expert on language design, FORTRAN programs execute more efficiently than programs written in languages many years its junior (e.g., Pascal, Ada, APL).[12] This efficiency is an outgrowth of the pervading challenge to those early programming theorists, best expressed by Grace Hopper,

There were beginning to be more and more people who wanted to solve problems . . . . They wanted an easier way of getting the answers out of the computer. So the primary purposes were not to develop a programming language, and we didn't give a hoot about commas and colons. We were after getting correct programs written faster, and getting answers for people faster . . . . We were trying to solve problems and get answers."[13]

If FORTRAN is less user friendly than BASIC or Logo, it is worth remembering that the original goal was to prove that automatic programming was possible and not to produce a programming language that a layperson could understand.

Another reason for FORTRAN's longevity is that its designers knew who their intended audience was (scientists and engineers) and designed the language to meet their specific needs. FORTRAN may not support a lot of different data structures or string-handling operations, but it does allow four different kinds of numbers (integer, real, double precision, complex), supports an extensive set of arithmetic operations and mathematical functions, and has some special arithmetic control statements (e.g., the IF line in the sample program means that when $BIGA - A(I)$ is negative, control is transferred to line 10; when it is 0, control is transferred to line 20; and when it is positive, control is transferred to line 20.) Furthermore, for the first two decades of FORTRAN's existence, before the era of microcomputers, it was precisely these scientists and engineers who were the main computer users. Therefore, because FORTRAN was in use by the majority of computer users, it was taught in universities; and because it was widely taught in universities, the new majority of computer users learned to use it.

Finally, FORTRAN's designers also knew that much of scientific computing involved using the same programs to solve standard, mathematical problems (e.g., differentiation, integration, and even the trajectory of a weapon projectile). In order to facilitate this repetitive aspect of computing, in order to prevent the constant reinvention of the wheel, FORTRAN has a simple subroutine procedure that allows tested programs to be melded into new programs.

By compiling subroutines separately, FORTRAN made it easy to debug only the new part of any program. More importantly, as an explanation of its staying power, the library of FORTRAN subroutines grew into the thousands so that programming in FORTRAN became largely a matter of writing a simple input/output program to go with an already proven subroutine. With its impressive library, replacing FORTRAN with a new, improved language is like trying to replace books with a new, improved technology (e.g., computers, video discs, microfiche). Put simply, the market (i.e., computer manufacturers, programmers, scientists, and engineers) has a lot invested in FORTRAN that it does not wish to lose.

All of the programming languages discussed in this chapter— those few out of the hundreds that have survived and left their mark—share at least one common trait: a well-defined *raison d'être*. This is no less true for FORTRAN, with its major goal lucidly expressed in the original *Programmer's Reference Manual*:

> The FORTRAN language is intended to be capable of expressing any problem of numerical computation. In particular, it deals easily with problems containing large sets of formulae and many variables, and it permits any variable to have up to three independent subscripts. However, for problems in which machine words have a logical rather than a numerical meaning it is less satisfactory, and it may fail entirely to express some such problems."[14]

Quite clearly, FORTRAN's developers had a keen sense of both their objectives and their limitations.

FORTRAN may seem primitive by today's standards. In fact, 15 years ago Jean Sammet, this country's foremost historian of programming languages, declared that "Because it was designed so early, better ways have been found to do almost everything that is currently in FORTRAN."[15] But FORTRAN's conceptual and structural clarity is a near-perfect match for the jobs it was intended to perform; FORTRAN is a classic example of designing the right tool for the job.

INDUSTRIAL STRENGTH COMPUTING—COBOL

[T]here was still the major difficulty of the data processors. Working with the people that I had worked with in data processing, I found very few of them were symbol-oriented; very few of them were mathematically trained. They were business trained, and they were word-manipulators rather than mathematics people. There was something else that was true of the data processing world: whereas in the mathematical-engineering world, we had a well-defined, well-known language; everybody knew what—if you said "SIN" everybody knew it meant "sine"—they knew exactly what you meant, whether you were in Berlin or Tokyo, or anywhere in between. It was fully defined, already there. Everybody knew it. But there wasn't any such language for data processing. We took something over 500 data processing programs and sat down to write out what people were doing when they did data processing. We finally identified about 30 verbs which seemed to be operators of data processing.[16]

Data processing (DP) is the blue-collar work of computing. It may not possess the pure intellectual stimulation of scientific computing or the exciting innovation of work in artificial intelligence, but more computers and computer programmers earn their living figuring payrolls or billing customers than by any other computer application. The potential of this DP boom was not lost on the early computer manufacturers, and in the mid to late 1950s all the major players in the infant computer industry were busy developing their own business programming languages and compilers.

Remington Rand's UNIVAC, with the legendary Grace Hopper at the helm, was the first company with a true business language, which they called FLOW-MATIC. (Actually, the development staff had called it B-0, but the marketing people readily perceived that designation's lack of cachet and had renamed it for marketing purposes.) What made FLOW-MATIC the first business language and not just a scientific language applied to business problems was Hopper's understanding of both the nature of business communication and the nature of business computing.

Since there was no universal business language in the sense that mathematics was the universal language of science, FLOW-MATIC introduced the idea of using English words as commands (e.g., ADD, COUNT, EXECUTE) rather than scientific abbreviations or symbols. This enabled programs to begin to look like part of the natural business flow (e.g., INPUT INVENTORY FILE, MOVE UNIT PRICE) instead of a mathematician's nightmare.

Hopper also realized that actual business computing procedures (e.g., salary and commission calculations) were quite simple, but that the data for these calculations were often complex (e.g., thousands of employees in hundreds of different categories). In order to ensure the ultimate flexibility of FLOW-MATIC, it was designed so that the data were written completely independently of the algorithms. This meant that the same computing procedures could be used with an ever-changing stream of data.

FLOW-MATIC was hardly the first contribution of Grace Murray Hopper to the burgeoning world of computers. She was the third programmer on the MARK I [the first (nonelectronic) digital computer], wrote the software prototypes for the first compiler, and designed the first English-like command language. Now almost 80, Commodore Hopper, the navy's oldest officer until her retirement in 1986, is still plugging for creative change in the computing establishment. Traveling about 300 days a year to give speeches and presentations, she tells every audience, "If during the next 12 months any of you say, 'but we've always done it this way,' I will instantly appear in front of you and I will haunt you for 24 hours."[17]

It was that kind of forward thinking that motivated Hopper, almost 30 years ago, to begin considering a standardized business language. In addition to FLOW-MATIC, IBM had COMTRAN (later called Commercial Translator), and Honeywell had FACT. In an attempt to stem this anarchic tide and bring some order to business computing, Hopper began explaining to anyone who would listen (chief executive officers of all the major computer manufacturers, representatives from the Bureau of Standards, top ranking military officers) that having everybody writing programs in different languages just wasn't going to work.

As the result of Hopper's efforts, a meeting was held on April 9, 1959, with the objective being "to plan a formal meeting involving both users and manufacturers where plans could be prepared to develop the specifications for a common business language for automatic digital computers."[18] It is an interesting historical exercise to compare the efforts of the business community with those of the scientific community, which had met a few years earlier in a failed attempt to standardize the programming languages used for scientific computing. The remarkably different results of the two groups lead to some interesting speculations about the differences between scientists and businesspeople.

One month later, in May 1959, the formal meeting was convened with representatives from the government (e.g., army, air force, navy, Bureau of Standards), industry users, (e.g., U.S. Steel, Westinghouse, DuPont, Metropolitan Life), and computer manufacturers (e.g., IBM, Remington Rand, Honeywell, Burroughs, RCA, GE, NCR, Philco, and Sylvania). The meeting established an executive committee known as CODASYL (Committee on Data Systems Languages) and three working committees and produced the following list of desired characteristics for the proposed Common Business Language (CBL):

a. Majority of group favored maximum use of simple English language; even though some participants suggested there might be advantage from using the mathematical symbolism.
b. A minority suggested that we steer away from problem-oriented language because English language is not a panacea as it cannot be manipulated as algebraic expressions can.
c. The need is for a programming language that is *easier to use*, even if somewhat less powerful.
d. We need to broaden the base of those who can state problems to computers.
e. The CBL should not be biased by present compiler problems.[19]

Most of the work of meeting these objectives fell to the Short-Range Language Committee chaired by Jean Sammet. Their charge was:

> To report by September 1, 1959, the results of its study of the strengths and weaknesses of existing automatic compilers (especially AIMACO, FLOW-MATIC, and COMTRAN); and to recommend a short-range composite approach (good for at least the next year or two) to a common business language for programming digital computers. This group will explore a "problem-oriented but machine-independent language." This is defined as: "A language which will permit the description of the problem in such precise terms as to convey the management needs and objectives while providing a regimented and firm basis for the exploration of these objectives in a language which would not be geared to a specific data processing system, but to which each data processing system might be applied to provide for the accomplishment of the objective in the most practical manner."[20]

The parenthetical remark, "(good for at least the next year or two)," turned out to be one of the classic understatements in the history of computing. Within 6 months Sammet's committee produced the full-blown language COBOL—Common Business Oriented Language—that has been the acknowledged standard for DP work for the past 25 years.

Working within such a short time frame was just one of the constraints the committee labored under. Perhaps the most important constraint was political—the need to produce a language that did not give an unfair advantage to any one manufacturer. This requirement meant that some obvious choices could not be made (e.g., DO could not be used to control loops since it was used in IBM's FORTRAN), while other choices had to be taken so that everyone was equally offended. As Sammet explains, the choice of 18 decimal digits as the maximum to be used in any data field "was chosen for the simple reason that it was *dis*advantageous to every computer thought to be a potential candidate for having a COBOL compiler."[21] In a certain sense, design by committee means that COBOL is the camel of programming languages.

A third important constraint concerned the abilities of COBOL's intended users—the business community. A majority of the committee argued that business users could not, or at least should not, be required to deal with even the simplest mathematical formulas (e.g., 2 + 2). Because of this view, COBOL contains the four arithmetic verbs ADD, SUBTRACT, MULTIPLY, and DIVIDE so that simple formulas may be expressed in English (e.g., ADD 2 2). The minority view held that at least some of the business community could handle formulas, and they should not be penalized by a "glaring" educational deficiency in others. The compromise was to include the mathematical symbols $+$, $-$, $\times$, $/$ but to require that they be prefaced by the English word COMPUTE (e.g., COMPUTE 2 + 2). We need only reflect a moment on the current state of business acumen regarding quantification—sophisticated mathematical models, widespread use of electronic spreadsheets, MBA curriculum requiring computer projects—for an object lesson about how computers have changed our lives.

As it turned out, these three constraints (viz., time, politics, user skills) forced the committee to make some very intelligent decisions. Because of time pressure, they could not develop a language *de novo* but instead had to appropriate the best features of the already existing languages: the use of full data names instead of short symbolic codes, the use of full English words for key commands, and the separation of the data descriptions from the procedural instructions. Because of politics and the need to design a language that was transportable (i.e., machine independent), the committee decided that every COBOL program should include a separate Environment Division that would isolate all the machine-dependent features (e.g., allocation of data tapes, hardware switches, and specific computer configurations). (Compare this objective with FORTRAN's machine-specific goals.) This allowed COBOL programs to run on different machines as long as a new Environment Division was inserted. The Environment Division also included information that eased training problems, helped to improve readability, and provided built-in documentation.

Finally, because of the presumed background of its intended users, COBOL programs were written in a four-division, outline form—Identification, Environment, Data, and Procedure, which legions of COBOL students remembered with the mnemonic device I Enjoy Data Processing—with the individual program lines beginning with an English verb, ending with a period, and closely approximating the syntax of natural language.

As the result of these constrained decisions, the Short-Range Committee produced a programming language with two main features: English-like readability and an emphasis on data rather than algorithms. In many ways, COBOL is more of a business language than a computer language. Words may be up to 30 characters long (e.g., SOCIAL-SECURITY-NUMBER) so there's never a need to try to decipher some cryptic code (e.g., SOCSEN). COBOL thoughts are put into English-like sentences that end with periods (e.g., IF HOURS-WORKED IS GREATER THAN 40, THEN PERFORM OVERTIME-ROUTINE.), and related sentences are grouped together to form paragraphs. Finally, the entire COBOL program is structured into divisions so that different functions (data, procedures, etc.) are isolated.

These features give COBOL programs their characteristic form:

```
IDENTIFICATION DIVISION.

     PROGRAM-ID.
        COBOL Demo.
     AUTHOR.
        Howard Levine.

ENVIRONMENT DIVISION.
```

```
CONFIGURATION SECTION.

    SOURCE-COMPUTER.
        MD3.
    OBJECT-COMPUTER.
        MD3.

DATA DIVISION.

    WORKING-STORAGE SECTION.
    01  K PICTURE IS XXXXX.

PROCEDURE DIVISION.

    START.
    DISPLAY "This is the COBOL Demo Program".
    MOVE "Hello" TO K.
    DISPLAY K.
    STOP RUN.
```

This program prints the two lines, "This is the COBOL Demo Program" and "Hello". Line 01 simply says that K is a variable of five characters, and the MOVE statement assigns the string Hello to K.

This ease of readability is important for two reasons. First, it allows managers, and not just programmers, to understand the functions of a given program. Second, it facilitates program maintenance, that is, debugging, data updates, and adding new routines. Business computing usually involves large programs (i.e., thousands of lines) that remain useful for a long period of time (i.e., 5 years). This means that more time is spent maintaining a program than writing it, and often many different programmers will be involved. The self-documenting nature of COBOL is critical for functioning in the business environment.

COBOL's emphasis on data over algorithms is another reflection of its intended use: The typical business task involves a relatively straightforward computation (e.g., salary) on a large, varied data base (e.g., full-time, part-time, salaried, commission). Because of this, almost half of the language is dedicated to methods of data handling: COBOL files may be accessed sequentially (e.g., each record in order), directly (e.g., access to any file based on its identifier such as worker #555), or through a user-selected index (e.g., based on a special value in the file, such as all workers earning more than $2000 a month). COBOL also has a SORT module that allows reorganization of data files according to user-defined parameters, such as alphabetical order. In addition, COBOL has a COPY statement that allows the transfer of data from program to program. This encourages different operations on the same data base—the beginning of today's sophisticated data base management systems (DBMS). Finally, COBOL has a wide range of options, such as adding dollar signs, suppressing leading zeros, and putting in commas, for displaying its data. Many of these features would strike the scientist as useless frippery, but they all meet a recognized business need.

Having designed the language within its 6-month deadline, the Short-Range Committee presented its report to CODASYL and dissolved. Its work was immediately accepted with the following endorsement:

> That Basic COBOL as recommended in the Short Range Committee's report would be accepted as the minimum that would be required from all computer manufacturers; i.e., no computer manufacturer could correctly claim that his computer accepts COBOL unless he provides a compiler that will deal with every element included in Basic COBOL, as defined."[22]

Then, as so often is the case in the history of programming languages, the market made the crucial decision. The Department of Defense, which had been peripherally involved from the beginning, announced that it would only buy computers capable of running COBOL unless a compelling case could be made that a particular computer was unsuited for COBOL application. (After all, who else has a bigger payroll to process than the army?) A year later, in 1961, Westinghouse made a similar announcement and other private companies followed. The manufacturers really had no other choice but to embrace COBOL and get to work designing compilers.

Today, COBOL is big business. More than $100 billion is invested in COBOL applications worldwide and it has its own journal, the *COBOL Journal of Development*. Although the Short-Range Committee is ancient history, CODASYL still meets six times a year to review amendments to COBOL. The current ANSI version of COBOL, COBOL 74, consists of 12 modules, each handling different

COBOL features such as sorting and report writing, which can be implemented at two different levels. In fact, COBOL has become so feature rich that one computer expert claims that no computer can fully understand COBOL 74.[23] At the other extreme, the minimum COBOL compiler must contain three modules: NUCLEUS, TABLE-HANDLING, and SEQUENTIAL I/O implemented at Level I. The idea is that all the different versions of COBOL fit together like a nested series of Russian dolls—anything written in a simpler COBOL will be able to run on a computer with a bigger, more complex COBOL compiler.

Twenty-five years later, the work of the Short-Range Committee is still going strong as the industry standard. And so is Grace Hopper. For all of her numerous accomplishments, Grace Hopper is best known as the Mother of COBOL.

COMPUTING GOES TO COLLEGE—BASIC

We at Dartmouth envisaged the possibility of millions of people writing their own computer programs. Therefore, we decided to design a new computer language that would be accessible to typical college students. This is how the language called BASIC was created. Profiting from years of experience with FORTRAN, we designed a new language that was particularly easy for the layman to learn and that facilitated communication between man and machine.[24]

Dartmouth is a small Ivy League university tucked away in Hanover, New Hampshire. Although it has an enviable academic record, it is perhaps best known for its Winter Carnival and "animal house" social life. Fortunately, its people also find time for a lot of serious academic work, and Dartmouth is the site of three important milestones in the history of computing: In 1940, the first remote use of a computer over communications lines was demonstrated; in 1956, a summer conference on artificial intelligence (the first known use of this phrase) that led to the LISP programming language was convened; and finally, at 4 A.M. on May 1, 1964, BASIC was born to parents John G. Kemeny and Thomas E. Kurtz. With this last notable achievement, Dartmouth became the first university to take the idea of computer literacy for all its students seriously. The birth of

BASIC meant that the days of the computer priesthood were numbered; computer programming was no longer the exclusive property of a small enclave of specialists, but a powerful tool that was available to assist thinkers in any field of intellectual inquiry.

Although Kemeny and Kurtz were both mathematicians, they realized that only 25 percent of the Dartmouth student body majored in science or engineering. Clearly, meeting their goal of developing a computer system that would give all Dartmouth students an opportunity to learn about computers would require bringing computers to the students rather than the other way around. They knew, quite rightly, that the average fine arts major was not going to wade through the snow to the computer office, hand in a bunch of punched cards, and wait 2 hours for the results of a program to generate the Fibbonaci sequence of numbers. Computing at Dartmouth had to put the student first, and they adopted a four-part plan to meet this goal:

1. Because the computer system would have to be "friendly, easy to learn and use, and not require students to go out of their way,"[25] Dartmouth adopted time-sharing with remote terminals. (Along with MIT, Dartmouth's was one of the first installations to experiment with a time-sharing system). Because the computer's operating system parceled out the computer's resources to many different programs at once instead of feeding the programs to the computer one at a time, it became possible to eliminate the batch processing ritual that had previously intervened between the programmer and the computer. Gone were the treks to the central computer with a handful of cards. Computing was now interactive from many locations.

2. Because most students did not want to take computer classes, computing was integrated into the curriculum. Students were introduced to computers as tools for solving problems that arose naturally out of their course work.

3. Because tools are only used to the extent that they are available, Dartmouth adopted a policy of open access to computers. Previously, campus computer centers were treated as inner sanctums, accessible only to the highest initiates in the programming hierarchy. At Dartmouth, students were given the same free access to computers that they had to books in the library.

4. Finally, because the current generation of computer languages was difficult to learn, a new computer language was devel-

oped—BASIC, Beginner's All-purpose Symbolic Instruction
Code—that was both easy to learn and easy to use.

Since time-sharing technology was available and curriculum integration and open access were policy objectives, the new wrinkle in
the plan was BASIC. Could Kemeny and Kurtz develop a new programming language that was both sophisticated enough to allow serious computing to take place and simple enough so that the fine arts
major wouldn't be intimidated by it?

Of course, BASIC didn't just appear out of thin air. It had its
ancestors, most notably FORTRAN, from which it borrowed a means
of controlling loops by specifying the starting (or initial) value, the
final value, and the value of the increments or steps (e.g., FOR I = 1
to 10 STEP 2: PRINT I: NEXT would output the values 1,3,5,7,9),
and ALGOL, from which it borrowed the commands FOR and STEP.
Yet these languages required a precise and unforgiving syntax, careful attention to the types of variables used, and a complex programming structure that prohibited novice experimentation. BASIC
emphasized just the opposite traits: a flexible syntax that allowed a
certain amount of free expression, unrestricted, simple variables,
and a programming structure that encouraged students to learn as
they go along, that is, actually to interact with the computer, try different ideas, and expand their simple program notions as they became more fluent in the language.

Kemeny and Kurtz succeeded because they managed to strip
away all the nonessentials from their programming language. BASIC
was simply a listing of instructions, with each instruction consisting
of three parts: the instruction number (this was crucial in early versions of BASIC so that the main computer running the time-sharing
terminals could distinguish program lines and sort them), the operation or command, and the operand, or data, to be manipulated. This
scheme is so simple and elegant that you need know nothing about
computers to understand the first BASIC program ever published:[26]

Instruction No.	Operation	Operand
10	LET	X = (7 + 8)/3
20	PRINT	X
30	END	

Dartmouth BASIC has undergone at least six revisions, referred to as editions because of the numbers of the manuals, since 1964; but the elements that led to its success have remained more or less constant:

1. Command names such as LET, PRINT, FOR, NEXT, GOTO and END that do exactly as speakers of English would expect
2. Function names such as SIN, COS, SQR, ABS, INT that are reminiscent of the mathematical operations they perform
3. Algebraic means for expressing formulas [e.g., $X = (7+8)/3$] that are familiar to anyone with a high-school education
4. Unstructured variables that free the programmer from worrying about whether the value is an integer (5) or a real (5.0)
5. Automatic numerical formatting so that BASIC decides if a number is best represented as an integer, as a real, or in exponential notation (e.g., 1.23E-06).

Simply said in the words of Thomas E. Kurtz, BASIC has succeeded

because there are more people in the world than there are programmers. If ordinary persons are to use a computer, there must be simple computer languages for them. BASIC caters to this need by removing unnecessary technical distinctions (such as integer versus real), and by providing defaults (for declarations, dimensioning, output formats) where the user probably doesn't care. BASIC also shows that simple line-oriented languages allow compact and fast compilers and interpreters, and that error messages can be made understandable.[27]

The success of BASIC also dramatically demonstrates something important about market forces in the computer industry: Software may *be* the computer, but people start out by buying the hardware. If you can link (the marketing word is *bundle*) your software with a manufacturer's hardware, you can become a dominant force in the computer world. When BASIC was invented in 1964, no one had heard of personal or microcomputers. All computing was done on expensive mainframe and minicomputers owned by companies or universities. Computer programming was an occupation for an elite group of professionals, and few had heard of BASIC outside of the profession. BASIC was still considered a success, but it was a success within a limited circle.

That circle would widen significantly in 1974 with the invention of the first *microcomputer*—a small, personal computer whose entire central processing unit was on a single, silicon chip; it was the Altair by Micro Instrumentation and Telemetry System (MITS). Although the machine was incredibly limited in memory (256 bytes of main memory) and programming capability (input was done by hand-setting switches, as in the first ENIAC, and output was little more than a few flashing lights), it met the needs of an expanding group of hobbyists who understood computing and were not put off by its primitive nature.

The microcomputer hobbyists who experimented with the Altair weren't interested in word processing, or ordering airline tickets, or playing chess. They just wanted their own computer so that they could program. Initially, all this programming had to take place in machine language; but in 1975 MITS licensed Bill Gates and Paul Allen to produce a BASIC interpreter for the Altair.

The difference between the BASIC created by Kemeny and Kurtz and that produced by Gates and Allen was not so much in the specification of the language itself as in the way the machine-specific interpreter was constructed. A computer language is a formalism suitable for expressing algorithms and data structures based on a system of formal definitions. The specific version of a language, the mechanism for a machine's interpretation of programs based on this formalism, is known as its *implementation*; and although computer languages are not themselves patentable, implementations are. Each implementation is a program, written in the machine language of the target computer, that enables programmers to write and execute high-level programs on the target computer. Like any other program, an implementation can run faster or slower, have few or many features, be easy or difficult to use; it all depends on how well it was designed and coded.

Gates and Allen formed their company, Microsoft, and within a year over 10,000 Altairs had been sold with the Microsoft implementation of BASIC known as MBASIC. Within a few years, Microsoft had licensed MBASIC to Commodore, Tandy (Radio Shack), Apple, and IBM, and the industry standard was born. With over 2 million computers running MBASIC by 1985, the market has done what the computer professionals at ANSI could not: it agreed on the generic implementation of BASIC.

Even though MBASIC has dominated the scene for what in computer industry terms is a few life times (actually 10 years), BASIC continues to be a living language with a steady stream of proposed revisions. In fact, with a potential market of more than 2 million users and a need to retrofit BASIC with all the new techniques and capabilities developed since 1964, the next 20 years of BASIC's evolution promise to be just as interesting as the first 20.

Compared with some of the newer, compiler-based languages, BASIC is often denigrated as being too slow in its execution of programs. This may be a valid criticism of MBASIC and other interpreted implementations of BASIC, but there is no formal, intrinsic reason why BASIC must be interpreted. In fact, the original Dartmouth BASIC was compiled. Now, with the invention of a new type of compiler, called the *incremental compiler*, many programmer designers envision a compiler-based BASIC that preserves its interactivity and immediate error checking while running as fast as the competition.

BASIC is also criticized for having a restricted vocabulary. It requires you, as one critic put it, to say everything you might ever want to say using the same 50 words over and over again. Newer BASICs will meet this criticism from two directions. First, they will add considerably to the primitive BASIC vocabulary. For example, control structures will be expanded from the traditional FOR/NEXT loop to include a multiline IF/THEN/ELSE/ENDIF to allow you to execute as many statements as you wish as long as a stipulated condition remains true or false. Also, the traditional ON/GOSUB for subroutines will be replaced by a flexible SELECT CASE/END CASE construct, enabling you to transfer program control based on the value of a given expression. Second, and more importantly, newer BASICs will be extensible; that is, they will have the capability of allowing the programmer to define new key words which will become a permanent part of the language.

A third, and perhaps most influential criticism of BASIC, is that although it is easy to learn, it is difficult to use for all but the most trivial applications. According to computer guru Edgser Dijkstra, one of the key proponents of structured programming, "It is practically impossible to teach good programming to students that have had a prior exposure to BASIC; as potential programmers they are mentally mutilated beyond hope of regeneration."[28] Dijkstra's main complaint is that BASIC's trial-and-error approach leads to spaghetti code—an ill-thought-out, jumbled program with added *ad hoc* lines, no consistent use of variables, frequent use of GOTO statements causing the program to jump about without explanation, and, as a result, a tangled mess that even the programmer can't explain.

The proposed solution to this so-called spaghetti code is structured programming—a programming philosophy best exemplified by Pascal, that wasn't even invented back in 1964. The key idea is a simple one: Plan the entire project first by breaking the program into individual modules with each module expressing a complete thought (e.g., input module, computation module, output module) and then organizing the modules in a logical way to show the structure of the complete program. Although this philosophy can be followed with BASIC, structures such as GOTO and GOSUB allow long, unstructured programs to grow like topsy. Newer BASICs encourage structure by providing facilities for typing variables (e.g., integer, real, string), inserting descriptive names of variables (e.g., LET COUNTER = 5 instead of LET C = 5), and eliminating line numbers to facilitate modularization.

Finally, because computer hardware has changed even more than the software, newer BASICs have been designed to take advantage of developments such as greatly expanded memory, superb graphics, and screen windows to display both the program and its output at the same time. Just how far BASIC can change and still remain recognizable is a question for programming language philologists, but this much is clear: All programming languages involve trade-offs, and BASIC is no different. If BASIC came bundled with your computer, it provides a good opportunity to familiarize yourself with some of the general skills involved with computer programming. On the other hand, if you expect to write any complicated programs, BASIC may not be the language of choice.

THE LINGUA FRANCA OF THE ARTIFICIAL INTELLIGENTSIA— LISP

From childhood we are exposed to numbers and to ways of processing numerical data, such as basic arithmetic and solutions to algebraic equations. This exposure is based upon a well-established and rigorously formalized science of dealing with numbers. We are also exposed to symbolic data—such as names, labels, and words— and to ways of processing such data when we sort, alphabetize, file, or give and take directions. Yet the processing of symbolic data is not a well-established science. In learning an algebraic programming language, such as FORTRAN or ALGOL, we call upon our experience with numbers to help us understand the structure and meaning (syntax and semantics) of the language.

In learning a symbolic programming language such as LISP, however, we cannot call upon our experience, because the formalism of symbolic data processing is not part of this experience. Thus, we have the added task of learning a basic set of formal skills for representing and manipulating symbolic data before we can study the syntax and semantics of the LISP 1.5 programming language.[29]

Fueled by science-fiction speculation about thinking machines and Sunday-supplement prognostication about giant brains, the lay public and many scientists expected the first computers to match, and perhaps surpass, human reasoning capabilities. As it turned out, it took more than a decade before these devices were even able to accomplish such mundane tasks as payroll computations. The computers of the 1940s lacked both the software and hardware for even the most elementary experiments in thought-like computation.

Despite the failure of the first generations of computers to wrest control of planet earth from their human creators, the rapid advances in computer technology that took place in the forties and fifties stimulated the growth of a scientific field devoted to the creation of true machine intelligence. In 1956, this field was given its name—artificial intelligence, or AI—by John McCarthy, the man who soon thereafter created LISP. After 30 years of work, AI has still not achieved the grandiose goals envisioned by its pioneers, but LISP is still a living computer language—a subject of controversy in some quarters and an object of veneration in others.

Theoretically, LISP (an acronym for LISt Processing) is rooted in the abstract mathematical realm of recursive function theory—the same subject area that Turing, Gödel, and Church were exploring in the 1930s when they invented the theoretical basis of computation. On the practical side, LISP is naturally suited for the kind of programming necessary for exploring natural language, game playing, robotics, and other concerns of AI researchers.

The first organized study of AI took place at Dartmouth University during the summer of 1956, when McCarthy met with a small number of other mathematicians and electrical engineers who specialized in computer programming (computer science was not yet a recognized discipline). The AI pioneers hoped to map out a plan for constructing a program that could accomplish some task that heretofore had been exclusively within the province of human reasoning, such as proving theorems in logic. It came as a surprise when three of the participants, Allen Newell, Herbert Simon, and Cliff Shaw, presented a program known as Logic Theorist, that did just that.[30]

The computer on which Logic Theorist was implemented, the Rand Corporation's JOHNNIAC, was one of the first stored-program computers. Logic Theorist managed to apply a set of rules of inference to a small number of axioms and generate proofs of theorems, a skill that had previously been exclusively human. It was an impressive accomplishment, not only because it achieved one of the higher-level goals of the AI pioneers but also because the programmers had to invent their own programming language for JOHNNIAC. The first high-level language, FORTRAN, was still an IBM research project when the Rand programmers undertook their ambitious task.

Logic Theorist was written in IPL-2 (which stood for Information Processing Language) and used a theoretical scheme known as list processing that worked on symbolic as well as numerical expressions. After the 1956 conference, McCarthy, who had started his academic career as a mathematician, began working on the theoretical bases of a list-processing language for the IBM 704 computer.[31]

McCarthy and his colleague Marvin Minsky were interested in creating an AI program that would represent information about the world in terms of sentences in a formal language and would decide appropriate answers to queries by making logical inferences. Lists seemed to be the natural data structure for representing sentences, and a list-processing language appeared to be similarly appropriate for programming deductive operations. McCarthy and Minsky were also interested in chess-playing programs, and the representation of the treelike hierarchy of potential chess moves was best suited to list-based data structures and algorithms.

McCarthy also wanted two capabilities that were, at that time, lacking in other languages: conditional expressions (such as If-Then operations) and recursion (procedures that could call themselves). He invented conditional expressions—surely one of the most powerful features of all modern high-level languages—while writing chess-playing routines for the IBM 704 at MIT in 1957-1958. (FORTRAN's IF statement did not, at that time, provide efficient conditional branching.) But these innovations were more than improvements on existing languages; they were the first steps toward the creation of an entirely new kind of computer language. During the summer of 1958, McCarthy created the theoretical foundations of LISP when he put conditional expressions together with recursive function definitions. In the fall of 1958, McCarthy and Minsky started the MIT Artificial Intelligence Project. One of their first projects was planning a compiler program for LISP.

The implementation of recursive subroutines was theoretically attractive to McCarthy because they made LISP a far more efficient formal language than Turing machines as a tool for describing computable functions. The mathematicians who followed up on Turing's work on recursive function theory were concerned with computable functions strictly as theoretical entities and didn't mind the fact that Turing machines were unwieldy and inefficient ways to write programs. LISP not only fit the strict definition of a Turing machine, but it promised to be an efficient high-level language for performing actual machine computations as well.

Another practical result was that the LISP function EVAL made it possible to write a LISP interpreter in LISP. This was noted by Stephen Russell, one of the gifted young programmers who had gravitated toward Minsky and McCarthy's AI laboratory. Russell coded the interpreter, and LISP was suddenly a usable programming language as well as a theoretical *tour de force*.

By 1960, not only had the AI lab attracted a community of programmers who turned McCarthy's original, rather unwieldy language into a functional, elegant, programming tool, but the evolution of time-sharing gave LISP even more power. The MIT group was generously funded by the government to create the software for the new multiuser computers and it was the recipient of one of the first minicomputers manufactured by the Digital Equipment Company—the PDP-1. In 1963, a child prodigy by the name of Peter Deutsch implemented the first interactive LISP on the PDP-1, a seminal act that gave the MIT hackers a means of building further improvements into McCarthy's invention.

The IBM 704, with its unwieldy hardware and software, was soon left behind as LISP was implemented on successively more sophisticated machines. And along with more powerful hardware came a spate of sophisticated AI programs for playing chess, interpreting natural language, and commanding robots. Just as FORTRAN boosted the capabilities of the scientific community and was, in turn, improved by the suggestions of the large population of FORTRAN users and COBOL was similarly bootstrapped by the data-processing users, LISP coevolved with the discipline of AI research.

From the beginning, the fundamental data abstractions of LISP were wordlike objects known as *atoms*, which could be combined into sentencelike objects known as *lists*. Lists were planned to be similarly modular so that they could be chunked together to form hierarchies of lists. Atoms and lists are collectively known as *symbolic expressions*, or simply *expressions*, and the vocabulary of primitive LISP commands are meant to manipulate expressions.

All of the following examples are LISP atoms: numbers such as 15 or 1.5 (known as *numeric atoms*), operators such as $+$ and $*$, and alphabetic and alphanumeric combinations such as FOOBAR, WORD, and R385 (known as *symbolic atoms*). A list consists of a left parenthesis, followed by zero or more atoms or lists, followed by a right parenthesis: (THIS IS A LIST) (AND SO IS 3.5). An expression that is meant to be evaluated, usually beginning with an operator, is known as a *form*. The expression $(+\ 3\ 5)$, for example, is a form that yields the atom 8 upon evaluation. *Evaluation* is the name for the process by which the value of a form is computed. The result, like 8 in the previous example, is often referred to as the value *returned* by the procedure that is specified by the form.

Lists can consist of lists, and expressions can be nested within each other. All of the following examples are legitimate lists: (THIS LIST HAS FIVE ELEMENTS) (3 (A) (B C D) (E (F)) G); is a list; (3.14159) and (PI) are both lists; ( ) is the empty list, and (THIS LIST HAS (FOUR ELEMENTS)) is a list that contains a list as one of its elements.

Since LISP data and LISP programs are both represented in the form of lists, programs can become data for other programs. Because hierarchies of lists can be created, levels of abstraction are easily represented. Lists can be nested within other lists. The parentheses demarcate the levels of nesting. To many people who see LISP for the first time, the multiple parentheses look strange. But they are supremely useful when it comes to figuring out the various depths of nested expressions in complex lists.

LISP was created as a list-processing language because its creators perceived lists to be a natural data structure for representing abstractions about the real world. And because lists are the language's basis structure, LISP requires primitive operations for building lists and taking them apart in various ways. New lists are constructed by using the LISP function CONS to add new elements to a list, starting from an empty list. Lists are taken apart by using the primitive operations CAR and CDR. The nonmnemonic names for the commands CAR and CDR are artifacts of LISP's early history: CAR stands for Contents of the Address part of the Register, a reference to the hardware of the IBM 704, and CDR stands for Contents of the Decrement part of the Register. Nobody ever thinks about IBM 704 registers when using these primitives, but the names have stuck.

CAR is simply a command for breaking off the first element of a list, and CDR represents the part of the list that is left when the first element is removed. For example, suppose you want to separate the first element of the list (THIS SENTENCE IS A LIST). You can do this by using the function (CAR '(THIS SENTENCE IS A LIST)), which returns the value THIS. Similarly, (CDR '(THIS SENTENCE IS A LIST)) returns the value (SENTENCE IS A LIST).

Arithmetic operations are evaluated according to the syntax of *Cambridge Polish notation*. LISP uses *prefix notation*, in which the operator precedes the arguments, as opposed to the kind of *infix notation* people normally used when doing arithmetic by hand. In prefix notation, the value of $(+ \ (* \ 2 \ 6) \ (* \ 2 \ 2))$ is 16, because 2 is first multiplied by 6 to yield 12, then 2 is multiplied by 2 to yield 4; once the inner expressions are evaluated, they are returned to the next highest level, where they are added together to return a value of 16.

The value of a list is usually the result of applying an operation such as CDR or $+$ (included as the first element of the list) to the rest of the elements of the list. A value for a symbol is established by an *assignment* operation which, as in other languages, links that symbol with an address in memory in which a symbolic or numeric value is stored.

Any procedure that computes a value based strictly on its arguments is called a *function*. As an example of a procedure that returns a value, consider the following expression: $(+ \ (* \ 3 \ 4) \ (- \ 8 \ 5))$. The $+$ function is supposed to add two numbers. But the arguments to the function are lists, not numbers, which means they cannot be added. Therefore, the lists must be evaluated. First, $(* \ 3 \ 4)$ is evaluated, generating the value 12, which is substituted for the list (* 3 4) as the first argument to +. Second, (− 8 5) is evaluated, generating the value 3, which is substituted for the second argument to +. Third, (+ 12 3) is evaluated, returning the value 15. Saying that a function returns a value means that (* 3 4) generates a value of 12, which is then substituted for the list (* 3 4) in the operation (+ (* 3 4) (− 8 5)).

As an example of how a programmer can use LISP list-manipulating operations to perform some useful programming task, consider a list that represents information about these same (list-manipulating) operations:

```
(SETQ lisplist '(some-primitive-lisp-functions (CAR selector)
                                               (CDR selector)
                                               (APPEND constructor)
                                               (LIST constructor)
                                               (CONS constructor)
                                               (SETQ assignment)))
```

The list is indented in order to make levels of nesting more clear. The procedure, known as *prettyprinting*, does not alter the expression: It would have the same meaning if it were written as one long line. In each of the pairs of words, the first is a name of a LISP function, and the second describes what kind of function it is (e.g., CDR is a selector function and SETQ is an assignment function).

Suppose we want to find out what kind of operation LIST is. Knowing what the data structure looks like, we can use the selector functions to extract the sublist that describes the LIST function. We know that the sublist we want is the fifth element of the list named lisplist. To extract the fifth element of lisplist, we need to take four successive CDRs in order to strip off all the elements preceding the one we want. This strips the first element off the list and returns the rest of the list. Next, we need to take the first element (using CAR) of the list that is left:

```
(SETQ extractlist (CAR (CDR (CDR (CDR (CDR lisplist))))))
```

Then, knowing that the second element of the list that describes the LIST function is the one we want, we need to extract that element:

```
(SETQ kind-of-function (CAR (CDR extractlist)))
```

Putting it all together, we extracted the second element of the fifth list. This is a simple example of one way that LISP functions can be used to store knowledge about the real world in the form of data structures and then extract various pieces of that knowledge.

Like Logo, FORTH, and other modern languages such as C, LISP is *extensible*; that is, LISP contains procedures for easily building new procedures out of old ones and adding them to the language's basic repertoire. Once a programmer combines a collection of lower-level procedures into a new superprocedure, the new abstraction becomes a part of the language and the programmer no longer has to think about the lower-level details that went into building the abstraction. The new abstraction can then be used as a building block for even higher-level procedures.

Although the small programs we presented thus far don't resemble anything that could be called artificial intelligence, they are examples of the kind of software tools LISP programmers can use to investigate computer simulation of human reasoning processes. Before any programs can be written to simulate reasoning, problem solving, or logic, a fundamental problem known as *knowledge representation* has to be solved: We know that people know many things about the real world and that this knowledge is somehow stored in the human brain. How then can an approximation of human knowledge be stored in a computer?

One aspect of human knowledge concerns the linkage of things in the real world to various abstract attributes. In some manner that is far from understood by psychologists, human memory establishes linkages between things and attributes. For example, most people know that an oak is a tree. Tree is an attribute of oak; so are has-leaves, needs-water, grows-in-temperate-climates, and a large number of other attributes. On a very sophisticated level, programs for representing knowledge in machine-readable form use high-level structures such as frames and scripts to represent networks of connections between objects and attributes. But these high-level structures are no more than very complex programs, and like all other programs, they are constructed from simpler building blocks. The following example illustrates an elementary kind of building block for a knowledge structure.

The goal of this exercise is to create a data structure that allows the representation of attributes (and the values of those attributes) and their association with appropriate symbols. The domain chosen is the realm of programming languages, and the specific instance is the programming language LISP. The first task is to define a function that adds an attribute-value pair to an attribute list associated with a symbol. The next task is to define a function that finds the value of a given attribute for the symbol in question.

When we put the first function to work to create a list of attribute-value pairs for the symbol lisp, we get a series of states like the following, which builds the list:

```
(SETQ lisp
    (add-attribute-value-pair-to-symbol lisp '(level high)))
(SETQ lisp
    (add-attribute-value-pair-to-symbol lisp '(recursive yes)))
(SETQ lisp
    (add-attribute-value-pair-to-symbol lisp '(extensible yes)))
(SETQ lisp
    (add-attribute-value-pair-to-symbol lisp '(primary-application AI)))
(SETQ lisp
    (add-attribute-value-pair-to-symbol lisp '(invented-by J-McCarthy)))
```

Given the above data structure, queries can be addressed to it by using the second function, which has to be defined. Suppose you want to know what the primary application of lisp happens to be. The defined second function, (find-value-for-attribute lisp 'primary-application), will then return the value AI.

Although this is a very simple example, it is similar to more elaborate knowledge-representing data structures and functions that are used to create programs that can play games, solve problems, and perform logical manipulations. In the future, new languages specifically invented to help solve knowledge-representation problems will extend AI research into more sophisticated realms. But the fundamental research that had to precede these new languages was conducted by means of complex LISP programs built from elements like the ones demonstrated here.

POWERFUL IDEAS AND
OBJECTS TO THINK WITH—
LOGO

In a computer-rich world, computer languages that simultaneously provide a means of control over the computer and offer new and powerful descriptive languages for thinking will undoubtedly be carried into the general culture. They will have a particular effect on our language for describing ourselves and our learning . . . . Thus we look at programming as a source of descriptive devices, that is to say as a means of strengthening language.[32]

Everybody knows that computer languages are tools, but can they be toys? Can young children learn to program computers? There are methodologies such as structured programming to guide the design of computer programs, but are there general principles of human thinking that might guide the design of computer languages? Speculations such as those regarding the relationships between play and learning, thinking and programming, young children and high-level language design led to the language Logo. The designers of Logo, as one of them attests, were after something much more ambitious than a new formalism for manipulating algorithms and data structures. Their goal was nothing less than a revolution in the way people learn to think:

> Stated most simply, my conjecture is that the computer can concretize (and personalize) the formal. Seen in this light, it is not just another powerful educational tool. It is unique in providing us with the means for addressing what Piaget and many others see as the obstacle which is overcome in the passage from child to adult thinking. I believe that it can allow us to shift the boundary separating concrete and formal. Knowledge that was accessible only through formal processes can now be approached concretely. And the real magic comes from the fact that this knowledge includes those elements one needs to become a formal thinker.
>
> . . . .
> . . . What matters most is that by growing up with a few very powerful theorems one comes to appreciate how certain ideas can be used as tools to think with over a lifetime. One learns to enjoy and to respect the power of powerful ideas. One learns that the most powerful idea is the idea of powerful ideas.[33]

Seymour Papert, author of the bold statement quoted above, was one of the earliest advocates of the idea that computer languages, because they link the thinking capacities of the human mind with the symbol-processing capacities of the computer, are not only handy devices for performing computations but also are potentially powerful tools for amplifying the power of thought. Twenty years ago Papert was a key member of a team of educators, computer scientists, and psychologists who created a computer language specifically designed to help teach people how to think. Wallace Feurzeig, founder of the research project and codesigner of the language, even named their creation Logo after the Greek word for "thought."

The birthplace of Logo was a private consulting firm near Boston named Bolt, Beranek, and Newman (B.B.&N.); it was a remarkable organization that has been virtually unknown outside the computer science community but that contributed a large proportion of the ideas that led to personal computers—from time-sharing, interactive programming, and CRT-screen graphics to new languages such as LISP and Logo. B.B.&N. was one node of a network of researchers funded throughout the 1960s by the Defense Department's Advanced Research Projects Agency.

Before the electronic revolution made low-cost, high-power computers possible, computer languages were designed to fulfill the requirements of computing machines rather than meet the needs of the people who used the language. The fact that the first programming languages had to be adapted to the physical limitations of computers had the unintended side effect of making the notation of computer languages incomprehensible to nonexperts. This led to the myth that computer programming is a mysterious and mathematical activity that only a few highly trained experts could hope to master. Even scientists looked at the first programmers as a kind of technological priesthood.

But not everyone agreed with the computer elitists. A small minority of computer researchers were exploring ways to expand the limits of computer capabilities, and a minority within that minority were convinced that programming was actually a process of creative problem solving—literally, a skill that schoolchildren can master. By the mid-sixties, a few of these radical explorers of computational frontiers were ready to bring their knowledge to the wider world of computer users. As one of the members of the Logo team described the situation two decades later:

> If we can dispel the delusion that learning about computers should
> be an activity of fiddling with array indexes and worrying whether X is
> an integer or a real number, we can begin to focus on programming as a
> source of *ideas*. For programming is an activity of *describing* things.
> The descriptions are phrased so that they can be interpreted by a com-
> puter, but that is really not so important. Computational descriptions,
> like those of science or mathematics, provide a perspective, a collec-
> tion of "tools of thought," such as procedural organization, hierarchical
> structure, and recursive formulations. Logo, and languages like it, will
> help make these tools available to everyone.[34]

The Logo project grew out of research Wallace Feurzeig organized in 1965. The original idea was to use the newly created time-
sharing technology and a new, interactive computer language,
TELCOMP, to teach mathematical concepts to schoolchildren. A
team of researchers with an unusually eclectic collection of qualifica-
tions in artificial intelligence research, computer language design,
education, and psychology joined Feurzeig in the B.B.&N.-spon-
sored project. Among them was Seymour Papert, a mathematician
who had recently arrived at MIT after 5 years of research with the
educational psychologist Jean Piaget.

The Logo project members weren't just another group of people
designing a programming language for the new generation of computers. The fundamental difference between them and other language
designers was that they concentrated on affecting the minds of future
programmers instead of catering to the constraints of contemporary
computer hardware. Their project was not directed at the small
number of computer programmers and computer scientists but at a
large proportion of the world's future population—the millions of
people whose thoughts and lives would be enhanced by access to
personal computers.

Logo was a deliberate attempt to influence the way new computer users—especially children—learn to understand and interact
with computers. Because a special kind of self-evident, self-amplify-
ing human-machine communication was the goal of the Logo creators, the logical architecture and engineering details of creating a
programming language and implementing it on the computer had to
mesh with solutions to the problems of how people learn, how people
learn to think, and how the formal properties of the computer can be
made concrete.

Inventing an entirely new kind of computer language that could be learned by young children was a difficult programming goal in itself, technically speaking, but deciding precisely *which* theory described how people learn and think was, and still is a particularly thorny political matter (e.g., is knowledge encoded in frames or scripts?). In terms of theoretical background, the presence of Seymour Papert brought the Logo group into contact with several new branches of education, psychology, and computer science. In particular, Papert was interested in bringing the seminal thinking of John Dewey and Jean Piaget into the age of the microprocessor.

Dewey, whose work encouraged generations of progressive educators, stressed that important learning occurs during aimless play. Psychologist Piaget agreed and saw play as a spontaneous and potent form of research. According to Piaget, the chief talent and dominant drive of every child is to *know* about the world. Young minds create knowledge by continually formulating hypotheses about how the world works and then revising these mental models when they are proved false.

Papert showed how Piaget's view of the learning process could help the Logo designers create a tool to help humans solve problems. If play is a form of research, the computer could become the world's most versatile sandbox and toy chest. The main goal of the Logo creators was to plan a *computational environment*—a little world on the computer screen—that was simple and responsive enough to encourage children to explore and learn on their own but which had enough potential computational power to give the mature Logo programmer the scope and flexibility of thought available to FORTRAN, BASIC and LISP programmers.

The turtle, a perfect example of what Piaget would call a *transitional object*, was the solution to the problem of introducing young children to the high-level abstractions necessary for computer programming. Children wouldn't set out to learn mathematics; rather, they were given the tools for drawing purple triangles on green backgrounds. The mathematical concepts were embedded in the nature of the thinking the child was led to do in order to instruct the turtle to draw the colored geometric figures.

The second goal, that of giving the language power as well as making it easy to learn, was achieved by basing the underlying structure of Logo on LISP. By making Logo a subset of LISP, the Logo team ensured that whereas kindergarten students could draw fascinating designs on their screens, computer scientists could use the same language to explore list processing and other advanced programming domains.

The turtle, what Papert would call "an object to think with," was originally a hemispherical robot on wheels that was connected by a wire to a computer that controlled its movements. By entering the proper commands into the computer, children could cause the turtle to draw designs on paper with a pen that could be lowered and raised as the turtle moved. Interactive video graphics were just coming into use when the first Logo experiments took place, so the turtle-on-wheels-with-a-pen evolved into a turtle-on-the-screen-with-glowing-trail-of-light.

A Logo screen has a small area in which keyboard commands can be seen, but most of the screen is occupied by a kind of electronic chalkboard. The turtle is represented by a triangle that always starts out in the center of the computer screen, with the pointed end aimed toward the top of the screen.

If you had a computer running Logo in front of you and could use the keyboard to type FORWARD 50, for example, the turtle on the screen would move directly up the screen, leaving a line behind it. This is illustrated in Figure 5.1.

If you then gave the command RIGHT 90, the turtle would stay in the same position it attained with your first command, but it would turn to face 90 degrees to the right. The numbers 50 and 90 are *inputs* to the commands FORWARD (or FD) and RIGHT (or RT), respectively.

If you next repeated your first command, FORWARD 50, the turtle would draw another line, thereby making a right angle (two thirds of a right triangle or half a square) on the screen. Figure 5.2 shows what the screen would look like after the three commands were given.

Now, if you repeated both commands two times each, in the same order, you would have drawn a square, as illustrated in Figure 5.3. As we see, the turtle can go backward and forward, can turn to the left and to the right, can draw lines of different lengths, and can rotate through an infinity of angles.

But Logo has an easier way to draw a square. Besides making square building far easier, this new procedure is a simple, straightforward introduction to *iteration*, one of the three tools no algorithm builder can do without. (Logo frequently replaces iteration with a special kind of

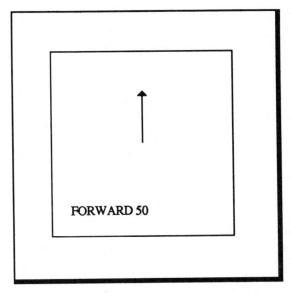

Figure 5.1 Logo Screen: Forward 50

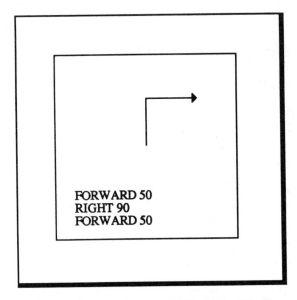

Figure 5.2 Logo Screen: Forward 50, Right 90, Forward 50

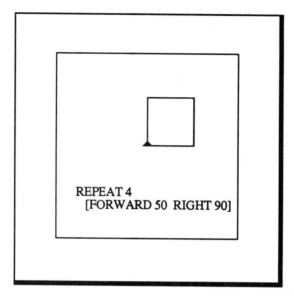

Figure 5.3 Turtle with Full Square and Listed Directions

iteration called *recursion.* See Chapter 4.) Instead of typing identical commands four times, all you have to do is type this one line:

```
?REPEAT 4 [FD 50 RT 90]
```

When you press the ENTER key, the turtle instantly responds by drawing a square, 50 units on a side.

The next level of abstraction is a simple but crucial one. It enables you to use the editor to "teach the turtle a new word" so you won't have to type instructions every time you want the turtle to do something, such as draw a square. This metaphor for programming—creating new command words and combinations of command words for a hypothetical agent like the turtle—is more than a device for teaching programming languages to children; it moves one step forward from the primitive code-based languages and one step closer to natural language, the one we use to think with.

To teach the turtle how to draw a square at the command "square," type this on the keyboard:

```
?TO SQUARE
>REPEAT 4 [FD 50 RT 90]
>END
```

The next time you want a square, you just type the word "square." (The > symbol that replaces Logo's customary ? in the listing indicates that you are using Logo's *editor*, a tool for writing Logo programs, rather than Logo's *interpreter*, a tool for executing Logo programs.)

The simple Logo instructions presented thus far have covered many of the essential elements of programming in any language, from building abstractions to iteration to program structure to the kind of direct involvement with the problem that the Logo researchers called "thinking like a turtle." The first command of FORWARD 50 was an example of one of Logo's primitive commands—the basic letters of every programming language's alphabet.

Combining the primitive commands FD 50 and RT 90 with the iterative command REPEAT, created a *procedure*—the fundamental building block of the Logo language. Procedure definition is a powerful concept. A procedure can be any small program or part of a program that is defined once, stored in memory, and thereafter can be invoked from many different parts of a program. Whenever a defined procedure is called by a larger program, the sequence of instruction-execution transfers to that part of memory in which the procedure is stored and then returns to the next instruction in the main program. If the called procedure produces a value that is returned to the main program, it is known as a *function*.

But this level of abstraction is only the beginning. If you want your computer to remember how to perform your square program the next time you turn your computer on, you can save it from the temporary workspace of the computer's main memory to permanent storage on a secondary medium such as disk or tape. You can also use Logo's editor to modify the procedure to give it more power. For example, you might want to make a different size square, or many squares of different sizes. Our original program specifies a square 50 units on a side; you could change that program so that the turtle would draw a square 40 units on a side simply by changing the 50 to a 40.

Another way to change the input, which involves another powerful programming and problem-solving idea, is by using the concept of a *variable*. Suppose that instead of commanding the turtle to travel 50 units forward, you could tell it to travel forward by the number of units specified by the number stored in the memory location named SIZE. You could use Logo's editor to modify your original SQUARE program so that it would look like this:

```
?TO SQUARE :SIZE
>REPEAT 4 [FD :SIZE RT 90]
>END
```

Now, if you want a square 100 units on a side, you enter the command SQUARE 100; similarly, SQUARE 10 would produce a square 10 units on a side.

Logo was designed with the principles of structured programming in mind. Like Pascal and FORTH, Logo allows each programmer to create a list of procedures such as SQUARE, which can then be used as building blocks for more complex procedures. The building blocks are called *subprocedures* and the compound programs are called *superprocedures*. For example, consider the procedure SPIN-SQUARE created by the program specification:

```
?TO SPINSQUARE :SIZE :ANGLE
>SQUARE :SIZE
>RIGHT :ANGLE
>SPINSQUARE :SIZE :ANGLE
>END
```

A natural language translation of these instructions to the turtle is as follows: Create a square of the size specified by the value of the variable SIZE, turn right by the amount specified by the value of the variable ANGLE, then go to the top of the list and follow both steps again. Return to the top of the list and repeat the procedure indefinitely. By calling the procedure SPINSQUARE and providing two inputs, it is possible to create designs such as those shown in Figure 5.4.

In SPINSQUARE the instruction that appears just before the instruction END is crucial, because SPINSQUARE calls one of its own procedures as its final procedure. This technique, known as *tail recursion*, is one of the most powerful tools in the Logo toolkit. Recursion is also a significant characteristic of LISP, Logo's mother language. This type of instruction occurs at the end of the program and returns the program to the beginning, which makes it tail recursion. But the recursive command can also occur earlier in the list of instructions.

The creators of Logo used the metaphor of an "agent" or an "electronic servant" who carries the instructions from the programmer to the turtle—an anthropomorphized model of the way values and variables are passed from one procedure to another. In SPIN-

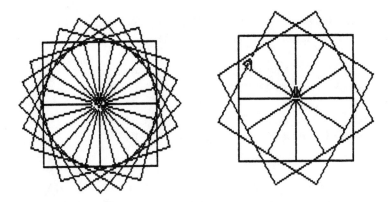

Figure 5.4 Screen Dumps of Two Different SPINSQUARE Designs

SQUARE, the servant first takes the value specified for SIZE and submits it to the subprocedure SQUARE; it then submits the value of ANGLE to the primitive RIGHT. Next, the servant returns to the top of the list of instructions and repeats the whole process in precise detail; it does this over and over again.

Consider one more turtle-based procedure. This time we'll reverse the usual presentation and look at the results, shown in Figure 5.5, before we examine the way the procedure was created.

Figure 5.5 Screen Dumps of POLYSPI 1 122 1.5; POLYSPI 5 75 1; POLYSPI 2 90 2

The procedure that created the designs in Figure 5.5 is just one step more complicated than SPINSQUARE:

```
?TO POLYSPI :DISTANCE :ANGLE :CHANGE
>FORWARD :DISTANCE
>RIGHT :ANGLE
>MAKE "DISTANCE :DISTANCE + :CHANGE
>POLYSPI :DISTANCE :ANGLE :CHANGE
>END
```

POLYSPI has three variables: The variable named CHANGE is of particular interest because it is a way to cause a recursive procedure to increase one of its dimensions regularly—in this case, the DISTANCE the turtle travels each time it loops through the procedure. The new primitive command MAKE in the third line is a Logo *assignment statement*, which assigns a new value to the variable named DISTANCE. Each time the electronic servant reaches this point in the program, it adds the value of the variable named CHANGE to the previous value of DISTANCE to create the new value of DISTANCE.

POLYSPI illustrates the same mathematical principle underlying spirals in nature, from galaxies to pine cones, as well as in the Logo microworld. And the use of :DISTANCE illustrates another thinking tool common to all programming languages—stepping variables. As R.W. Lawler, another early Logo educator and researcher, pointed out:

> The POLYSPI microworld reveals the stepping of variables as a powerful idea. By stepping variables I mean identifying one variable as a dimension of examination and holding all other variables constant while the chosen one is varied incrementally. In short, this microworld provides a clear model of how particular things may be generated through their intersecting dimensions of variation. Piaget judged variable-stepping to be an essential component of formal operational thought. The idea is a powerful one because it is almost universally useful; it is crucial to the process of scientific investigation."[35]

Procedures based on turtle graphics illustrate most of the powerful tools that Logo provides for algorithm building. But computer programs need data structures to provide grist for the algorithmic mill.

Since Logo is a subset of LISP, the list is Logo's primary method for handling collections of data. A Logo list, like a LISP list, is a sequence of data objects; for example, [this is a list of 8 data objects] and [4, 2, thirty, 6, 546] are lists.

The individual elements of Logo lists, again as in LISP, can themselves be lists; for example, [a little man named [John Q. Farnsworthy]] is a list consisting of five elements, one of which is a list consisting of three elements. A list that consists of lists, which in turn can consist of lists, is a simple way of representing hierarchical structures; and by this time, we've seen a few examples of the power of hierarchical structures.

Several primitive (fundamental) Logo commands manipulate lists. For example, FIRST outputs the first element of a list. The result of the command FIRST [this is a list] would be [this]. Similarly, the command LAST returns the last element of a list. The command SENTENCE combines lists such as [this small clause,] [for example] into a sentence such as "this small clause, for example." BUTFIRST returns all the elements of a list except for the first: BUTFIRST [1 2 3 4] would return [2 3 4]. BUTLAST similarly returns all the elements of a list except for the last. EMPTYP returns the value true if the specified list is empty, that is, if it has no elements.

Logo has become part of an educational movement and is being taught in elementary schools across the country. One of the original Logo group, Andrea diSessa, has been creating an even more powerful and easily learnable successor to Logo, known as Boxer. Clearly, an entire lineage of new programming languages, suitable for both education and computer science, is branching from the movement that started with Logo. Further successors to Logo, such as Smalltalk, are discussed in Chapter 6, "The Future of Programming Languages."

STRUCTURED PROGRAMS AND DATA STRUCTURES—PASCAL

[Structured programming] . . . is the expression of a conviction that the programmers' knowledge must not consist of a bag of tricks and trade secrets, but of a general intellectual ability to tackle problems systematically, and that techniques should be replaced (or augmented) by a method. At its heart lies an *attitude* rather than a recipe: the admission of the limitations of our minds. The recognition of these limitations can be used to our advantage, if we carefully restrict ourselves to writing programs which we can manage intellectually, where we fully understand the totality of their implications.[36]

One of the major boasts of the computer industry is that if the cost of automobiles had decreased as much as the cost of computers in the last 30 years, we'd all be driving around in our $17 Rolls-Royces. (And if the power of automotive technology had kept pace with the power of computers, our $17 Rolls would cruise at 1000 miles an hour.) Whether or not the boast is an exaggeration, there can be no doubt that the hardware side of the computer industry now routinely produces home computers for a few hundred dollars that would have been the envy of research scientists not too long ago. The electronic miniaturization revolution made possible order of magnitude gains in computer power, as well as equally impressive price drops.

Unfortunately, this impressive productivity gain in terms of hardware only made an emerging problem in software development more apparent: As computers have grown more powerful and sophisticated, they have become more capable of running ever larger, more comprehensive software packages. But there have seemed to be no comparable gains in programmer productivity to match the breakthroughs in hardware engineering. In fact, the larger programs become, the more difficult they are to write, debug, and revise. Without the tools to construct complex, powerful, programs, all future hardware breakthroughs will be worthless.

Although important groundwork in automatic programming had been accomplished by several programming groups in the early 1950s, the first real leap forward in programming occurred in 1957, with the introduction of FORTRAN. This granddaddy of high-level programming languages freed the programmer from the 1s and 0s of machine code. With FORTRAN, most of the housekeeping chores of programming were done automatically by the compiler, and programmers could devote their attention to issues of algorithmic and program design rather than machine-related issues (e.g., what the contents of register 9084 were and how to get it to the accumulator). This revolution in programming led to a change in the way programmers looked at their role; they now used languages instead of code.

The revolution also opened up the floodgates for an abundance of new FORTRAN-like languages. In short order, MATHMATIC, BACAIC, IT, and FORTRANSIT joined the scene. The programmers' joy over the power and ease of high-level languages was balanced by the dismay of the people who managed large software projects, because it soon appeared that everyone would end up speaking his or her own language. Fearing that the art and science of programming was heading for a cybernetic Tower of Babel, computer scientists decided to hold an international conference with the goal of developing a universal language—an Esperanto for computers. The agenda for the conference was put forward in a letter from GAMM, the German computer science group, to John W. Carr III, president of the American Association for Computing Machinery (ACM):

1. None of the existing languages appears to overshadow the others sufficiently to warrant it being chosen as the universal language.
2. The situation would not be improved by the creation of still another nonideal language.
3. Each passing month will bring a large increase in the number of installations using existing languages, and thus increase the difficulty in arriving at a uniform formula language that will be widely used.
4. How can the logical structure of existing languages be adjusted to conform to a recommended common formula language?[37]

Two conferences were held to address these issues, and in 1960 the group published its results—ALGOL 60. ALGOL contained many improvements over FORTRAN, making it an easier, more productive language to program:

1. ALGOL variable names could be of any length, making them much more descriptive than those allowed by FORTRAN, which limited names to six characters.
2. ALGOL was indifferent to fixed numbers (such as 2) and floating-point numbers (such as 2.0), whereas FORTRAN placed great emphasis on the form of the numbers used.
3. Many ALGOL key words such as IF..THEN..ELSE and FOR, had much more flexibility and utility than their FORTRAN counterparts.

Perhaps the most obvious difference between FORTRAN and ALGOL was that ALGOL programs had to start with the word BEGIN and finish with the word END. Although the addition of these words may seem like a trivial annoyance, it was actually the opening wedge of the second important revolution in programming productivity—the concept and implementation of structured programming. By using BEGIN and END as vertical delimiters within a program, it became possible to modularize any large program; that is, to break it into smaller, simpler, virtually self-contained subprograms.

Modularization was more than an efficient way to write programs; in conjunction with the programming strategy of *stepwise refinement*, modularization was an all-purpose problem-solving tool. Stepwise refinement and modularization made it possible to conceptualize any large project as an integrated hierarchy of smaller, more manageable programs. Writing, debugging, and revising could now be efficiently carried out by teams of programmers, each having its own module responsibility.

With all these advantages, ALGOL naturally took the computer world by storm. Well, not quite. In fact, not even close. Once again, the marketplace had another idea. Initially, the outlook for ALGOL was bright. European programmers began using it immediately, and the ACM decreed that all programs in its journal should be written in ALGOL. The fly in the ointment (bug in the computer?) was that IBM, which had developed FORTRAN, would not put ALGOL on its computers. Since most people in the United States used IBM computers, the ACM dictum resulted in a translation nightmare reminiscent of the old party game where a joke is whispered down a line of guests and slowly metamorphosizes into a new joke unrecognizable by the original joke teller: Programmers wrote their programs in FORTRAN and then translated them into ALGOL to meet the ACM guidelines. Readers then took the ALGOL listings and translated them back into FORTRAN to run them on their computers. Eventually, the ACM realized the foolishness of the situation and returned to FORTRAN, IBM penetrated the European market, and FORTRAN returned to a position similar to its corporate inventor—the environment within which other languages were allowed to function.

Such setbacks did not deter ALGOL's adherents. During the 1960s, ALGOL continued to be the focus of study and numerous ALGOL-like languages such as ALGOL 68, Euler, and GPL were developed. One of the experts who worked with the ALGOL 68 committee was the Swiss scientist Niklaus Wirth. Unfortunately, it often seemed to Wirth as if the committee was working against him. To programmers, and especially to computer language designers, issues like structured programming can be matters of strong—some might say theological—beliefs. Because of this friction, Wirth left the committee and published the specification for his own ALGOL-like language, Pascal, in 1971.

As befits a man whose programming language emphasized clarity of structure, Wirth was exceedingly clear about his aims for Pascal:

> Pascal . . . was developed on the basis of ALGOL 60. Compared to ALGOL 60, its range of applicability is considerably increased due to a variety of data structuring facilities. In view of its intended usage both as a convenient basis to teach programming and as an efficient tool to write large programs, emphasis was placed on keeping the number of fundamental concepts reasonably small, on a simple and systematic language structure, and on efficient implementability."[38]

In order to achieve his intended usage, Wirth designed Pascal to adhere strictly to the tenets of structured programming that had developed since the publication of ALGOL 60:

1. Individual program routines are presented in modular form, with each module representing a complete logical thought. You can think of a module as a well-constructed paragraph in an essay (program).
2. The modules are to be hierarchically organized so that each unit within a module is itself logical and structured. You can think of a module's building components as the sentences in a paragraph.
3. Finally, the individual syntactic components are chosen for their straightforward meaning and ease of reading. You can think of this program level as the words in a sentence.

Exactly how Wirth implemented these general guidelines can be seen in the following two examples. The first is the Pascal version of the BASIC program listed earlier in this chapter:

```
PROGRAM Compute_X;
VAR X: REAL;
BEGIN
   X:= (7+8)/3;
   WRITELN(X);
END.
```

This simple program demonstrates some of the structuring features of Pascal. First, all Pascal programs are composed of three parts: (1) the *header*, which begins with the reserved word PROGRAM and is used to name the program; (2) the *variable declaration* section in which the data type and name of each variable in the program must be declared; and (3) the *body* of the program, which is delimited by the reserved words BEGIN and END. Other features that help to make the program intelligible include the use of all uppercase letters for reserved or key words, uppercase and lowercase letters for nonreserved or key words, and indenting to help the eye group the various logical levels.

The second program, which is slightly more complex, demonstrates the use of programming with self-contained modules:

```
PROGRAM Module_Demo;
VAR Num,Numsquare,Numroot: REAL;

PROCEDURE Input_Num;
BEGIN
   WRITELN('Enter a positive number. Pascal will
provide its square and square root.');
   READLN(Num);
END;

PROCEDURE Square_Num;
BEGIN
   Numsquare:=Num*Num;
END;

PROCEDURE Squareroot_Num;
BEGIN
   Numroot:=SQRT(Num);
END;
```

```
PROCEDURE Output_Num;
BEGIN
    WRITELN(Numsquare, ' is the square of ', Num);
    WRITELN(Numroot, ' is the square root of ', Num);
END;

BEGIN {Main Program}
    Input_Num;
    Square_Num;
    Squareroot_Num;
    Output_Num;
END.
```

Pascal programs are bottom heavy, with the main program coming last. As such, it is one of the programming languages in which the programmer is encouraged to build tools (such as subprocedures and data structures), then use the tools to solve the problem. In our example, PROGRAM Module_Demo, the main program consists of four modules; each, in turn, allows a number to be input, computes that number's square, computes its square root, and finally outputs the results in human-readable form. Each module is totally self-contained, starting with its own name following the reserved word PROCEDURE. It is thereafter delimited by the BEGIN...END construction.

Well-structured programs such as these have at least five advantages over programs created with a language that does not require precise structuring:

1. Structured programs are created with fewer errors because they require thinking before programming rather than encouraging an ad hoc, trial-and-error approach to programming.
2. Should errors arise in structured programs, they are easier to locate and fix because the logical connections are clearly stated and the modules isolate problem areas.
3. Structured programs are quicker to get up and running because there is less time spent debugging.
4. Structured programs are easier to revise since individual modules can be added, deleted, or changed without affecting the rest of the program.
5. Since good modules are portable, a programmer can build a library of modules that he or she can just drop into a new program.

If Pascal's only contribution to the theory of programming had been a superb implementation of the theory of structured programming, it would still rank as an intellectual achievement of the first order. But Wirth was also concerned about Pascal's range of applicability:

> The main extensions relative to ALGOL 60 lie in the domain of data structuring facilities, since their lack in ALGOL 60 was considered as the prime cause for its relatively narrow range of applicability. The introduction of record and file structures should make it possible to solve commercial type problems with Pascal, or at least to employ it successfully to demonstrate such problems in a programming course. *This should help erase the mystical belief in the segregation between scientific and commercial programming methods.* [emphasis added][39]

Wirth's goal appeared to be nothing less than the elusive, universal programming language. In order to accomplish this, he designed Pascal with the richest possible mix of data types. If programmers could conceive of a problem, they could find a Pascal data type that would meet their needs. The language supported five simple data types: BOOLEAN (true and false), CHAR (individual characters), INTEGER (such as 3, 15), REAL (such as 3.0, 15.35), and in later implementations, STRING (such as 'This is a string').

Structured data types were created by using the simple data types as building blocks. Pascal allowed four structured data types: *arrays* (groupings of the same simple type defined by the order or position of each element), *sets* (groupings of the same simple type defined by inclusion or exclusion of an element), *records* (a data structure that may contain elements of different types), and *files* (a data structure whose elements all conform to the same structure (e.g., a file of records). Finally, Wirth defined a new data type, called *pointers*, that could be used with dynamic data structures—those that changed their size during a program run.

As it turned out, Wirth was also something of a student of human nature. He realized that no matter how many data types were provided, someone would always want more. In order to accommodate such individuals, Wirth took the ultimate step in data-type flexibility—programmer-defined data types. Using a simple construct such as

```
TYPE dog = (beagle, collie, poodle)
```

programmers can create data types that may then be used to define a variable as follows

```
VAR spot: DOG
```

and to have values of that type assigned to it as follows

```
spot:= collie.
```

By allowing programmers to create new data types, Pascal automatically guards against the unwanted mixing of data types (you wouldn't want your dog to end up being named 3.17!). This is just one more example of the ways in which Pascal enforces clearly thought-out, well-structured programs.

In addition to being a student of computers, Wirth is also a student of history. Learning from the ALGOL 60 experience, he understood that a programming language, no matter how elegant, was ultimately at the mercy of the marketplace. Unless the language was implemented and made available for the current generation of computers, it would remain just an esoteric topic of discussion among professionals. To avoid this fate for Pascal, Wirth avowed a final goal:

> To develop implementations of this language which are both reliable and efficient on presently available computers, dispelling the commonly accepted notion that useful languages must either be slow to compile or slow to execute, and the belief that any nontrivial system is bound to contain mistakes forever.[40]

Wirth was successful in meeting this goal, but a barrier still remained to the widespread adoption of Pascal—the creation of a Pascal compiler for each of the dozens of new microcomputers that were flooding the market in the mid-1970s. Constructing a separate Pascal compiler for each new CPU would require years of work. Kenneth Bowles, a devotee of Pascal at the University of California at San Diego, however, devised an elegant solution to this problem. Rather than build a full-fledged compiler for each CPU, he proposed building a pseudocompiler (P-compiler) that would produce the same pseudocode (P-code), instead of pure machine code, for every processor. The fact that these P-compilers ran more slowly than true compilers was not viewed as a major problem.

In addition to the P-compiler, each implementation would also need an interpreter to turn the P-code into machine code that matched the idiosyncrasies of the individual CPUs. It turned out that these P-code interpreters were easy to write because they only had to interpret the predigested output from the P-compiler. By choosing a strategy of divide and conquer, Bowles was able to make Pascal available for all computers.

With the question of implementation resolved, decisions about the use of Pascal could be made on the merits of the language alone. Colleges and universities adopted Pascal as *the* language to teach programming, thereby ensuring that future computer professionals would use it. And the College Entrance Examination Board decreed that Pascal would be the language used on its Advanced Placement Exam in computer science, thereby ensuring that it would be taught in the high schools. Both Texas Instruments and Apple decided that Pascal was the language to use in the creation of their microcomputer software. Finally, as a result of all this support for the language within the computer industry, Pascal was made commercially available for most computers.

Pascal, more than any other language, represents not just the proposed solution to a class of programming problems (e.g., "a convenient basis to teach programming and an efficient tool to write large programs"), it is also the concrete instantiation of a programming philosophy—structured programming. Because of this peculiar role as standard bearer, any assessment of Pascal must proceed on two levels. First, is structured programming an important breakthrough in programming methodology? Second, is Pascal an important implementation of that methodology?

The market has already answered the first question affirmatively. Earlier languages such as FORTRAN and BASIC have appeared in structured versions, and Pascal has spawned new structured languages such as Wirth's own Modula-2 and the Department of Defense's ADA. The success of structured programming is really a response to what is generally perceived as the negative features of the GOTO statement, that is, the order of statements need not correspond to the order of program execution, and of flat programs, in which the overall structure is totally obscured. As an aside, most structured programming languages, including Pascal, contain provisions for the use of GOTO statements—old ideas die hard, even in the computer age. But they are eschewed by purists, and used sparingly by non-doctrinal programmers and only in specific situations.

The market has also answered the second question in the affirmative and that means that Wirth's original goals have been met— Pascal is an important teaching language (viz. the College Entrance Examination Board decision) and is being used to develop large programs (viz. the Apple computer decision). Why has Pascal succeeded while other structured languages (e.g., extended ALGOL, Euler, ALGOL 68) have not fared as well? The keys are conceptual and structural clarity. By providing a rich mix of data types and control structures, Wirth has provided the programmer with all the tools needed for conceptual clarity; by forcing the programmer to use structured programming techniques (e.g., strong data typing, declaration of all variables and constants, modularity), he has ensured structural clarity.

There is no doubt that Pascal is worth learning for the professional, or would-be professional, programmer. Yet what about the personal computer owner who only intends to write an occasional small program and whose machine came with BASIC? For this user, Pascal has a number of deficiencies: First, simple BASIC programs may be three times as long when written in Pascal. Second, because Pascal is generally compiled (Macintosh Pascal is an interesting exception), Pascal programs can be more trouble to write and edit. Third, Pascal's syntax is pickier and unforgiving of data-type errors. Finally, Pascal programs require a lot of forethought (e.g., declaring variables and thinking out overall structure), whereas BASIC allows you to get started immediately and make changes and decision on the fly.

Ultimately, learning Pascal is like learning a mental discipline. For some, learning the discipline will be an important goal even if they never intend to use it. For other, more utilitarian, souls, whose goal is simply to write a running program, BASIC is adequate to the task.

A LANGUAGE FOR CREATING
LANGUAGES—FORTH

Programming computers can be crazy-making. Other professions give you the luxury of seeing tangible proof of your efforts. A watchmaker can watch the cogs and wheels; a seamstress can watch the seams come together with each stitch. But programmers design, build, and repair the stuff of imagination, ghostly mechanisms that escape the senses. Our work takes place not in RAM, not in an editor, but within our minds.

Building models in the mind is both the challenge and the joy of programming. How should we prepare for it? Arm ourselves with better debuggers, compilers, and disassemblers? They help, but our most essential tools and techniques are mental. We need a consistent and practical methodology for *Thinking about* software problems . . . .

. . . .

FORTH is a language, an operating system, a set of tools, and a philosophy. It is an ideal means for thinking because it corresponds to the way our minds work.[41]

FORTRAN was invented by a group of IBM employees, and COBOL was created by a committee of government and industry representatives. LISP was devised by a mathematician who wanted to explore artificial intelligence research, and Pascal was constructed by a computer scientist who was concerned with teaching good programming style. One of today's most unusual languages was also a one-man product, but it wasn't originally intended to be a programming language.

Since FORTRAN is best suited for scientific applications, and COBOL is tailored for business applications, the ideal language might be one that is created specifically for the application area in which the programmer is working. If you want to program a graphic display, you need a graphic display language. If your goal is to control the processes in a chemical plant, the ideal language would be a chemical-plant-process-control language. Of course, such a proliferation of languages would create an incredible tower of Babel problem. But what if one language could provide programmers with the means of creating a specialized language for each application?

FORTH was invented by a person who was more interested (at first) in galaxies and planets than in the characteristics of computer languages. But that's the way inventions often happen. The person who invented the wheel probably had no intention of benefiting humankind.

FORTH is an example of one man's tool that grew into a full-fledged programming cult. Charles H. Moore, the person who invented the language, was not a computer scientist or even a professional programmer when he started experimenting with his new approach to software abstractions. He was an astronomer, and his initial goal was to find an easier way to use computers to control the motions of telescopes.[42]

Moore first became acquainted with computers in the 1950s, when he was an undergraduate physics student at MIT, working part-time at the Smithsonian Astrophysical Observatory. He was one of the first astronomers to explore the ways computers could be used to control telescopes. In tracking the motions of satellites, for example, very precise and complex adjustments have to be made in order to keep telescopes aimed and focused at precisely the right spot in the sky. At that time, the only high-level programming language was FORTRAN, so Moore learned it.

Moore's career brought him into contact with a number of different computer applications at such diverse institutions as the Stanford Linear Accelerator and a carpet manufacturer in New York. As he was applying his programming skills to a variety of different jobs, he experimented with ways of increasing his productivity as a programmer. By the late 1960s, his experiments with programming tools became something that needed a name. At that time he was working on a third generation IBM 1130 computer. He believed that his language-in-the-making was truly a fourth-generation language, so he decided to call it FOURTH. Since the IBM 1130 would only accept five-letter identifiers, the name became FORTH.

In the 1970s, Moore, by then a full-fledged astronomer and free-lance programmer, began to use his language to control the 36-foot radio telescope at Kitt Peak National Observatory in Arizona. He estimated that his private programming tool increased his productivity tenfold over his ability to create applications in FORTRAN. Other astronomers began to ask him how they could apply his invention, so Moore placed his language in the public domain in order to encourage its adoption. A colleague at Kitt Peak, Elizabeth Rather, became the world's second FORTH programmer and, in 1973, helped him start FORTH, Inc., to create new FORTH applications and spread the word about his language.

It soon became evident that astronomy was not the only field in which FORTH could be applied profitably. The kind of programming involved in controlling telescopes was similar to the kind of programming used in any industrial or scientific process that involved direct computer control of complex instrumentation and real-time processes—the field known as *process control*. Portable heart monitors and other biomedical equipment, automatic radar systems, and automated movie cameras for special-effects sequences, as well as most of the astronomical observatories in the world, now use FORTH as a process-control language.

The way in which FORTH has diffused into the general computer community is another way in which this language differs from others. The refinement of the language and its introduction to new application areas have not been supported by large computer manufacturers, as in the case of IBM's FORTRAN, or promoted by government agencies, as in the case of COBOL, or taught to undergraduates, like BASIC and Pascal. The growth of FORTH has been nurtured by the efforts of a small group of devotees who call themselves the FORTH community; thus, FORTH became the first language to attract attention through the efforts of a grass-roots movement.

Kim Harris, a software engineer for a Silicon Valley company, was initially skeptical about the wild claims made by the devotees of this new language but was converted to FORTH when he saw a FORTH programmer develop a music-playing program in 15 minutes—a task that an assembly-language programmer of Harris's acquaintance had been working on for more than a year. Harris convinced his company to invest in a FORTH system. At that time, the language was running on minicomputers and mainframes. But a new kind of computer—the first microprocessor-based personal computers—was already in the hands of hobbyists.

In 1977, Harris and four others formed FIG—the FORTH Interest Group. By this time, the microcomputer age had arrived, and the FIG founders came from the same hobbyist community that spawned successful microcomputer hardware manufacturers such as Apple and microcomputer software companies such as Microsoft. The five founding members of FIG, with the help of seven volunteers, wrote a microcomputer version of FORTH known as FIG FORTH. In 1979 they began to sell printed source-code listing and installation manuals for $20—essentially, giving it away.

With the availability of FIG FORTH, the FORTH cult began to gain adherents in the hobbyist community, which by 1979 had grown into an industry. With its cryptic notation, the new language was definitely not a favorite among amateur programmers. But microcomputer programmers who were tired of the slowness and relative clumsiness of BASIC programming began to use FORTH. The most attractive features of the language were its execution speed, its compactness, the power over the workings of the hardware it gave programmers, and its extensibility.

Execution speed is particularly important to programmers who intend to create saleable programs for microcomputers, particularly if graphic effects are involved. Assembly language is the only way to write fast-executing code, but the fine detail work required by assembly-language programming slows down development time—a crucial factor in a fast-moving market like microcomputer software. FORTH programs can run as fast as comparable assembly-language programs, but FORTH wizards claim their versions can be written as quickly as comparable BASIC programs.

When microcomputers first fell into the hands of amateur programmers, the amount of main memory in most machines was restricted to no more than 16 kilobytes. This meant that many applications simply could not be programmed for microcomputers: The programming language (including the computer's operating system and the language's editor and interpreter or compiler program) took up too much memory, and the applications themselves were too bulky. A FORTH system, including operating system, editor, compiler, and interpreter (FORTH is both compiled and interpreted), however, can fit into less than 8 kilobytes. An efficiently constructed FORTH application program can fit into less than 1 kilobyte.

FORTH programmers also like the way the language gives them direct access to the operations of the hardware machine. Hierarchical layers of virtual machines make abstractions easier to construct but restrict fine-level control of registers and main memory activities. FORTH offers a window to lower levels. The attraction of this kind of power to an experienced programmer is like the attraction of a manual transmission rather than automatic transmission to an experienced automobile driver: The machine is more responsive, but it takes more work and close attention and is less forgiving of mistakes.

The extensibility of the language is the key feature that makes FORTH highly attractive to its devotees and that promises a great deal of power to less-expert programmers who are willing to learn FORTH's unorthodox notation and data structures. Like Logo and other extensible languages, FORTH allows programmers to create their own subroutines, which can become building blocks for more complex programs. In Logo, these subroutines are known as *procedures*; in FORTH they are known as *words*.

The core program that is furnished with a FORTH system includes a number of primitive words (not to be confused with memory words) that are listed in the system's dictionary. (The word for multiplication, for example, is * and the word for addition is +.) These dictionary entries are actually pointers to locations in memory where the machine-language equivalents of these words are stored. A programmer combines these primitive words into various combinations (also known as words), which are then entered into the dictionary in compiled form. A FORTH program consists of a series of definitions of progressively more complex words built from combinations of simpler ones.[43]

In FORTH, new words are defined by preceding the name of the definition with a colon (:) and ending the definition with a semicolon (;). For example, assume that you want to print a hollow box by printing the capital letter X an appropriate number of times in a square pattern on the computer screen. You would start out by using the primitive FORTH word EMIT, which prints a designated character, and the number 88, which is the ASCII designation for a capital X. A word for printing a single X would be:

```
: X    88 EMIT ;
```

As soon as you press the carriage return, the system responds with the word ok at the end of the line, signifying that the word named X was defined. When you press the carriage return, the FORTH interpreter recognizes the colon as the command to define a new word, then scans the rest of the line for words that have already been defined; according to the built-in dictionary, the combination of 88 and EMIT means "print a capital X." The new word X is then compiled in your computer's machine language and stored in the dictionary.

Once you have defined X, you can type the word X, followed by a carriage return, and an X will be printed on the screen, followed by FORTH's ok. When you enter a word followed by a carriage return, the FORTH word INTERPRET is activated; the text interpreter scans the characters you entered, compares it with the words in the dictionary, and if it finds a correspondence, passes the defined word to the word EXECUTE, which then executes the machine-language command that corresponds to the dictionary word X.

To print a horizontal line of Xs followed by a carriage return and line feed, your next word would be:

```
: LINE   X X X X X X carriage return ;
```

Another way to do this would be:

```
: LINE   DO X LOOP carriage return ;
```

The DO...LOOP construction is the same kind of iterative procedure used in other programming languages. If you want to print 6 Xs in a horizontal line using the loop, all you have to do is define LINE and enter 6 LINE followed by a carriage return. When you execute LINE, the computer will print:

```
XXXXX      (for convenience we'll omit the ok prompt)
```

In order to create the second through fifth lines of a six-by-six X square, another definition is needed to cause one X to be printed, followed by four spaces, followed by another X, followed by a carriage return:

```
: PAIR   X 4 SPACES X carriage return ;
```

When you execute PAIR, the result looks like this:

```
X    X
```

Putting all these words together into a word called BOX results in:

```
: BOX LINE PAIR PAIR PAIR PAIR LINE ;
```

When you execute BOX, the result is the following:

```
XXXXX    (LINE) (These comments would not be printed.)
X    X   (PAIR)
X    X   (PAIR)
X    X   (PAIR)
X    X   (PAIR)
XXXXX    (LINE)
```

The listing for this program would look like this:

```
0  (  A box made of Xs)
1  :  X 88 EMIT ;
2  :  LINE X X X X X X carriage return ;
3  :  PAIR X 4 SPACES carriage return ;
4  :  BOX LINE PAIR PAIR PAIR PAIR LINE ;
```

The first line, enclosed in parentheses, is a comment that is ignored by FORTH's interpreter-compiler. The first parentheses is a word that means comment follows, so it is followed by a space, as are all FORTH words. The second parenthesis, however, is a delimiter, not a word, so no space is required. You could also create words such as 2BOXES; each new word can be used as a building block for more complex words. Although more complicated considerations enter the process, all FORTH programs are similar to this example insofar as they consist of a series of progressively more complex word definitions.

Forth's extensibility allows programmers to create their own data types and data structures. If your version doesn't have provisions for floating-point numbers or string variables, for example, you can make them up yourself by defining new words to perform the operations you need. But FORTH's extensibility doesn't stop with operations or data structures. The language itself can be customized by advanced programmers. Except for the primitive words and a small machine-language program known as the *inner interpreter*, the entire FORTH system is written in FORTH and is accessible to the FORTH programmer. The text editor, the assembler, and the compiler all can be customized.

In order to deal with numbers and calculations, the FORTH programmer must make use of two concepts that are often confusing to beginning programmers—postfix, or reverse Polish notation, and the data structure known as the stack.

Postfix notation looks strange to everybody at first because we learn to perform mathematical calculations using infix notation. For example, everybody knows what 2 + 3 means. In postfix notation, however, this calculation would be written 2 3 +. Although this way of representing a calculation seems unusually complicated to a human, it is easier to implement for interpreters or compilers. Certain kinds of electronic calculators, such as those manufactured by Hewlett-Packard, use postfix notation. Because the FORTH compiler doesn't have to perform the more complex parsing required for interpretation of infix notation, postfix notation is one of the reasons the FORTH compiler is more compact than other language compilers.

Postfix notation is intimately related to the data structure that is most closely associated with FORTH and that gives beginning programmers the most trouble—*the stack*. Although FORTH's stack is used as part of a different computational scheme, it is similar to the stack data structures used by other languages. A stack is a group of memory cells organized as a last-in first-out (LIFO) data structure. In FORTH, numbers (which can represent many different kinds of parameters, including alphabetic characters and dots of light on a screen) are treated like trays in a cafeteria or tennis balls in a can. That is, the numbers are pushed onto the top of the stack and pulled off of it in reverse order to the one in which they were pushed on in the first place. (Actually, the values on the stack do not move, a *pointer* moves; but it is easier to visualize a moving stack than a pointer.)

The FORTH interpreter-compiler program evaluates arithmetic expressions according to two rules: If it recognizes a number, that number is pushed onto the top of the stack; if it recognizes an operator like * or +, it pops the top two numbers off the stack, applies the operation to the numbers, then pushes the result back on the stack. An expression like 2 3 +, then, would result in the number 2 being pushed onto the stack, after which 3 would be pushed onto the stack; then the numbers would be popped off the stack and added together, and the result (5) would be pushed onto the stack.

When the operator pulls the two numbers off the stack, those entries are discarded. The result is a stack with one number on it— 5. The same rules are applied to multiple operators and numbers, two at a time.

Postfix notation and stack effects get tricky when the operations become more complex than very simple arithmetic. For example, in order to solve the problem (X − Y) / Z, a special kind of word, known as a *stack manipulation operator*, is required. In this case, the word is SWAP, which switches the order of the top two numbers on the stack. SWAP 1 2 takes a stack with 2 on the top and 1 on the bottom and turns it into a stack with 1 on the top and 2 on the bottom. By using SWAP, X − Y / Z can be solved by converting it to the form Z X Y − SWAP /.

First, Y and X are popped off the top of the stack, Y is subtracted from X, and the result is pushed onto the stack. Then, the remaining values are swapped, the top (rightmost) value is divided by the bottom (leftmost) value, and the result is pushed onto the stack. People trained in orthodox infix arithmetic have to practice this style of operation before it becomes comfortable.

Although we used the term "the stack," the structure discussed above is the *parameter stack* because it holds parameters (also known as arguments in other languages) that are passed from one word to another. There is actually a second stack, known as the return stack, which holds pointers that are used by FORTH to keep track of words that are executing other words—a place to store values temporarily while operations are performed on the parameter stack. The *return stack* is also a LIFO structure, capable of storing many values; however, anything that is put on the return stack must be removed before the end of a definition is executed (signaled by a semicolon). Parameters cannot be passed from one word to another by means of the return stack.

FORTH allows decision-making conditional operators, in its own peculiar way. Suppose you are programming a tennis ball can-stuffing machine and you want the machine to put a lid on the can when 5 balls are stuffed. The FORTH phrase

```
5 = IF PUT-LID THEN
```

would test whether the number of balls in the can is equal to 5 (5 =); If it is, the word PUT-LID is executed. If it is not, execution moves to the words that follow THEN. The word = takes two values off the stack (the number of balls in the can and the number 5), compares them, and if the comparison is true, puts a value on the stack known as a FLAG. A FLAG is a value that one part of a program leaves on the stack as a signal for another part of a program. Traditionally, 0 is the flag for false, and 1 (or any other nonzero number) is the flag for true.

The comparison operators $<$ (less than) and $>$ (greater than) familiar to programmers who use other languages are also used in FORTH. FORTH also uses $0 =$ (zero equal), $0<$ (zero less than), and $0>$ (zero greater than). It also allows IF...THEN...ELSE statements, as in the following:

```
5 = IF PUT-LID ELSE STUFF-BALL THEN
```

As in other languages, these constructions cause conditional branching—a rerouting of the path of execution of instructions. Also like other languages, FORTH allows a special kind of word definition in which execution can branch back to an earlier part of the same definition until a certain condition is satisfied—a *loop*.

FORTH was an instance of a breakthrough idea—that programmers should create their own special languages, tailored to each task—but it is hardly the last word in languages. An entirely new phase in the history of programming languages is now underway—the creation of very high-level languages, programming environments, and new computational metaphors. The next chapter, "The Future of Programming Languages," surveys these developments, which promise to be the most dramatic forward leaps in the history of computerized thought tools.

6

The Future of
Programming Languages

*The adaptation of machinery can only be perfected by him
who, as it were, enters into it, making it an incarnation of
himself, an enlargement of his own organism. Oliver Wendell
Holmes has described the putting of his life into a rowing
boat—his every volition extending as perfectly into his oars as
if his spinal column ran down the center of the keel. So the
thoughtful locomotive driver is clothed with all the attributes
of a power superior to his own, except volition. Every faculty is
stimulated and every sense exalted.*[1]

THE COGNITIVE CONNECTION

The use of language is a social skill. Although philosophers argue
over the possibility of a private language, billions of people exercise
their linguistic skill to accomplish everything from saying "good morn-
ing" to writing books to explaining how to program a computer. But
language was not always such an all-purpose tool. It took tens of
thousands of years for natural thought to give rise to natural language,
which then increased the range and power of thought, leading to symbolic language, science, and ultimately computers. Now, with an incredible burst of acceleration, the same evolutionary process is
transforming computer hardware and software with astonishing rapidity.

At the software level, primitive, plug-programmed computers
gave rise to stored programs and internal machine language, which
engendered assembly language, which begat higher-level languages.
At the same time that software was evolving, the speed and capacity
of computer hardware was increasing by orders of magnitude. As the
power of computing machines increased, so did the need for more

powerful and efficient languages with which to program them. Powerful languages help us program powerful new machines, which in turn help us design even more powerful machines. This process of self-transformation has led to a new generation of computer and software every 5 years, and the end is nowhere in sight.

The theory of computation took no more than 30 years to evolve from the abstract solution to a 2500-year-old problem into a game for schoolchildren—from Turing machines in the 1930s to turtle graphics in the 1960s. Judging from current research efforts into very high-level languages, we can expect computer systems of the 1990s to bring enormous amounts of thinking power to an increasing number of people. When these new metalanguages graduate from the research laboratories and spread through the general population, today's relatively small group of programmers will expand into a large community.

The historical trend is clear: With every past breakthrough in human-computer communications, the availability of intellectual augmentation tools has been extended to a larger proportion of the population. The cycle started in the 1940s, when the first computer language breakthrough (stored programs) brought sizable calculating power to mathematicians. Then, in the 1950s, high-level languages extended the mental horizons of scientists and accountants. In the 1960s, time-sharing brought new thought tools to college students, engineers, and business administrators. In the 1970s, desktop computers triggered the office automation revolution and ushered in the age of the knowledge worker. By the mid-1980s, personal computers had been used by tens of millions of people in offices, classrooms, and homes.

By the dawn of the twenty-first century, the terms "programmer" and "programming language" will probably be inadequate descriptions of the human-computer relationship (just as "code" and "coder" disappeared with the advent of languages like FORTRAN). J.C.R. Licklider, one of the people who first foresaw the evolution of very-high-level software, declared, back in 1960:

> The hope is that, in not too many years, human brains and computing machines will be coupled together very tightly, and that the resulting partnership will think as no human brain has ever thought and process data in a way not approached by the information-handling machines we know today.[2]

This predicted amplification of human cognitive power will not come about because of any radical changes in our basic thinking apparatus but will result from changes in the way human-computer communications are carried out. These changes are propelling today's computer languages in two directions: Improved human-machine interfaces and more sophisticated programming metaphors will bring the power of programming within range of ever-larger nonexpert populations; at the same time, development of new, advanced programming tools and languages will give programming specialists a great deal more power than they have today.

The evolution of more easily learnable programming languages for nonspecialists and the design of more powerful programming tools for expert programmers are intimately related to one another. Expert programmers will use high-level software tools to free themselves from lower-level tasks such as translating algorithms into code and keeping tabs on syntax in order to devote their thoughts to creative problem solving. And the most important problem they are out to solve is the question of how to make powerful computers available to nonprogrammers. Novices will use the new languages created by experts to amplify their own capabilities to solve problems, the most important of which is the question of how to use computers to help augment their own thinking.

The idea that computers could augment the intellectual capabilities of nonprogrammers originated in the Defense Department's Advanced Research Projects Agency (ARPA) in the early 1960s, and the future of programming languages is being built today on foundations laid down by the ARPA-funded research community decades ago. Licklider, who was the director of ARPA's Information Processing Techniques Office, believed that the future development of sophisticated human-computer communications was integral to the management of our increasingly complex civilization; to that end, he funded selected groups of researchers around the country in order to create what he then called Man-Computer Symbiosis. Before Licklider's effort, the main thrust of computer research was aimed at automating various human activities—turning them over to machines. In contrast, symbiosis was based on a kind of partnership in which human minds could provide the guidance for powerful but unimaginative information-processing tools and the computers could provide power and speed for the creative but computationally limited capabilities of human cognition.

Before such lofty goals as true symbiosis could be achieved, however, fundamental changes had to be implemented in the way computers were designed and used. ARPA supported projects that promised dramatic leaps beyond current technologies. The development of interactive, time-sharing computers, the use of graphic displays as computer output devices and keyboards and mice as input devices, the acceleration of research into AI languages and programs, and the invention of computer networks were among the more notable achievements of the ARPA-funded efforts of the 1960s.[3]

One of the visionaries funded by Licklider's office was Douglas Engelbart, who had been convinced since the late 1950s that a properly designed and programmed computer system could be used as a kind of intellectual amplifier. When ARPA provided him the funding, Engelbart wrote a now-classic paper, "A Conceptual Framework for the Augmentation of Man's Intellect," in which he pointed out that all humans have the same "hardware," even though human cultures differ widely in their material or spiritual development. Individuals in a civilized society, for example, differ from members of a primitive society by virtue of the different frameworks their cultures give them for augmenting basic human intellectual powers.

This framework is a kind of cultural software that is not inherent in the human brain but is provided when the culture educates its members; it consists of language, artifacts (such as books or wheels), training (such as in the skill of reading), and methodology (such as the scientific method). Engelbart proposed that each component of such a framework, and the system as a whole, could be powerfully amplified by the application of specially modified computer systems.[4]

Engelbart and his colleagues at the Augmentation Research Center (ARC) achieved several spectacular successes, the effects of which have taken decades to diffuse into the general computer-using population. One of ARC's first innovations was to put words on televisionlike screens and use computers to manipulate those words—the first implementation of what is now known as word processing. Although this use of computers is now commonplace, it was considered bold and purely experimental when it was first developed at ARC in the late 1960s.

The other significant contributions of Engelbart's ARC team were the pointing device known as the mouse, a small object that fits in the user's hand and moves a pointer around the computer display screen when the object is rolled on a desk, and windows on the display screen that gives the user several different views of different kinds of material (two different sections of text, for example). The key idea behind ARC was similar to that of Licklider's symbiosis model: Rather than *replacing* humans, computers were seen to be ideally suited for *increasing the power* of individuals and groups to solve complex problems.

Licklider, Engelbart, and their proteges at Xerox Corporation's Palo Alto Research Center (PARC) knew that if these machines were to become practical tools for anyone other than programming wizards, the way humans and computers communicate with one another would have to be radically redesigned. The part of the human-computer system they chose to concentrate upon first was that aspect of computing that had been widely ignored by earlier generations of computer designers—the *human-computer interface*—the software and input-output devices that mediated between brains and central processing units. The goal was to adapt computers to the way people think rather than to adapt ways of thinking to the peculiarities of computers.

To meet this goal, the researchers at PARC based their formal design methodology on a number of findings about the way human brains process information. Some of these findings had been known to psychologists but ignored by computer designers. For example, the inherent limitation of the human short-term memory—"The Magical Number Seven, Plus or Minus Two"—had been discovered in the 1950s.[5] Ten years after they started, when several members of the PARC team published their design methodology, they discussed the psychological principles upon which they based their design approach. The Star to which they refer is the name of the product that was eventually based on PARC's prototype machine, the Alto:

Some types of concepts are inherently difficult for people to grasp. Without being too formal about it, our experience before and during the Star design led us to the following classification:

Easy	Hard
concrete	abstract
visible	invisible
copying	creating
choosing	filling in
recognizing	generating
editing	programming
interactive	batch

The characteristics on the left were incorporated into the Star user's conceptual model. The characteristics on the right we attempted to avoid.[6]

When they talked about the "user's conceptual model," the Star designers were acknowledging the Janus-faced nature of the human interface: One aspect of the interface, the part that "faces" the computer, is more closely related to traditional operating systems; the more important, and heretofore neglected part of the interface, however, was the part that connects directly with the conceptual models in the minds of computer users. The display media through which the computer makes information available to users, the input devices people use to convey their commands to the computer, the language in which those commands are communicated, the user's conceptual models of how the computer works, and the interactions among these factors are all part of the interface.

By relating each of the pairs of easy-hard concepts to the ideas people use when they explain to themselves how computer systems operate, the designers came up with a new model of the human-computer interface, incorporating, among other design criteria, the principles of *a familiar conceptual model for users, the desktop metaphor,* and *seeing and pointing rather than remembering and typing.*

A "familiar conceptual model" is a way of presenting the computer's operations to people in a way that makes use of people's prior knowledge of familiar tools; the prior knowledge helps introduce new kinds of knowledge about the computer versions of these tools. Instead of facing an enigmatic and unfamiliar environment, the users of this new kind of computer would immediately perceive many references to well-known operations.

An example of a conceptual model is the idea of a push-down stack, the abstraction used so much in the high-level language FORTH. Although the stack is nothing more than a collection of memory addresses, most programmers find it easy to visualize it in terms of a cafeteria-tray metaphor. The PARC interface based its metaphor for information manipulation on the familiar physical objects used in an office: paper folders, file cabinets, in baskets and out baskets, and garbage cans. The electronic desktop was designed to make the new way of working less alien and forbidding and to link users' conceptual models with the way computers actually operate.

Personal computers built on the Alto-Star-Macintosh paradigm are bringing programming skills to millions of nonspecialists. At the same time, the interface has been built into high-performance computers, such as machines that execute LISP as their machine language, used by expert programmers. Specialized tools important to experts, such as debuggers, compilers, and editors, have been adapted for more efficient use with this new interface. In the 1980s, both novices and experts are using mouse-driven systems with windows, bit-mapped screens (in which individual picture elements on the screen are directly connected to the computer's memory cells, making it possible to issue commands to the computer via visual representations on the screen), and other elements of the PARC interface as general programming tools.

As a new generation of programming students begins to learn how to control computers via the new interface, the old style of programming is becoming as outmoded as teletype printers and punched-card programs. A high-level language is a virtual machine that makes it easier for programmers to manipulate lower-level virtual machines such as assembly language and machine language; a programming *environment* (as a collection of programming tools is known) based on the new interface is a higher-level virtual machine that makes it even easier to manipulate high-level languages—a very-high-level language, if you will.

Even very-high-level languages are not the ultimate peak of the hierarchy of abstractions. The PARC interface became a foundation for a whole new level of graphical, metaphorical, intuitively learnable programming systems. Indeed, as computer and display hardware continues to become faster, more powerful, and less expensive, programming systems based on the PARC principles now are increasingly being used to experiment with new programming metaphors and human-computer interface systems that may eventually replace PARC's version.

ALTERNATE MODELS: SMALLTALK AND OBJECT-ORIENTED LANGUAGES

The purpose of the Smalltalk project is to provide computer support for the creative spirit in everyone . . . . We have chosen to concentrate on two principal areas of research: a language of description (programming language) that serves as an interface between the models in the human mind and those in computing hardware, and a language of interaction (user interface) that matches the human communication system to that of the computer . . . .

. . . .

. . . Instead of a bit-grinding processor raping and plundering data structures, we have a universe of well-behaved objects that courteously ask each other to carry out their various desires.[7]

The first software breakthrough in the 1940s, the concept of stored-program computers, allowed computers to store and retrieve both data (information) and programs (instructions about how to manipulate that data) in the computer's internal memory. This breakthrough had the beneficial effect of speeding up computation time, as well as the negative effect of convincing programmers that a program is a sequence of instructions that operates upon data and that data is an inert raw material stored in the computer's memory locations.

Traditional software systems, no matter how much they differed on other issues, all treated these two components in the same manner—as totally separate entities. Indeed, mechanisms such as data typing have been added to high-level languages to make sure that programmers choose data representations that are appropriate for the kinds of computing procedures assigned to operate upon them. Thus, the procedural model has dominated thought about software architecture across all programming languages, just as the von-Neumann machine has dominated computer hardware architecture.

There is nothing in the Turing machine definition of computation that requires computer software to conform to the von-Neumann or procedural models; it was simply easier to do things that way in the early days of computer hardware. Old habits are particularly pernicious in the software realm, where people become inordinately attached to the first thought tools they happened to learn. Unfortunately for programmers who aren't mentally flexible, new tools tend to come along quickly. But computer science is a rather unique forum for proving the power of new metaphors or discarding trivial ones, because it is rather quickly evident whether or not a new model enables people to do something new with computers or to do old tasks in better ways.

Smalltalk was one of the first and most spectacular creations of the generation of programmers who had grown up using interactive programming, ever-faster transistorized components, and ever-growing memory capacities rather than the old batch-processed, tube-based, limited-capacity computers of the FORTRAN and COBOL era. With Smalltalk came a new metaphor of computation as a system of software objects, all containing their own data and instructions and carrying on computations by exchanging messages rather than by performing instructions. Smalltalk was more than another computer language. It was a portal to a whole new way to think about what computation is and what it can do.

Alan Kay, the originator and guiding spirit of the Smalltalk group at PARC, had been profoundly influenced by three programming innovations. As a computer science student at the University of Utah, he had been part of the community of ARPA researchers during the late 1960s; the ARPA culture led him to the Sketchpad program and the language Logo. As a graduate student, one of Kay's tasks was to decipher some program listings of Simula, a language first developed in Norway that used a new abstraction—software objects. Kay used parts of Sketchpad, Logo, and Simula as tools to craft the ideas that became the language Smalltalk.

As one of the first to attempt to design and build a personal computer—the FLEX machine—in the late 1960s, Kay was looking for programming tools to make the next generations of computers comprehensible to nonexperts. From Sketchpad came the idea of graphical interaction—the notion that dynamic visual representation is an important medium for human-machine communication and that the internal contents of the computer can be altered by changing the screen representation with a light pen. From Logo came the idea of powerful ideas that are learned by direct interaction with a simulated microworld, as in the metaphor of "teaching the turtle a new word" as a way of writing a program. The turtle itself, aside from its psychological power as "an object to think with," was one model for a computer's version of an object.

Simula 67, the Norwegian language that contributed Smalltalk's object-oriented underpinning, was derived from Algol 60 by Ole-Johan Dahl and Kristen Nygaard of the Norwegian Computing Center. The language was particularly well suited to real-time simulation programs, which is precisely the kind of power we would want in a language designed to be a kind of microworld construction kit. And it introduced the idea of a *software object*, a new entity that was not strictly a data structure and not strictly an algorithm, but a hybrid of the two.

In the early 1970s, Kay and his PARC colleagues managed to extend Simula's notion of objects, combine it with high-resolution graphics, add a command interface organized around mouse-based point-and-select operations upon browsers, pop-up menus, and graphical icons, and imbed the language into an integrated environment in which the operating system, source program, interpreter, compiler, editor, and debugger are all visible on the screen at the same time and can all be interactively controlled by the programmer.

The Smalltalk paradigm of message-passing between hybrid data-procedure entities was described by Kay in 1977:

> Both data and procedures can be replaced by the single idea of "activities," computerlike entities that exhibit behavior when they are sent an appropriate message. There are no nouns and verbs in such a language, only dynamically communicating activities. Every transaction, description and control process is thought of as sending messages to and receiving messages from activities in the system . . . .
>
> . . . .
>
> The host computer is in effect divided into thousands of computers, each with the capabilities of the whole. The message-activity approach therefore enables one to dynamically represent a system at many levels of organization from the atomic to the macroscopic, but with a "skin" of protection at each qualitative level of detail through which negotiative messages must be sent and checked. This level of complexity can be safely handled because the language severely limits the kinds of interactions between activities, allowing only those that are appropriate, much as a hormone is allowed to interact with only a few specifically responsive target cells.[8]

Logo's turtle is a crude example of the kind of entity Kay was proposing. The turtle takes certain messages from the programmer, such as FORWARD 50, and knows what procedures to follow: It recognizes a basic lexicon of replies to such messages, and it can be taught new procedures based on combinations of those primitive building blocks. The meaning of high-level messages can be changed by altering their submessages. In comparison to true Smalltalk objects, however, a turtle is just one, not very complicated instance of an entire hierarchy of objects.

In Smalltalk, *everything* is an object; numbers, control structures, strings, complex data structures, procedures are all objects.

An arithmetic object can send a message to the object 6, asking it to add itself to 2. A graphic object can perform all the calculations, computations, and operating system procedure calls necessary to maintain its own screen representation and to transform itself to other representations upon command: When the user of an icon-based system moves the mouse, places the cursor on an icon, presses a button, and watches the icon expand into a page of a document, all the icon objects, system objects, document objects, and file objects exchange messages with one another.

The powers of Smalltalk objects as building blocks for higher-level abstractions are as important as their internal powers. Everything in Smalltalk is an *instance* of a *class* and is the *superclass* of its own instances. A turtle object might be an instance of the class ObjectsToThinkWith (Smalltalk syntax runs multiple-word names together, using initial caps as delimiters). And ObjectsToThinkWith might be part of a larger class, MindTools. The hierarchical arrangement of message-exchanging entities is one of the keys to Smalltalk's power through a mechanism called *inheritance*. Every object automatically inherits the properties of its superclass and is differentiated from the superclass by its *instance variables*—the pieces of information that instances of that class are allowed to possess.

All the appropriate levels of this software hierarchy are visible to the programmer by means of the hierarchical menu structures know as *browsers*. A class is described by creating or editing its *class template*. A small slice of class template for a turtle would look like this:

```
class name; Turtle
superclass: ObjectToThinkWith
instance variable names: position, heading, color
```

When Smalltalk programmers create new classes, they have to specify how instances of that class react when they receive messages. *Method* is the name for the lists of instructions that describe an instance's reaction to a message. A new object can instantly inherit all the instance variables of its superclass but can very quickly be modified to define a new instance—a powerful idea that enables programmers to create new objects, in essence, by saying it's like this other object, except for X, thereby delegating all the laborious copying of shared subroutines to a lower level.

A basic Smalltalk system contains several thousand objects; more elaborate applications can be much larger. The hierarchical layering of objects, classes, and instances is the abstraction tool that tames this complexity; it does so by selecting essential features to highlight on each level, allowing the operational details to sink out of sight into lower levels. The user or programmer can always navigate because the total system is structured in the same way as the basic objects. Smalltalk's tool for describing new structures is recursive on all levels: A programmer can redesign the entire system and a user can customize the appearance of an icon in essentially the same way.

The power of these recursive description tools lies in the way a new user can add new knowledge of the system in a modular way, expanding on what has already been learned. Once a level has been mastered, the intermediate Smalltalk user can take a look at the level below—to use the browsers as their inventor intended them to be used. A programmer or user can explore deeper levels of the system by moving the mouse up or down a menu and clicking a button, then perhaps typing a few words from a keyboard or copying the required command sequence from a piece of preexisting code at a lower level (look for something like the thing you want, then modify it) and watching what happens.

Instead of choosing algorithms and data structures, mapping out the flow of control, putting together modules that pass information in sequential order, and writing the code for each operation, the Smalltalk programmer chooses a class, begins editing it by adding and deleting instance variables, roaming up and down the hierarchy of abstractions to collect snippets of code and useful objects, and then putting the components together. The debugging operation, by which subtle programming errors are corrected, is also facilitated by Smalltalk's hierarchical structure and recursive tools.

The watching what happens part of Smalltalk (the environment) is at least as important as the what happens part (the societies of objects passing messages to one another). The original PARC interface, using windows, icons, menus, and mouse selection, evolved from the Smalltalk environment created in the early 1970s for the first Altos. The structure of the language requires an equally powerful interface in which the programmer's actions and the computer's activities are visible and the tools are handy. Smalltalk's text editor, file system, and compiler are written in Smalltalk, so they can be inspected and changed; the capability of overlapping windows eliminates modes (as in editing mode or compile mode) and makes the screen a visual cache of abstractions, freeing the programmer's attention for higher-level problems.

Smalltalk's major drawback has been its general lack of availability. For over a decade, it would only run on one of Xerox PARC's high-performance machines; as the first publicly available versions became available in the mid-1980s, they still required expensive, high-performance systems such as the Sun terminal. Although Smalltalk itself is relatively compact as languages go, its environment and the universe of microworlds created by each programmer put a strain on the capabilities of today's less-expensive personal computers. With the advent of the Macintosh and the adaptation of the PARC interface to other personal computers, several new object-oriented languages have begun to emerge.

NEON, a language for the Macintosh, is an object-oriented language that puts a Smalltalk-like shell around, of all things, a FORTH-like core. The Smalltalk environment eliminates some of FORTH's uglier features, such as its incomprehensible syntax, and although the stack is still there, it is in a more easily visualized form. Smalltalk structures—objects, messages, classes, instances, and so on—are intact, but NEON shares FORTH's virtues of being compact and quickly executable.

Another experimental language that is under development at Apple Corporation is Clascal, an object-oriented language based on Pascal. Undoubtedly, these are only the first of a new generation of Smalltalk variations that will become available to personal computer users in the next few years.

EMERGING NEW METAPHORS: MODELING, SIMULATION, AND PROGRAMMING BY REHEARSAL

When faced with the problem of exploring the possible ways in which some situation might evolve in the future, one of the most highly developed tools that an analyst has is to set up an analog of the real world which may then be manipulated to discover how it works under new conditions. This analog or *model* represents, in a simplified form, the processes of some aspect of the real world, such as the movement of people in the city or a political conflict. Operating the model by manipulation of its elements by means of humans, computers, or both, in order to see how it reacts (and by analogy how the real world should react), is termed *simulation* . . . .

. . . .

Models may be used to describe a situation at a given point in time. These are called *descriptive models*. Or, if they contain time-dependent variables, they may be used to predict what happens at some future time. These are called *predictive models*. Manipulation of the variables in a model, or simulation, is intended to provide answers to the critical question, *"what would happen if."*[9]

The graphical interfaces and programming environments created at PARC led other researchers to use these new programming tools to explore yet higher levels of metaphor. But at this higher level, one layer of abstraction above the very-high-level interfaces, all those lower portions of the software hierarchy are working together behind the scenes to manipulate millions of chunked abstractions per second, and the emerging metaphors look a lot less like programming languages and a lot more like small simulated worlds on the computer screen—*microworlds* that use dynamic imagery to couple computational processes with human cognitions.

At PARC, one of the first new metaphors was explored in an experimental programming system called Pygmalion, written in Smalltalk for the Alto by David Canfield Smith, one of the original codifiers of the Star design principles. Smith's goal was to create a system capable of reflecting and assisting the mental processes underlying creative thinking—a thought tool for programmers.[10] He concluded that a graphic display was necessary to act as a high-bandwidth communication channel between mind and machine, that the system must provide rapid interactive feedback to the person using it, and that commands should emphasize doing rather than telling—as in pointing at an icon and selecting it with a mouse instead of typing a memorized command string. Pygmalion offered student programmers a way of creating workable programs by designing and editing graphical icons. Every programming operation is done by creating and manipulating icons that affect both the visual display and the internal state of the machine.

Programming in Pygmalion departs from the standard paradigm of procedural programming, in which algorithms are translated into step-by-step instructions, because the Pygmalion programmer uses the icons to *demonstrate* steps of a computation by simulating the results of various input values; the Smalltalk-implemented virtual machine behind the scenes in Pygmalion constructs the sequence of operations needed in order to perform the specified computation on new values. If, for example, you were to demonstrate that an operation would return an output of 2 for an input of 1, an output of 4 for an input of 2, and an output of 6 for an input of 3, the Pygmalion system would transform an input of 4 into an output of 8.

Programming-by-demonstration, as such systems are called, is one of the alternatives to the procedural paradigm. The metaphor presupposes some intelligence built into the programming environment. Programming-by-demonstration involves the performance of examples of the desired computation; the interpreter in such a system generalizes from those examples to create a rule. So the ultimate demonstration system would not simply mimic procedures but would perform simple *induction*, the human reasoning faculty that Francis Bacon was convinced would democratize the production of knowledge.

Pygmalion was a step toward iconic programming languages, but it was aimed at augmenting a specialized skill—the ability to program a computer. Others experimented with metaphors that non-specialists might use. Instructors in elementary schools and colleges, for example, could be provided with magic blackboards that would enable them to create educational media of unprecedented effectiveness.

One of the earliest such attempts at a general teaching tool based on the Smalltalk interface was a prototype of a simulation kit for science teachers—Alan Borning's ThingLab.[11] Borning called ThingLab, which was also written in Smalltalk for the Alto, a "constraint-oriented simulation laboratory." He meant that the graphical objects in this Smalltalk microworld can be used as building blocks for simulations, controlled by a set of user-manipulable constraints or rules for operation.

A constraint, by Smith's definition,

specifies a relation that must be maintained. Examples of constraints that have been defined in ThingLab include a constraint that a line be horizontal, a constraint that a resistor obey Ohm's law, and a constraint that the digits in an editable paragraph correspond to the height of a bar in a bar chart.[12]

In other words, constraints are ThingLab's tool for constructing simulations out of icons.

A dynamic, high-resolution, interactive simulation is one of the most powerful capabilities of digital computers: Computers can create, display, and rapidly update lifelike visual and auditory representations of worlds that exist in nature or imagination. Every interactive simulation consists of two aspects: a representation that is sensed and manipulated by a person via displays and input devices and an internal representation that is manipulated by the machine according to a person's commands.

By performing rapid and voluminous calculations on an elaborate mathematical model of a specified world (the internal representation), such as a geometric world of lines and polygons, a world of electronic components like resistors and transistors, a fleet of spaceships, or an ecological model of a marine environment, and then displaying the results in real-time graphic displays, simulations can serve as a kind of teaching device that never existed before. Because an interactive simulation can be altered and observed by the person who uses it, it furnishes a means of experimenting with concrete models of abstract entities directly.

ThingLab, Borning wrote, "is a kind of kit-building kit . . . . The kernel system doesn't have any knowledge about specific domains in which ThingLab can be used, such as geometry or electrical circuits. Rather, it provides tools that make it easy to construct objects that contain such knowledge."[13]

The instructor who uses ThingLab defines the graphic building blocks for a given educational domain by drawing the icons and specifying the constraints that govern their behavior. The constraints determine how objects on the screen are represented, how they change when their input changes, and how they react when they are connected with other objects. Representations of transistors, wires, and other electronic components can be specified with the same constraints that govern electronic circuits. Students can then build simulated circuits, observe their effects, and tinker with them.

The ability to change small elements of a simulation system and then observe the global results, sometimes known as asking what-if questions, is currently exploited by popular spreadsheet programs for microcomputers. Whereas spreadsheet programs are limited to numerical calculations, they are examples of the kind of change-and-observe process that a kit-building program such as ThingLab can simulate. The phenomenal popularity of spreadsheet programs was not due to their usefulness as bookkeeping tools, as their inventors intended, but to a result of their *forecasting* (e.g., simulation and experimentation) capabilities that allow financial planners to model different alternatives.

Two other PARC researchers, Laura Gould and William Finzer, were also concerned about providing tools for educators and students. In 1980, they implemented a system called TRIP, which conveyed an intuitive understanding of algebra word problems. TRIP allowed students to construct graphic representations of problems by arranging a small set of icons. When students correctly completed each set of icons, they could watch the simulation in action via clock, moving icons, and odometers.

When Gould and Finzer finished TRIP, they started designing a computer environment curriculum that designers could use to create their own simulations. Their goal was to find a way in which teachers could specify their problems pictorially, just as students had done in TRIP, by placing icons into an ordered sequence. In order to implement any iconic system, a tool known as a *graphical editor* must be used. TRIP's designers realized that these tools could be used to reverse the usual roles of computer and programmer: In traditional applications, the computer presents graphical displays for the user to analyze; with the graphical editor, the user can present graphical information for the computer to analyze. Would it be possible for such a tool to "watch" the user arrange a sequence of iconic actions and then create a program based on that demonstration?

By the time Gould and Finzer started implementing their new system, programming by demonstration wasn't a totally new concept, but the specific way in which the system watched the user's actions was a ripe area for innovation. Several related ideas, based on Smalltalk, ThingLab, and other experiments, gradually developed into the new metaphor of programming by rehearsal. Instead of a toolkit for building toolkits, this new metaphor presented a stage upon which teachers could audition icon-like objects known as *performers* (which respond to cues) in order to find out what they do, then rehearse them for the specific production the teacher had in mind. By asking the system to "watch" the production, the teacher could translate the resulting simulation into programming code.

The theater metaphor emerged as a natural extension of the Smalltalk 80 system in which the Rehearsal World was implemented.

Indeed, although the Rehearsal World was built as a tool for curriculum designers, it is a visual metaphor for Smalltalk. Like ThingLab, the Rehearsal World is a Smalltalk program. Whereas the original Smalltalk designers used objects and messages as higher-level metaphors for data structures and algorithms, the Rehearsal World designers used visible *performers* that respond to concrete *cues*. Figure 6.1 illustrates programming by rehearsal.

Figure 6.1 Programming by Rehearsal
(Courtesy of Laura Gould)

The effects of sending and receiving cues are immediately visible on the screen. Each aspect of the Rehearsal World concretizes a programming abstraction. The World itself, to expand upon Shakespeare, is a *theater*. *Productions* (programs) don't take place somewhere in the computer, but on a visible *stage*, and several stages can occupy the theater at the same time. Similar performers are organized into *troupes*, which the *designer* (programmer) can *audition* by sending them cues and observing their responses.

The Rehearsal World comes equipped with a set of predefined, primitive performers (which include predefined sets of cues), grouped together in *Central Casting*. A designer begins to create a program by auditioning performers; this is done by selecting (via mouse and menus) that primitive performer's cues and observing the performer's responses. Then the chosen performer is copied and placed on a stage. The production is *blocked* by resizing and moving the performers and is rehearsed by showing each performer what actions it should take in response to cues from users or other performers.

The Rehearsal World, like other powerful high-level languages, is extensible: Designers can create *composite performers* and teach them new cues. The programming protocol (the method for creating composite performers and teaching them new cues) is based on the Smalltalk system of selecting items from pop-up menus that appear at the programmer's command.

The method in which the designer's production is transformed into machine-executable Smalltalk code is also an innovation of the Rehearsal World. Next to every parameter line of a cue is a small icon representing a closed eye. When the designer selects the closed-eye icon, the eye opens, signaling that the system is watching. The designer then sends the appropriate cue or string of cues to the performer by selecting them with the mouse. The appropriate Smalltalk code appears within the square brackets of the parameter line; then the eye closes.

The Rehearsal World's ability to watch eliminates a great deal of the designer's syntactic burden: The designer decides what needs to happen, and the system provides syntactically correct code. With this programming method, the shift between editing mode and running mode is not perceptible to the designer, who instantly sees the results of all actions.

The Rehearsal World abstraction, unlike almost every other higher-level metaphor, offers two-way access between the higher- and lower-level virtual machines. Whereas performers and cues can act as metaphors for Smalltalk's objects and messages, the Rehearsal World also offers a trapdoor through which curious advanced users can gain direct access to the underlying Smalltalk program. Smalltalk code can be typed directly onto parameter lines, or copied from existing code, instead of being rehearsed. The Rehearsal World provides a "familiar conceptual model" for moving into the Smalltalk world of objects and messages.

Programming by rehearsal was developed from 1981 to 1984. By 1985, another PARC researcher, Randy Smith, started working on yet another Smalltalk-based metaphor that he calls ARK—for Alternate Reality Kit. It appears that further refinements of kit-building kits and iconic-textual programming will continue to emerge from the Smalltalk research community. But the Smalltalk interface is not the only basis for creating iconic programming languages and systems such as Pygmalion, ThingLab, and Rehearsal World, which mix both text and graphics, are not the only way to use graphics as programming tools.

Programming languages based entirely on iconic manipulation and using a variety of different interfaces also are being explored. Advocates of this approach claim that purely graphical systems have more potential power than systems that make use of old-fashioned text-based commands, even if they are selected from menus instead of entered as command strings.

ICONIC PROGRAMMING: SKETCHPAD, PICT, MANDALA, AND BEYOND

Sketchpad lets you try things out before deciding. Instead of making you position a line in one specific way, it was set up to allow you to try a number of different positions and arrangements, with the ease of moving cut-outs around on a table.

It allowed room for human vagueness and judgment. Instead of forcing the user to divide things into sharp categories, or requiring the data to be precise from the beginning—all those stiff restrictions people say "the computer requires"—it let you slide things around to your heart's content. You could rearrange till you got what you wanted, no matter for what reason you wanted it.

Sketchpad was historic in its simplicity . . . . It was, in short, an innocent program, showing how easy human work could be if a computer were set up to be really helpful.[14]

The first breakthrough in iconic programming—the idea that computers can be controlled by manipulating graphic symbols—occurred in the early 1960s, when a computer prodigy by the name of Ivan Sutherland created a remarkable program called Sketchpad.

Like the first computers, the earliest graphic display systems were the products of military-sponsored research. Video display screens and light pens, the necessary tools for iconic programmers, were invented in the 1950s as part of a crash program to computerize the U.S. air-defense system. By plugging radar systems into computers, putting the displays on large television-like screens, and allowing operators to manipulate the displays by touching the screens with light pens, the air force brought the nation's air defenses into the missile age.

The Artificial Intelligence laboratory at MIT didn't even exist in the 1950s, when the center of computer display technology research was Lincoln Laboratory, a top-secret MIT-affiliated institution outside Boston. The presentation group at Lincoln looked closely at the field then known as "human factors in electronic systems." One of the members of the presentation group, J.C.R. Licklider, inadvertently opened the era of computer graphics when he invited a bright young graduate student to one of the group's conferences.

The leading experts of the late 1950s had been experimenting with one of the first transistor-based computers—the TX-2—connected to other components of a screen-oriented computer system. Because they were working at different locations on different aspects of human-computer communications, the leaders of the research groups around the country met annually to discuss their findings. Ivan Sutherland, the graduate student invited by Licklider, wasn't on the formal agenda, but he brought slides of his doctoral dissertation project. When he showed them, it was clear to the experts that this student had leaped ahead of them into a new paradigm for human-computer communications systems.

Sketchpad enabled people to create patterns on a display screen, using a light pen—a device that looked like a fountain-pen-sized flashlight, connected to a computer by a wire. This device, along with Sketchpad, allowed users actually to draw patterns on the screen, which would be stored digitally in the computer's memory, just like any other data, and manipulated in various ways, just like any other collection of bits. Graphic manipulation commands made the computerized representations something more than electronic versions of human drawings; Sketchpad users could do things with their graphical information that only computers could do.

Pictures drawn on a Sketchpad screen could be copied, rearranged, telescoped, and microscoped. A user could draw a picture of a kitchen counter, then draw a picture of a toaster, then instantly put tiny toasters all over the kitchen counter, or, if you preferred, put tiny kitchen counters all over the toaster. The scope of Sketchpad's internal representation was not limited by the size of the screen, so a user could expand a picture of a computer to see tiny pictures of microprocessors hidden within it, then magnify the microprocessors to look at the details of their chip design, then zoom back to the level of the picture of the computer, then put the computer inside an even bigger picture of a moon rocket launch control center.

You could also edit parts of drawings or edit a graphical object that acts as a component of a larger graphical object—like the tiny toasters on the counter—and expect all the copies of the object to change instantly. The key concept of iconic programming—that it is possible to change data structures in the computer's memory by editing graphical objects on a screen—was contained in Sketchpad's editing capabilities. Sketchpad allowed designers to alter their pictorial designs—whether they were blueprints, circuit diagrams, or city plans—and try out many alternate versions on the screen.

Sketchpad was not just a drawing tool for architects and engineers. It had been deliberately designed as a demonstration of what computers could do besides crunching numbers—if you built the right kind of human interface. In 1964, at the age of 26, Sutherland succeeded Licklider at the ARPA post and moved beyond Sketchpad to work on computerized flight simulation and other projects. The iconic programming languages of the 1980s are just beginning to take up where Sketchpad left off 20 years ago.

In 1984, two computer scientists at the University of Washington, Ephraim Glinert and Steven L. Tanimoto, reviewed the field of iconic programming and designed a programming methodology that would take advantage of the discoveries made by their colleagues at ARPA and PARC. They started their investigation by asking, "Why do programmers—especially novices—often encounter difficulties when they attempt to transform the human mind's *multidimensional, visual,* and often *dynamic* conception of a problem's solution into the *one-dimensional, textual,* and *static* representation required by traditional programming languages?"[15]

Glinert and Tanimoto concluded that the types of variable names used in programs are less like symbols and more like signs that do not resemble their values and that the von Neumann paradigm of procedural programming, although suitable for fitting solutions into the peculiarities of computer processing, was not amenable to the normal mode of operation of the human brain's innate problem-solving apparatus. They believed that a radical departure from previous programming styles would be necessary to permit humans to apply their native intelligence to the task of using computers to solve problems.

After surveying the various kinds of available programming languages, including visual and iconic systems, Glinert and Tanimoto[16] concluded that the dominant paradigm for implementing an algorithm in a programming language consisted of four steps:

*Select signs for the data structures and needed variables . . . .
*Encode the algorithm as a linear text string that conforms to certain syntactic and semantic rules . . . .
*Run the program and wait for results . . . .
*If the results seem incorrect, try to figure out where the "bugs" are. Then, modify the program and go back to the previous step.

In terms of a purely iconic system—one in which programming consists of selecting and/or composing graphic icons and juxtaposing them on a screen—they concluded that a more natural, easily learnable paradigm for implementing a program would proceed in a different manner:

*Select images that *visually represent* the data structures and variables needed.
Draw the desired algorithm as a logically structured, multidimensional picture.
Watch the program run and *see* the results being generated.
*If the program isn't doing what is expected, *see where* and *when* the error(s) occur.

Glinert and Tanimoto set out to remedy the deficiencies they saw in existing iconic systems. Their experimental language, Pict, doesn't require programmers to use letters, digits, or punctuation marks or to touch a keyboard; all programming is accomplished by drawing and editing icons using a joystick or other input device that controls the movement of a cursor on a screen. The drawings are like jigsaw puzzles, where predefined graphic elements are juxtaposed.

Animation, colors, and sound are used to make these representations of programming abstractions as concrete as possible. (The PARC systems were all in black and white.)

Communication with the Pict system is accomplished by pointing to icons on a menu tree, which is similar to a Smalltalk browser. Auditory cues signal the programmer whether or not a segment of the program is correct; when programs are ready to be tested, an animated version of the program is executed visibly, step by step. In general, Pict programs look a lot like flowcharts, with the exception that standard flowcharts are used as algorithmic maps to aid programmers in the construction of standard programs while Pict flowcharts are the programs themselves.

The experimental Pict system was first tested on novice undergraduates in computer science classes, and the preliminary results indicated that the iconic metaphor succeeded in conveying key programming concepts rapidly and painlessly. The authors are currently expanding their system into a full-fledged programming language that experts as well as novices will most likely find useful.

Pict is an experimental prototype that runs on a sophisticated minicomputer. Other authors of iconic systems are using microcomputers to develop similar graphic programming environments. One of the most unusual of these, which is also in its earliest stages of development, is Jaron Lanier's Mandala language. A colorful representation of a Mandala program was presented on the cover of the September 1984 issue of *Scientific American*. To those who didn't read the description of the cover, it probably didn't resemble anything like an orthodox computer program since Mandala uses icons of ice cubes, hearts, kangaroos, and other nonstandard images to encode algorithms and data structures.

Lanier's concerns are perhaps more far reaching than other designers of iconic systems since his project is based on his belief that "current programming languages are actually the larval forms of something far more interesting that will mature in the next ten years—a new form of communication on the same level as speaking and writing." Lanier claims,

> When you make a program and send it to somebody else, especially if that program is an interactive simulation, it is as if you are making a new world, a fusion of the symbolic and natural realms. Instead of communicating symbols like letters, numbers, pictures, or

musical notes, you are creating miniature universes that have their own internal states and mysteries to be discovered. You can have an empirical relationship with them, that is, you can learn about them by experimenting with them, but at the same time they are human artifacts and communications.[17]

For example, instead of describing a solar system or some theory about it, you might construct a computer simulation and allow people to discover their own theories by interacting with the simulation. Or instead of communicating a musical form by writing all the notes in sequence, you might make a simulation that improvises the essence of that musical style and includes musical principles with which your audience might play.

Whereas previous languages, iconic or otherwise, have been designed by computer scientists and technical programmers, Lanier's background as a free-lance video game designer for microcomputers led to an entirely different approach. His original intention was to make a music tool for personal computer users, using a form of simulation he calls *caricatures*. One of the aspects of computer simulations of complex behaviors is that the computer version is necessarily simpler than the human-originated version, which is why Lanier calls his simulations caricatures. His original goal was to create a caricature of a musical culture that could be manipulated in much the same way that video games are manipulated.

Instead of describing sounds in conventional terms of musical notes, Lanier thought in terms of designing instruments from graphical components and then training animated caricatures of animals to play the instruments. The animals could be assembled into a band, and the user could manipulate their behavior to create new forms of music. The result would be a caricature of a whole musical culture, rather than an editing tool for putting notes together.

Midway in his project, Lanier realized that his metaphors could be applied to a generalized programming language, one that could use purely iconic notation. Instead of using the procedural or algorithmic paradigms, Lanier based Mandala on the idea of dynamic representations. The language itself is a graphical simulation of the inside of the computer. The programmer can watch the computer's operations, at an appropriately high level of depiction, while programs are running, so the user is in continuous interaction with the internal state of the machine. The programmer interacts with the

Mandala representations through the use of a unique input device—a glove.

Some of the fundamental components of Mandala are called *proxies* if the programmer is an adult and *animals* if the programmer is a child. These entities have their own computation powers; for example, they can have their own keyboards or musical instruments. The programmer "trains" a proxy, somewhat like the way a performer is rehearsed in the Rehearsal World, by running the proxy through a behavior while the system is watching. Constraints, cues, messages, goals, and other internal attributes of the proxies can also be specified iconically.

Whenever a proxy is manipulated by the input device, the proxy can also use a caricature of that input device. The proxies operate upon the same tools that the programmer operates upon, a special kind of intelligent graphic editor. One of the capabilities of these tools is the ability to organize relationships between things, similar to ThingLab's constraints. A simple, old-fashioned programming task like sorting can be taught to a proxy, or made into an innate property of all proxies, by demonstrating to the proxy the alphabetic or numerical relationships the programmer wants to use to perform the sort.

Mandala has a set of primitive building blocks for constructing these relationships. A *sticky*, for example, has a sticky side to which objects (graphical representations or other data objects) can be made to adhere. Stickies can be arranged in rows and columns and automatically support insertion, deletion, and other editing operations. Text, for example, can be built by using stickies attached to characters. Another primitive, the *replacer*, changes its appearance according to the behavior state or object it represents. *Spiders* send out arms to other spiders to connect behaviors or objects, and *roamers* move around to represent some change of information.

A roamer can be used to teach a proxy how to sort items by assigning each roamer to each item to be sorted, then establishing the relationships between items (such as alphabetical or numerical order), and finally allowing the roamers to arrange themselves (and their attached items) into the right place. Proxies can be trained to sort according to different sorting algorithms by translating the algorithm into a form of proxy behavior.

"Mandala is a tool for expression," Lanier states, "and algorithms are only one of the things that it can be used to express. Theories of psychology or physics, cosmologies, music, and all sorts of things we haven't thought about yet ought to be expressible as interactive simulations."[18]

Mandala was not the first graphical interactive simulation to be implemented on microcomputers. In fact, although they were not concerned with constructing full-featured programming languages, several previous microcomputer programmers brought the idea of interactive graphical simulations and iconic manipulation to thousands of personal computer users who didn't know that they were using prototypes of futuristic programming languages.

In the late 1970s, Warren Robinett, a former game designer for Atari, teamed up with programmer Leslie Grimm and educational expert Ann Piestrup to create a revolutionary game called *Rocky's Boots*. The educational game was intended for children, who used graphical editors to assemble icon-like parts into various machines. The parts resembled and acted according to the rules governing Boolean operators—NOT, AND, and OR gates—and the machines were actually functional simulations of Boolean circuits. A more advanced sequel, *Robot Odyssey*, was written by Leslie Grimm and Michael Wallace; in this game, children learn to build robots on-screen in order to effect an escape from Robotopolis.

The robot metaphor is an effective simulation of procedural programming, since the user-programmer must instruct the robot in the sequences of actions necessary to negotiate the game domain successfully. A robot-programming game called *ChipWits* combines the robot metaphor with the Macintosh interface; in the process of programming robots to negotiate various environments, the user learns about conditional branching, stacks, subroutines, loops, debugging, and other elements of orthodox programming. It is likely that "games" such as these will evolve in the future to the point where very young children will be routinely learning the kinds of programming techniques that only college graduates are able to master today.

Graphical simulation games for children and iconic programming systems for novice programmers are indicative of one thrust in the development of future programming languages. But novices aren't the only programmers who will need new and more powerful tools as computer hardware and software grow more powerful and complex. Expert programmers—the ones who create tools such as iconic programming languages and programming games—can also look forward to a cornucopia of new tools, metaphors, languages, and environments.

Ironically, one branch of the future of programming languages turns back to the ancient quest for a logic machine, the intellectual pursuit that was overshadowed when it led, indirectly, to the invention of the theory of computation. One of the most powerful alternate paradigms for programming languages uses a metaphor based on logical relationships, rather than objects and messages, icons and spatial relationships, or instructions and procedural algorithms.

PROLOG TO THE FUTURE: THE ULTIMATE LOGIC MACHINE

I now regard all conventional languages (e.g., the FORTRANs, the ALGOLs, their successors and derivatives) as increasingly complex elaborations of the style of programming dictated by the von Neumann computer. These "von Neumann languages" create enormous, unnecessary intellectual roadblocks in thinking about programs and in creating the higher level combining forms required in a really powerful programming methodology. Von Neumann languages constantly keep our noses pressed in the dirt of address computation and the separate computation of single words, whereas we should be focusing on the form and content of the overall result we are trying to produce. We have come to regard the DO, FOR, WHILE statements and the like as powerful tools, whereas they are in fact weak palliatives that are necessary to make the primitive von Neumann style of programming viable at all . . . .

. . . .

My point is this: while it was perhaps natural and inevitable that languages like FORTRAN and its successors should have developed out of the concept of the von Neumann computer as they did, the fact that such languages have dominated our thinking for twenty years is unfortunate. It is unfortunate because their long-standing familiarity will make it hard for us to understand and adopt new programming styles which one day will offer far greater intellectual and computational power.[19]

With so many powerful ideas and languages pouring out of the software workshops, it is natural to ask whether there will ever be an industry-wide, standard programming language. Although the historical record is inconclusive—the business community achieved their Esperanto with COBOL, but the scientists failed with ALGOL—one lesson is clear: Market forces, even more than the elegance and power of the language, are the determining factors in language acceptance. And that is why scientific and industrial leaders, even governments, around the world were so interested by the announcement made by the all-powerful MITI (Japan's Ministry of International Trade and Industry) that PROLOG would be the standard language for their Fifth Generation Computer Project, the computer of the twenty-first century.[20]

Devotees of PROLOG (short for PROgramming LOGic) do not just view the logic machine as a metaphor for the computer: The PROLOG virtual computer is the actual embodiment of a logic machine. Whereas all the classic languages in Chapter 5 are called *procedural* because their programs must use precise algorithms to control the order and flow of operation, PROLOG is *nonprocedural*, or descriptive. A PROLOG program simply states relationships among data objects and specifies the desired result. The PROLOG virtual machine then uses its own internal logic to make inferences and solve for the requested result. Instead of using Logo, or BASIC, or Pascal to program a computer to make deductive associations, this capacity is built right into PROLOG.

The power of PROLOG can be demonstrated by recalling the syllogism example from Chapter 2:

All computers are machines

All machines are inanimate

All computers are inanimate

The syntax of PROLOG requires that the two premises be written as follows:

```
machines(Something):-computers(Something)
inanimate(Something):-machines(Something)
```

These statements are called *rules*, and they state that if something is a computer then it is a machine, and if something is a machine then it is inanimate. PROLOG syntax requires that "something" be capitalized to designate that it is a variable. The treatment of words such as all and something as variables is very similar to their treatment in the predicate calculus. Once the PRO-LOG virtual machine knows the rules, we simply ask, inanimate(What). The machine performs the logical reasoning and responds, What = computers. Of course, the more rules we input, the larger the information base and the greater the number of possible inferences.

At this stage, PROLOG may just look like a glorified data base. What sets it apart as a full-fledged programming language is its ability to write programs. PROLOG rules need not simply state individual, real-world connections. They can be used to represent mathematical relationships; and there is no end to the entities that can be described or modeled by mathematical relationships. For example, the program below uses recursion to set the rules for finding the factorial of a number (e.g., 4! = 4 x 3 x 2 x 1). Once the program is stored, the PROLOG virtual machine's capacity to generate factorials is constrained only by hardware considerations.

```
factorial (1 1)
factorial (x y) if 1 LESS x
    and SUM (z 1 x)
    and factorial (z y1)
    and TIMES (x y1 y)
```

The first line says that the factorial of 1 is 1. The second line is a beginning condition: Start the rule only if 1 is less than x. The third line subtracts 1 from x (z + 1 = x). The fourth line is the recursive condition sending z back to the top of the rule. The final line says that the factorial of x is equal to x times the factorial of x − 1 (e.g., 4! = 24, or 4 * 3! = 24). With this program in memory, you need only query PROLOG: which(y:factorial(4 y)—what is the value of y when it is equal to 4!)—to receive the answer 24.

Obviously PROLOG is extensible. We just taught it the word *factorial*. But extensibility means more in PROLOG. Its programs generally fail not because of some hard to trace logic bug, but because they lack information. When that happens, a query-the-user facility takes over, and the programmer is asked for more information. By teaching the PROLOG virtual machine new facts and rules, you solve the failure *and* increase the size of your data base. Add to that its capacity to manipulate lists, and it's easy to see why PROLOG first gained favor with AI researchers.

The amazing thing about so-called logic programming is that it is the computer that supplies the logic. Programming in PROLOG is really a declarative activity: First you tell the computer the facts [e.g., programlanguage(basic)—the constant basic has the attribute of being a programming language] and the relationships [e.g., language(Something) :- programlanguage(Something)—all programming languages are languages] you already know. Then you make a request, language(What). The method the computer uses to answer the query, the actual algorithms and data structures, is of no particular concern. In John Backus' phrase, PROLOG enables the users to get their noses out of the dirt of address computation and the separate computation of single words and focus on the form and content of the overall results they are trying to achieve.

Most virtual machines (certainly those classic languages in Chapter 5) require that even the simplest activities be spelled out in excruciating detail. In essence, much of procedural programming involves microdetailing the steps that humans take for granted. The goal of PROLOG and other logic languages is to do away entirely with such programming imperatives that tell the computer what to do. Algorithms are to be replaced by facts, rules, and queries; specifying a problem will be equivalent to solving it.

Although this objective is far from achieved, PROLOG has made some important contributions to the field of artificial intelligence. Because programming in PROLOG requires building a data base, it is not surprising to find PROLOG popular among those who work with *expert systems*—computer models (data + inference rules) of specific domains of human knowledge. But visionaries in this branch of artificial intelligence see expert systems as much more than passive repositories of information. Instead, they view them as a tool for understanding the nature of understanding:

A key idea in our current approach to building expert systems is that these programs should not only be able to apply the corpus of expert knowledge to specific problems, but they should also be able to interact with the users just as humans do when they learn, explain, and teach what they know . . . . These *transfer of expertise* (TOE) capabilities were originally necessitated by "human engineering" considerations—the people who build and use our systems needed a variety of "assistance" and "explanation" facilities. However, there is more of the idea of TOE than the implementation of needed user features: These social interactions—learning from experts, explaining one's reasoning, and teaching what one knows—are essential dimensions of human knowledge. They are as fundamental to the nature of intelligence as expert-level problem-solving, and they have changed our ideas about representation and about knowledge.[21]

Although the realization of full transfer of expertise capabilities still lies somewhere in the future, PROLOG-programmed expert systems are having an impact on the real world right now: Mecho solves mechanics problems stated in English, Chat answers complicated queries about international geography, and ORBI makes expert environmental resource evaluations.

The success of PROLOG in the AI field has reopened once again an argument that has its origins in the age of Aristotle and Euclid—the dispute between those who believe the logic machine is important because it tells us something about the workings of our own brain and those who believe it is important solely because it is an excellent way to generate new knowledge. Is PROLOG a model of a mind or simply a helpful thought tool? Recent theories and experiments would seem to confirm that it must be the latter:

> For many centuries, philosophers and others who have studied the human mind have believed that reasoning takes place according to the laws governing logic. Or rather, that it should, but regrettably often fails to do so. Ideal reasoning, they have held, is *deductive*: one starts with statements that are self-evidently true or taken to be true and, by means of logical processes, sees what other statements can be derived from them. When we violate the principles of logic, or when we reason *inductively*—moving from particular examples to a generalization that goes beyond them—we often fall into error or reach invalid conclusions.
>
> Such is the tradition that runs unbroken from Aristotle to Piaget. But the findings of cognitive science run counter to it: logical reasoning is not our usual—or natural—practice, and the technically invalid kinds of reasoning we generally employ work rather well in most of the everyday situations in which one might suppose rigorous deductive thinking was essential.[22]

But this conclusion in no way lessens the value of PROLOG. Its major value lies in its nonprocedural style, not in its application of deductive logic. It is possible to imagine a PROLOG-I that uses inductive logic or a PROLOG-P that uses probabilistic logic. If PRO-LOG is the ultimate deductive logic machine, it also may be the prototype for many different logic machines yet to come.

NEW COGNITIVE PARADIGMS

In the major challenge to computer scientists, that of enabling millions of people to program intelligent machines, discussions tend to focus on the significant improvements that have been made from early—and primitive—computer languages, or the relative merits of currently popular languages. I would like to focus the discussion instead on the emergence of *new types of concepts* within languages.

The early languages were designed to deal exclusively with arithmetic and primitive logic. As computers acquired large memories, they had to be able to read and write files. With the coming of time-sharing, users were able to interact with computers while their program was running; thus computer languages had to include commands that allowed two-way communication. Still later, when graphics terminals became easily available, concepts had to be added to languages for the drawing of pictures. I cite these developments because I believe that to enable computers to manipulate all kinds of machines, an entirely new set of concepts must be invented.[23]

If new languages make it possible for millions of people to program computers, will programmers become obsolete? The answer is yes—and no. If your definition of programmers is restricted to the software technicians who currently perform mundane tasks such as maintaining payroll and inventory programs for businesses or encoding algorithms for scientists, the answer is yes. By the time today's toddlers begin their adult careers, scientists, businesspeople, educators, students, and children will be able to perform for themselves most of the computing tasks that only programmers can handle today.

But if your definition of programmer includes the scientists, engineers, and artisans who extend the frontiers of computation, create tools for other software craftspeople, manage the evolution of the complex software that controls civilization's life-support systems, the answer is an emphatic no. An expanding population of programmers creates a demand for more powerful tools, and the management of large collections of software demands new programming methodologies; hence, the expert programmers of the future will require their own advanced languages. And we all better hope their tools are adequate to the task.

Who needs powerful, reliable, thought tools more than the people who build thought tools? Although the issue of software management is not as widely heralded as the arms race, population explosion, toxic pollution, or resource depletion crises, it is one of our most critical problems. As weapons become ever more powerful, the computer software that controls weaponry also grows more complex. Management of the global transportation and communication networks essential to supporting the world's population on a daily basis is equally dependent upon complicated software systems.

Computers were invented in the first place because our mathematical problems had become too complicated to solve without mechanical assistance. Now, new virtual machines must be invented to help handle the growing complexity of software systems. Software complexity is problematic because of all the unforeseen ways even simple programs can misbehave. Programs and software libraries are growing in size by orders of magnitude, and the complexity of a program increases enormously with increases in its size. A typical program for a microcomputer contains a few hundred lines of code. An ambitious AI program might run to more than 100 thousand lines of code. Large libraries of software, like those maintained by computer companies, are growing at the rate of 1 million lines of code per year.

It looks like the need for intellectual augmentation for programmers is finally upon us, just as Doug Engelbart predicted a quarter of a century ago. Although programmers will be the first to encounter this technology directly, it will also affect the design of computer systems used by nonexperts. Even before programming tools evolve to the point at which nonprogrammers can use them, they will be used by the programmers who write software for nonspecialists—the word processors, spreadsheets, data base management programs, educational software, and video games that transform today's relatively low-powered personal computers into valuable tools. The software workshops developed by high-performance teams will filter out to the third-party software developers who invent new virtual machines to empower our intellects and challenge our imaginations.

The computer research communities that are constructing today's and tomorrow's workshops are located in places such as PARC and Digital Equipment Company's Systems Research Center, IBM's and Bell Laboratories' research groups, Japan's MITI-sponsored fifth-generation complex outside Tokyo, and at similar institutions in Paris, Cambridge, Oslo, and Marseilles. A small subcommunity of tool builders has expanded into a worldwide computational culture. The major activity of these institutions is designing and producing prototype systems that provide interactive, personal computing services to their own communities of researchers.

Some of these hardware and software prototypes are short-lived experiments cooked up to test new ideas, and some grow into robust systems used by the entire community. The software management issue is of paramount importance when it applies to software architects; therefore, places such as PARC concentrate on building tools to enable them to conduct computing experiments quickly and at low cost:

> The software that we can produce, and the rate at which we can produce it, are too often limiting factors in our research . . . . We believe that it is increasingly desirable, feasible, and economic to use computers to directly assist the process of *experimental programming*. [By which we mean] . . . the production of moderate-sized systems that are usable by moderate numbers of people in order to test ideas about such systems.[24]

One of the most important tools an experimental programming community needs is an integrated programming environment—a system that includes high-quality, high-speed graphics, sophisticated editing and document preparation facilities, powerful debugging and program analysis tools, interpreters and compilers, all working together to facilitate the work of individual programmers and groups of programmers. The design of such an environment involves what software people call theological debate over which features are essential. At a place such as PARC, the design problem was particularly thorny because the programming environment had to meet the needs of three very different programming communities—the LISP programmers, the Smalltalk programmers, and the Mesa programmers.

The programming environment used at PARC was itself an experiment, a prototype of a tool-building toolkit. After the Altos were built, and the Smalltalk and Mesa languages were implemented, the next major step toward a high-performance integrated environment was the Cedar project, which started in 1978. One of its designers described it as follows:

. . . a programming environment designed to help programmers build experimental systems. It is the software equivalent of the kind of machine shop needed by an engineering laboratory, but unlike a machine shop, it does not represent a known technology: Cedar is itself an experimental system, and a very large one . . . . The main goal of Cedar is to increase programmer productivity . . . . The improvement will come from three main sources: a programming language that takes more responsibility for certain programming tasks, programming tools that make program development and debugging faster, and a package library that allows programmers to build upon one another's work.[25]

The task of maintaining an integrated workshop of software tools for software tool builders isn't easy, since the job of individuals within the tool-building community is to invent new tools that make the current ones obsolete. Computer Science Laboratory (CSL) and other experimental software institutions don't consist of 100 isolated programmers working in their cubicles on their pet projects; *communication* is the community equivalent of augmentation—a way of quickly distributing tools and ideas among individuals. The truly integrated software workshop must include a high-bandwidth communication medium, that is, one in which a large amount of information can flow quickly, and powerful communication tools for the use of the entire computation culture, as well as tools for improving the productivity of individual programmers.

The rest of the world will eventually catch up with the computational avant-garde, but until it does, thousands of programmers who use conventional languages will need tools to improve their own productivity. Some features of high-performance programming environments have been extended to the wider programming community by creating new integrated environments for older programming languages. A program development system call PECAN, developed by Steven P. Reiss of Brown University, extends the power of Pascal.

PECAN uses a PARC interface, with a bit-mapped display, icons, windows, browsers, and mouse point-and-select commands. But Reiss' system also includes visible views of many aspects of a program: Windows display the source text of the program, the source code for the part of the program currently being interpreted, the flowchart and other logical maps of the program, and visual representations of data structures such as trees and stacks.

The software tool builders are not the only members of the computer research community from whom language breakthroughs can be expected. While systems research groups concentrate on extending the power of programming teams, other computer researchers are using software to simulate aspects of human intelligence. Ever since John McCarthy invented LISP, the special needs of artificial intelligence researchers have stimulated important new developments in programming languages that have influenced the design of new languages for programmers outside the AI community.

LISP was the first, but won't be the last, programming innovation that was created in response to the needs of AI researchers. Recent studies in the AI subfields of knowledge representation, automatic programming, and robotics have led to the implementation of new features in the languages AI researchers use. Many of these features will be useful only to AI programmers; some of them are bound to influence languages used by all programmers. These features include new data types and memory management techniques, innovative control structures such as conditional interrupts (known as demons), pattern-matching techniques, and automatic deductive mechanisms.

The creation of a new data type extends the power of programming languages into fields in which computation was prohibitively difficult. The first programming languages permitted programmers to manipulate only numbers and mathematical relationships. The early symbol-manipulation languages, such as LISP and ALGOL, expanded the realm of computable problems by introducing symbolic data types such as strings, lists, and trees. For many years, these fundamental data types were adequate for AI research as well as for other kinds of programming. But as AI research has grown to include more complex problem domains, a richer variety of data types has become necessary. New additions to the general-purpose programming vocabulary of data types will emerge out of the current proliferation of special AI data types such as *items*, *sets*, *tuples*, *bags*, and *classes*.

New control structures are also beginning to emerge from specialized AI languages. One control structure in particular, known as the *conditional interrupt*, or *demon*, is a likely candidate for wide adaptation. A demon is a program or module that is dormant until certain conditions become true, at which point it becomes activated. Demons can be part of a larger program, or they can be independent programs that "sleep" in a computer's main memory or operating system until the right conditions awaken them.

A data-accessing function checks the input stream or the flow of instructions for sensitive data; when the specified condition occurs, a message from the demon to the current activity transfers control to the demon module, which performs its job and then transfers control to the main program. A demon might be instructed to awaken when nobody is using a particular computer, then perform a specified computation, beginning at the point it left off when it last went dormant, continuing until the next user logs onto that computer. Or a demon in a parser program might lie dormant until the parser is unable to find a subject for a particular sentence, at which point a subject-finding demon would awaken and begin searching previous sentences for the missing subject.

Pattern-matching techniques, first used extensively in string-manipulating languages, search for specific strings of characters or numbers. Complex data bases, logic-based programming, and natural-language programming can make use of this technique to speed up searches and sorts that might otherwise be too time consuming. Pattern-matching also can be a control mechanism for selecting the next subroutine by matching the arguments of available subroutines against the template provided by the computation in progress.

Deductive mechanisms from new AI languages may one day add intelligence to other programming languages; that is, deductive structures may provide a way for programmers to concentrate on higher levels of abstractions. Just as higher-level languages permit users to describe computations in terms of algebraic relationships and leave to the compiler the task of translating the relationships into machine code, deductive mechanisms allow programmers to concentrate on the higher-level concerns of complex problems, leaving lower level details to the programming language. In the words of two leading experts in AI languages:

> The extent to which a programmer may specify *what* he wants accomplished without detailing how it is to be done is one way of defining the *level* or *power* of a programming language . . . . The new languages go a step further. They permit the programming system to carry out certain activities, including modifying the data base and deciding which subroutines to run next, using only constraints and

guidelines the programmer sets up . . . . For example, the programmer can request a result, and the procedures which "match" the request will be tried by the system using a problem-solving mechanism working within the pre-established guidelines. The process of constructing a problem-solving program then becomes a matter of developing and modifying guidelines, and specifying matching criteria, rather than developing procedural algorithms. We call the semi-automatic search and data-construction features of these languages deductive because they bear some resemblance to so-called "theorem-proving programs" that attempt to deduce desired logical expressions (theorems) from previously specified expressions (axioms).[26]

How's that for a contemporary description of the ancient dream of a logic machine? What would Ramon Lull or George Boole have said about such a statement? Between the systems researcher communities and the AI laboratories, new developments in human-machine communications over the next 20 years are sure to happen at least as fast as the software innovations of the past 20 years.

To most people outside the programming community, the idea of tool builders who build tools for building better tools might sound solipsistic. But the most powerful tools that tool builders have created in the past have turned out to be widely adaptable to the needs of nonprogrammers. Communicators, artists, engineers, and educators have benefited from past adaptations of specialized software technologies such as word processing and document preparation programs, electronic painting and drawing software, computer-assisted design and engineering, interactive graphical simulations, telecommunications, and other formerly specialized tools.

With all the changes that have transformed computer technology again and again since it was invented, one thing has not changed: The conceptual model of the von Neumann computer, controlled by strictly ordered sets of procedural instructions, has been the dominant paradigm for computer language design at all levels for 40 years. But new alternatives to the procedural paradigm have begun to emerge. *Object-oriented* programming languages, *iconic* languages, and *logic-based* languages, to cite only three of the most successful recent examples, have created entirely new ways to look at and think about computers. On one level, these new ways of conceptualizing the organization of programs have given expert programmers a superb environment for practicing their craft; on another level, these new metaphors have unlocked for nonprogrammers the conceptual tool box that was formerly reserved for experts.

It is far too early to tell if Smalltalk, PROLOG, Mandala, Cedar, PECAN, and so on, will put an end to the programming language Tower of Babel. It is not too early, however, to see that these languages have the capacity to shape the way we think about the world. There is no doubt that natural language exerts a potent influence on our world view. Because the dominant programming languages of today (e.g., FORTRAN, COBOL, Basic) are based so strongly on the von Neumann procedural model, with its emphasis on serial, machine-like processes, they have relatively little effect on our world view. But when the programming languages of the future begin to foster metaphorical communications via systems of objects, or logic, or icons, they will begin to influence that world view, perhaps as profoundly as natural language has done.

Language will always be our most important thought tool. And as human-computer communication systems grow more sophisticated and more people become truly computer literate, language will include programming languages as well as natural languages. Computers may be the end of one quest (for the logic machine), but they are simply one more tool in the ultimate human quest—to give meaning and understanding to the world.

NOTES

FRONT MATTER

[1]Henri Bergson, *Creative Evolution*, trans. by Arthur Mitchell, New York: Henry Holt & Co., 1911, p. 139.

[2]J.C.R. Licklider, "Man-Computer Symbiosis," in *IRE Transactions on Human Factors in Electronics*, March 1960, vol. HFE-1, pp. 4-11.

INTRODUCTION

[1]Alan Kay, "Computer Software," *Scientific American*, September 1984, p. 59.

[2]Terry Winograd, "Computer Software for Working with Language," *Scientific American*, September 1984, p. 131.

CHAPTER 1

[1]Bertrand Russell, *Human Knowledge: Its Scope and Limits*, New York: Simon & Schuster, 1948, Part II.

[2]The story behind our use of "big numbers" is told in charming detail by George Gamow in *One, Two, Three . . . Infinity*, New York: Bantam, 1961, pp. 3-24.

[3]The relationship between thought and language is a crucial idea in both psychology and philosophy. For an early psychological perspective, see Lev Semenovich Vygotsky, *Thought and Language*, Cambridge: MIT Press, 1962. For an important philosophical perspective, see Bertrand Russell, *Human Knowledge: Its Scope and Limits*, New York: Simon & Schuster, 1948, part II. Recently, philosophers and psychologists have studied the issue as cognitive scientists. See the discussions with J. Bruner and J. Katz in Jonathan Miller, *States of Mind*, New York: Pantheon, 1983.

[4]The whole notion of symbol systems is elegantly discussed in Herbert A. Simon, *The Sciences of the Artificial*, Cambridge: MIT Press, 1981, 2nd edition; see especially pp. 22-28.

[5]Jane Muir, *Of Men and Numbers*, New York: Dodd Mead, 1966, p. 47.

[6]For a discussion of Descartes' dream and its impact on Western thought, see Willis Harman and Howard Rheingold, *Higher Creativity*, Los Angeles: Jeremy P. Tarcher, Inc., 1984.

[7]René Descartes, *Discourse on Method*, trans. by Laurence J. Lafleur, Indianapolis and New York: Bobbs-Merrill, 1960.

[8]For a fascinating and lyrical account of Bacon's ideas and their impact, see Loren Eiseley, *The Man Who Saw Through Time*, New York: Charles Scribner's Sons, 1961.

[9]J. Fodor and J. Katz, *The Structure of Language*, Englewood Cliffs, N.J.: Prentice-Hall, 1964, p. 19.

[10]The seminal work in this field is Noam Chomsky, *Syntactic Structures*, The Hague: Mouton & Co., 1957. A collection of important papers concerning syntax, semantics, and phonology is in Jerry A. Fodor and Jerrold J. Katz, *The Structure of Language*, Englewood Cliffs, N.J.: Prentice-Hall, 1964.

[11]John Dewey, *How We Think*, Lexington, Mass: D.C. Heath & Company, 1910, parts III, XIII, p. 175.

[12] Jerome Bruner, *Toward a Theory of Instruction*, Cambridge: Belknap Press, 1966, p. 107.

[13]Roman Jakobson, "Closing Statement: Linguistics and Poetics," in *Style in Language*, T.A. Sebeok, ed., New York: John Wiley & Sons, 1960, pp. 350-374.

[14]Alan Kay, "Computer Software," *Scientific American*, September 1984, p. 53.

[15]Jeremy Campbell, *Grammatical Man*, New York: Simon and Schuster, 1982, pp. 15-16.

[16]Claude Shannon, "A Mathematical Theory of Information," *Bell System Technical Journal*, 1948, 27:379-423, 623-656.

[17]Kuhn's influential ideas are lucidly explained in Thomas S. Kuhn, *The Structure of Scientific Revolutions*, Chicago: University of Chicago Press, 1970.

[18]The goals and methods of the cybernetic movement are described in W. Ross Ashby, *An Introduction to Cybernetics*, New York: John Wiley & Sons, 1963.

[19]An entertaining exposition of Shannon's ideas and their impact can be found in Pamela McCorduck, *Machines Who Think*, San Francisco: W.H. Freeman & Co., 1979, pp. 30-48, and Jeremy Campbell, *Grammatical Man*, New York: Simon & Schuster, 1982, pp. 15-80.

CHAPTER 2

[1]George Boole, *An Investigation of the Laws of Thought on which are Founded the Mathematical Theories of Logic and Probabilities*, New York: Dover, 1953, p. 1.

[2]Syllogistic logic is discussed in most logic texts. For a standard discussion, see Irving M. Copl, *Introduction to Logic*, New York: Macmillan, 1961, pp. 168-197.

[3]The influence of Moslem thought on Western science has been profound. For an exposition of the subject, see Thomas Goldstein, *Dawn of Modern Science*, Boston: Houghton Mifflin, 1980, pp. 92-130. For a discussion of the origins of algorithms, see Donald E. Knuth, *The Art of Computer Programming, Volume 1, Fundamental Algorithms*, Reading, Mass.: Addison-Wesley, 1968.

[4]Lull's device and several other logic machines are discussed in Martin Gardner, *Logic Machines and Diagrams*, New York: McGraw-Hill, 1958.

[5]Bertrand Russell, *A History of Western Philosophy*, New York: Simon & Schuster, 1972, p. 592.

[6]F.G. Heath, "Origins of the Binary Code," *Scientific American*, August 1972.

[7]George Boole, *An Investigation of the Laws of Thought on which are Founded the Mathematical Theories of Logic and Probabilities*, New York: Dover, 1854.

[8]F.G. Heath, "Origins of the Binary Code," *Scientific American*, August 1972.

[9]Henri Poincare, *Science and Method*, trans. by Francis Martland, New York: Dover, 1952, p. 147.

[10]Euclid's use of formal systems is explained by Raymond L. Wilder, "The Axiomatic Method," reprinted in *The Mathematical Way of Thinking*, James R. Newman, ed., New York: Simon & Schuster, 1956, pp. 1647-1667.

[11]Isaac Newton, *Philosophiae Naturalis Principia Mathematica*, Berkeley: University of California Press, 1934.

[12]Jacob Bronowski, *The Ascent of Man*, Boston: Little, Brown & Co., 1973, p. 233.

[13]*Geometrical Researches on the Theory of Parallels*, trans. by George B. Halsted, La Salle, Ill.: The Open Court Publishing Co., 1942, pp. 68-69.

[14]Non-Euclidean geometry is discussed in Peter Wolff, *Breakthroughs in Mathematics*, New York: New American Library, 1963, pp. 63-95. Extending geometry to the real world is the topic of Roger Penrose, "The Geometry of the Universe," in *Mathematics Today*, Lynn Arthur Steen, ed., New York: Springer-Verlag, 1978, pp. 83-126.

[15]George Boole, *An Investigation of the Laws of Thought on which are Founded the Mathematical Theories of Logic and Probabilities*, New York: Dover, 1958.

[16]Guiseppe Peano, *Formulaire de Mathematiques*, Torino, Italy: Bocca, 1895.

[17]Isaac Newton, *Philosophiae Naturalis Principia Mathematica*, Berkeley: University of California Press, 1934.

[18]David Hilbert, "Mathematical Problems," *Bulletin of the American Mathematical Society*, 1902, 8:444.

[19]David Hilbert, "On the Infinite," in *Philosophy of Mathematics: Selected Readings*, Paul Benacereff and Hilary Putnam, eds., Englewood Cliffs, N.J.: Prentice-Hall, 1964.

[20]Gottlob Frege, *Grundgesetze der Arithmetik*, 1903, vol. ii, appendix, p. 253; translated in *Philosophical Writings of Gottlob Frege*, Peter Geach and Max Black, Oxford: Basil Blackwell, 1966.

[21]Bertrand Russell, *Portraits from Memory*, New York: Simon & Schuster, 1956, pp. 54-55.

[22]Emil Post, "Introduction to a General Theory of Elementary Propositions," *Amer. J. Math*, 1921, 43:163-185.

[23]Kurt Gödel, "Die Völlstandigkeit Der Axiome Des Logischen Funktionenkalküls," *Monatsh. Math. Phys.*, 1930, 37: 349-360.

[24]The predicate calculus is generally the second course in the logic sequence. See Willard Van Orman Quine, *Methods of Logic*, New York: Holt, Rinehart, Winston, 1959.

[25]Kurt Gödel, "Ueber Formal Unentscheidbare Sätze Der Principia Mathematica Und Verwandter Systeme I, *Monatsh. Math. Phys.*, 1931, 38:173-198.

[26]The classic, popular explanation of Kurt Gödel's work is Ernest Nagel and James R. Newman, *Godel's Proof*, New York: New York University Press, 1958.

[27]Donald E. Knuth, "Algorithms," *Scientific American*, vol. 236, No. 4, April 1977, p. 63.

[28]Alan Turing, "On Computable Numbers with an Application to the Entscheidungsproblem," *Proc. London Math. Soc.*, 1936, 42:230-265; 1937, 43:544-546.

[29]The story of Turing's life and work is told by Andrew Hodges, *Alan Turing: The Enigma*, New York: Simon & Schuster, 1983.

[30]Robert Browning, *The Poetical Works of Robert Browning*, Boston: Houghton Mifflin, 1974, p. 384.

CHAPTER 3

[1]Peter J. Denning and Robert L. Brown, "Operating Systems," *Scientific American*, September 1984.

[2]Sir Francis Bacon, *De augmentis scientarum*, 1623, in F.G. Heath, "The Origins of the Binary Code," *Scientific American*, August 1972.

[3]Bateson was the only anthropologist in the original cybernetics group; one of his more recent and more accessible works is Gregory Bateson, *Mind and Nature*, New York: Bantam, 1980.

[4]Joseph Weizenbaum, *Computer Power and Human Reason*, San Francisco: W.H. Freeman, 1976, pp. 73-111.

[5]Claude Shannon, "A Symbolic Analysis of Relay and Switching Circuits," *Transactions of the American Institute of Electrical Engineers*, 1938, 57:713.

[6]Herbert A. Simon, *The Sciences of the Artificial*, Cambridge: MIT Press, 1981, 2nd edition, p. 195.

[7]Arthur W. Burks, Herman H. Goldstine, and John von Neumann, "Preliminary Discussion of the Logical Design of an Electronic Computing Instrument," original mimeographed report condensed and reprinted in *Datamation*, September-October 1962.

[8]A first-hand account of the invention of the stored-program concept is presented in Herman Goldstine, *The Computer from Pascal to von Neumann*, Princeton: Princeton University Press, 1972, pp. 12-225.

[9]Douglas R. Hofstadter, *Godel, Escher, Bach*, New York: Basic Books, 1979, pp. 287-288.

[10]An entertaining, popular-level rendition of the ENIAC story is Dirk Hanson, *The New Alchemists*, Boston: Little, Brown, 1982, pp. 39-69.

[11]David A. Patterson, "Microprogramming," *Scientific American*, March 1983, pp. 50-57.

CHAPTER 4

[1]Niklaus Wirth, "Data Structures and Algorithms," *Scientific American*, September 1984, p. 60.

[2]The intuitive notion of instruction tends to bog down quickly in the precise mathematics of algorithms. A good nonmathematical introduction to the concept is presented in T.E. Hull, *Introduction to Computing*, Englewood Cliffs, N.J.: Prentice-Hall, 1966, chap. 1. A more rigorous approach is taken by Donald Knuth, "Algorithms," *Scientific American*, April 1977. The full-blown mathematical theory is the topic of Harley Rogers, Jr., *Theory of Recursive Function and Effective Computability*, New York: McGraw-Hill, 1967.

[3]Zenon Pylyshyn, "Complexity and the Study of Artificial and Human Intelligence," in *Mind Design*, John Haugeland, ed., Cambridge: MIT Press, 1981.

[4]The design of algorithms is discussed in Niklaus Wirth, "Data Structures and Algorithms," *Scientific American*, September 1984, and Les Goldschlager and Andrew Lister, *Computer Science: A Modern Introduction*, Englewood Cliffs, N.J.: Prentice-Hall, 1982, chap. 2.

[5]Terrence W. Pratt, *Programming Languages: Design and Implementation*, Englewood Cliffs, N.J.: Prentice-Hall, 1984, pp. 350-352.

[6]All the major theorems of computability are proven in Hartley Rogers, Jr., *Theory of Recursive Functions and Effective Computability*, New York: McGraw-Hill, 1967. A more accessible discussion is Martin Davis, "What Is Computation?" in *Mathematics Today*, Lynn Arthur Steen, ed., New York: Springer-Verlag, 1978, 241-268.

[7]Claude Shannon, "A Chess-Playing Machine," *Scientific American*, February 1950.

[8]Most of the discussion about complexity theory are mired in difficult mathematical formalism. For an interesting exception that attempts to link complexity results to human rationality, see Christopher Cherniak, "Computational Complexity and the Universal

Acceptance of Logic," *Journal of Philosophy*, December 1984, LXXXI, No. 12:739-758.

[9]Niklaus Wirth, "Data Structures and Algorithms," *Scientific American*, September 1984, p. 64.

[10]See Niklaus Wirth, "Data Structures and Algorithms," *Scientific American*, September 1984, and Terrence W. Pratt; *Programming Languages: Design and Implementation*, Englewood Cliffs, N.J.: Prentice-Hall, 1984, chaps. 3-5.

[11]J. David Bolter, *Turing's Man: Western Culture in the Computer Age*, Chapel Hill: The University of North Carolina Press, 1984, pp. 186-187.

[12]Frederick P. Brooks, Jr., *The Mythical Man-Month*, Reading Mass.: Addison-Wesley, 1979, pp. 14-15.

[13]Herman H. Goldstine, *The Computer from Pascal to von Neumann*, Princeton, N.J.: Princeton University Press, 1972, pp. 266-267.

[14]Niklaus Wirth, "Program Development by Stepwise Refinement," *Communications of the ACM*, 1971, 14, no. 4:221-227.

[15]O.J. Dahl, E.W. Dijkstra, and C.A.R. Hoare, *Structured Programming*, London: Academic Press, 1972.

CHAPTER 5

[1]Lawrence G. Tesler, "Programming Languages," *Scientific American*, September 1984, p. 70.

[2]John Backus, "Programming in America in the 1950s—Some Personal Impressions," *A History of Computers in the Twentieth Century*, N. Metropolis et al., eds., New York: Academic Press, 1980, pp. 130-131.

[3]John Backus, in *History of Programming Languages*, Richard L. Wexelblat, ed., New York: Academic Press, 1981, p. 46.

[4]Grace Murray Hopper, in *History of Programming Languages*, Richard L. Wexelblat, ed., New York: Academic Press, 1981, p. 11.

[5]John Backus, in *History of Programming Languages*, Richard L. Wexelblat, ed., New York: Academic Press, 1981, p. 46.

[6]Donald E. Knuth and Luis Trabb Pardo, "The Early Development of Programming Languages," *Encyclopedia of Computer Science and Technology*, New York: Dekker, 1977, pp. 419-493.

[7]John Backus, "The History of FORTRAN I, II, and III," in *History of Programming Languages*, Richard L. Wexelblat, ed., New York: Academic Press, 1981, pp. 26-27.

[8]John Backus, "The History of FORTRAN I, II, and III," in *History of Programming Languages*, Richard L. Wexelblat, ed., New York: Academic Press, 1981, p. 30.

[9]John Backus, "The History of FORTRAN I, II, and III," in *History of Programming Languages*, Richard L. Wexelblat, ed., New York: Academic Press, 1981, pp. 28-29.

[10]*Specifications for the IBM Mathematical Formula Translating System*, New York: IBM Corporation, November 10, 1954.

[11]*Programmer's Reference Manual, The FORTRAN Automatic Coding System for the IBM 704 EDPM*, New York: IBM Corporation, October 15, 1956.

[12]Terrence W. Pratt, *Programming Languages: Design and Implementation*, Englewood Cliffs, N.J.: Prentice-Hall, 1984, p. 358.

[13]Grace Murray Hopper, in *History of Programming Languages*, Richard L. Wexelblat, ed., New York: Academic Press, 1981, pp. 10-11.

[14]J.W. Backus et al., *Programmer's Reference Manual, The FORTRAN Automatic Coding System for the IBM 704 EDPM*, New York: IBM Corporation, October 15, 1956, pp. 2-3.

[15]Jean Sammet, *Programming Languages: History and Fundamentals*, Englewood Cliffs, N.J.: Prentice-Hall, 1969, p. 169.

[16]Grace Murray Hopper, Keynote Address from the ACM SIG-PLAN History of Programming Languages Conference, printed in *History of Programming Languages*, Richard L. Wexelblat, ed., New York: Academic Press, 1981, p. 16.

[17]Gisela Meier, "Amazing Grace Hopper," *Micro Discovery*, July 1983.

[18]I.E. Block, *Report on Meeting Held at University of Pennsylvania Computing Center*, April 9, 1959.

[19]Charles A. Phillips, *Summary of Discussions at Conference on Automatic Programming of ADPS for Business-Type Applications*, The Pentagon, May 28-29, 1959.

[20]Charles A. Phillips, *Summary of Discussions at Conference on Automatic Programming of ADPS for Business-Type Applications*, The Pentagon, May 28-29, 1959.

[21]Jean E. Sammet, "The Early History of COBOL," in *History of Programming Languages*, Richard L. Wexelblat, ed., New York: Academic Press, 1981, p. 231.

[22]Jean E. Sammet, "The Early History of COBOL," in *History of Programming Languages*, Richard L. Wexelblat, ed., New York: Academic Press, 1981, p. 213.

[23]Russ Walter, *The Secret Guide to Computers*, Boston: Birkhauser Boston, Inc., 1984, p. 249.

[24]John G. Kemeny, *Man and the Computer*, New York: Charles Scribner's Sons, 1972, p. 30.

[25]Thomas E. Kurtz, "BASIC," in *History of Programming Languages*, Richard L. Wexelblat, ed., New York: Academic Press, 1981, p. 518.

[26]J.G. Kemeny and Thomas E. Kurtz, *BASIC Instruction Manual*, Hanover, N.H.: Dartmouth College Press, 1964, p. 4.

[27]Thomas E. Kurtz, "BASIC," in *History of Programming Languages*, Richard L. Wexelblat, ed., New York: Academic Press, 1981, p. 535.

[28]Jerry Pournelle, "User's Column," *Byte*, April 1983, p. 330.

[29]Clark Weissman, *LISP 1.5 Primer*, Belmont, Calif.: Dickenson Publishing Co., 1967, p. 1.

[30]An entertaining exposition of the origins of AI research can be found in Pamela McCorduck, *Machines Who Think*, San Francisco: W.H. Freeman, 1979.

[31]A profile of McCarthy can be found in Philip J. Hilts, *Scientific Temperaments*, New York: Simon & Schuster, 1982.

[32]Seymour Papert, *Mindstorms: Children, Computers, and Powerful Ideas*, New York: Basic Books, 1980, p. 98.

[33]Seymour Papert, *Mindstorms: Children, Computers, and Powerful Ideas*, New York: Basic Books, 1980, pp. 21, 76.

[34]Harold Abelson, "A Beginners Guide to Logo," *Byte*, August 1982, p. 112.

[35]R.W. Lawler, "Designing Computer-Based Microworlds," *Byte*, August 1982, p. 142.

[36]Niklaus Wirth, "From Programming Techniques to Programming Methods," *International Computing Symposium*, 1973, A. Gunther et al., eds, Amsterdam: North-Holland Publishing Co., 1974, p. 48.

[37]Alan J. Perlis, "The American Side of the Development of ALGOL," in *History of Programming Languages*, Richard L. Wexelblat, ed., New York: Academic Press, 1981, p. 77.

[38]Niklaus Wirth, "The Programming Language Pascal," *Acta Informatica*, 1971, 1:35.

[39]Niklaus Wirth, "The Programming Language Pascal," *Acta Informatica*, 1971, 1:36.

[40]Niklaus Wirth, "The Programming Language Pascal," *Acta Informatica*, 1971, 1:35.

[41]Leo Brodie, *Thinking FORTH*, Englewood Cliffs, N.J.: Prentice-Hall, 1984, p. xiii.

[42]A series of articles about the history and structure of FORTH can be found in *InfoWorld*, October 11, 1982, pp. 15-37.

[43]A highly readable introduction to this not-so-readable language is presented in Leo Brodie, *Starting FORTH*, Englewood Cliffs, N.J.: Prentice-Hall, 1981. A more advanced text is Leo Brodie, *Thinking FORTH: A Language and Philosophy for Solving Problems*, Englewood Cliffs, N.J.: Prentice-Hall, 1984.

CHAPTER 6

[1]Alexander Holley, "The Uncertain Relation Between Science, Engineering, and Art," 1876, quoted in Elting Morison, "The Uncertain Relation," *Daedalus*, winter 1980, 109, 1:179.

[2]J.C.R. Licklider, "Man-Computer Symbiosis," *IRE Transactions on Human Factors in Electronics*, March 1960, HFE-1:4-11.

[3]Howard Rheingold, *Tools for Thought*, New York: Simon & Schuster, 1985.

[4]Douglas Engelbart, "A Conceptual Framework for the Augmentation of Man's Intellect," in *Vistas in Information Handling*, Paul William Howerton and David C. Weeks, eds., Washington: Spartan Books, 1963, vol. 1, pp. 1-29.

[5]George Miller, "The Magical Number Seven, Plus or Minus Two: Some Limits on Our Capacity for Processing Information," in *The Psychology of Communication*, G. Miller, New York: Basic Books, 1967. An earlier version appeared in *Psychology Review*, 1956, 63, 2:81-97.

[6]David Canfield Smith, Charles Irby, Ralph Kimball, and Eric Harslem, "The Star User Interface: An Overview," *Office Systems Technology*, El Segundo, Calif.: Xerox Corporation, 1982.

[7]Daniel H. Ingalls, "Design Principles Behind Smalltalk," *Byte*, August 1981, p. 286.

[8]Alan Kay, "Microelectronics and the Personal Computer," *Scientific American*, September 1977.

[9]C.H. Waddington, *Tools for Thought*, New York: Basic Books, 1977, pp. 206-207.

[10]David Canfield Smith, *Pygmalion: A Creative Programming Environment*, PhD dissertation, Dept. of Computer Science, Stanford University (tech report STAN-CS-75-499), 1975.

[11]Alan Borning, "The Programming Language Aspects of ThingLab, A Constraint-Oriented Simulation Laboratory," *ACM Transactions in Programming Languages and Systems*, October 1981, vol. 3, no. 4, pp. 353-387.

[12]Alan Borning, "ThingLab," in Laura Gould and William Finzer, eds., *Programming by Rehearsal*, SCL-84-1, Xerox Corporation, Palo Alto Research Center, 1984, Appendix A, p. 114.

[13]Alan Borning, quoted in William Finzer and Laura Gould, "Programming by Rehearsal," *Byte*, June 1984, p. 192.

[14]Ted Nelson, *The Home Computer Revolution*, self-published, 1977, pp. 120-123.

[15]Ephraim P. Glinert and Steven L. Tanimoto, "PICT: An Interactive Graphical Programming Environment," *IEEE Computer*, November 1984, pp. 7-25.

[16]Ephraim P. Glinert and Steven L. Tanimoto, "PICT: An Interactive Graphical Programming Environment," *IEEE Computer*, November 1984, p. 9.

[17]Interview between Howard Rheingold and Jaron Lanier, 1985.

[18]Interview between Howard Rheingold and Jaron Lanier, 1985.

[19]John Backus, "The History of FORTRAN I, II, and III," in *History of Programming Languages*, Richard L. Wexelblat, ed., New York: Academic Press, 1981, p. 43.

[20]The story of the fifth-generation project and PROLOG's role in it is told in Edward A. Feigenbaum and Pamela McCorduck, *The Fifth Generation*, Reading, Mass.: Addison-Wesley, 1983.

[21]Avron Barr, J.S. Bennet, and C.W. Clancey, "Transfer of Expertise: A Theme of AI Research," Working Paper No. HPP-79-11, Stanford University, Heuristic Programming Project (1979), p. 1.

[22]Morton Hunt, *The Universe Within*, New York: Simon & Schuster, 1982, p. 121.

[23]John G. Kemeny, "The Case for Computer Literacy," *Daedalus*, Spring 1983, 112, no. 2:223-224.

[24]L. Peter Deutsch and Edward A. Taft, "Requirements for an Experimental Programming Environment," Xerox Palo Alto Research Center Report CSL-80-10, 1980.

[25]Warren Teitelman, *The Cedar Programming Environment: A Midterm Report and Examination*, Xerox Palo Alto Research Center Report CSL-83-11, June 1984.

[26]Daniel G. Bobrow and Bertram Raphael, "New Programming Languages for AI Research," *Computing Surveys*, 1974, 6, no. 3.

BIBLIOGRAPHY

BOOKS

Ashby, W. Ross. *An Introduction to Cybernetics*. New York: John Wiley & Sons, 1963.

Backus, J.W., et al. *Programmer's Reference Manual, The FORTRAN Automatic Coding System for the IBM 704 EDPM*. New York: IBM Corp., October, 1956.

Bateson, Gregory. *Mind and Nature*. New York: Bantam Books, 1980.

Benacereff, Paul, and Hilary Putnam, eds. *Philosophy of Mathematics: Selected Readings*. Englewood Cliffs, N.J.: Prentice-Hall, 1964.

Bergson, Henri. *Creative Evolution*. Trans. by Arthur Mitchell. New York: Henry Holt & Co., 1911.

Bolter, J. David. *Turing's Man: Western Culture in the Computer Age*. Chapel Hill: The University of North Carolina Press, 1984.

Boole, George. *An Investigation of the Laws of Thought on which are Founded the Mathematical Theories of Logic and Probabilities*. New York: Dover Publications, Inc., 1958.

Brodie, Leo. *Starting FORTH*. Englewood Cliffs, N.J.: Prentice-Hall, 1981.

Brodie, Leo. *Thinking FORTH*. Englewood Cliffs, N.J.: Prentice-Hall, 1984.

Bronowski, Jacob. *The Ascent of Man*. Boston: Little, Brown & Co., 1973.

Brooks, Frederick P. Jr. *The Mythical Man-Month*. Reading, Mass.: Addison-Wesley Publishing Co., 1979.

Bruner, Jerome. *Toward a Theory of Instruction*. Cambridge, Mass.: Belknap Press, 1966.

Campbell, Jeremy. *Grammatical Man*. New York: Simon & Schuster, 1982.

Copi, Irving M. *Introduction to Logic*. New York: Macmillan, 1961.

Chomsky, Noam. *Syntactic Structures*. The Hague: Mouton & Co., 1957.

Dahl, O.J., E.W. Dijkstra, and C.A.R. Hoare. *Structured Programming*. London: Academic Press, 1972.

Descartes, René. *Discourse on Method*. Trans. by Laurence J. Lafleur. Indianapolis and New York: Bobbs-Merrill Co., 1960.

Deutsch, L. Peter, and Edward A. Taft. *Requirements for an Experimental Programming Environment*. Xerox Palo Alto Research Center Report CSL-80-10.

Dewey, John. *How We Think*. Lexington, Mass.: D.C. Heath & Co., 1910.

Eiseley, Loren. *The Man Who Saw Through Time*. New York: Charles Scribner's Sons, 1961.

Feigenbaum, Edward A., and Pamela McCorduck. *The Fifth Generation*. Reading, Mass.: Addison-Wesley Publishing Co., 1983.

Fodor, Jerry A., and Jerrold J. Katz. *The Structure of Language*. Englewood Cliffs, N.J.: Prentice-Hall, 1964.

Frege, Gottlob. *Grundgesetze der Arithmetik*, Vol. ii, 1903. Trans. in Geach, Peter, and Max Black. *Philosophical Writings of Gottlob Frege*. Oxford: Basil Blackwell, 1966.

Gardner, Martin. *Logic Machines and Diagrams*. New York: McGraw-Hill, 1958.

Gamow, George. *One, Two, Three . . . Infinity*. New York: Bantam Books, 1961.

Goldschlager, Les, and Andrew Lister. *Computer Science: A Modern Introduction*. Englewood Cliffs, N.J.: Prentice-Hall, 1982.

Goldstein, Thomas. *Dawn of Modern Science*. Boston: Houghton Mifflin, 1980.

Goldstine, Herman. *The Computer from Pascal to von Neumann*. Princeton, N.J.: Princeton University Press, 1972.

Gould, Laura, and William Finzer. *Programming by Rehearsal*, SCL-84-1. Xerox Corporation, Palo Alto Research Center, 1984.

Gunther, A., et al., eds. *International Computing Symposium*, 1973. Amsterdam: North-Holland Publishing Co., 1974.

Halsted, George B., trans. *Geometrical Researches on the Theory of Parallels*. La Salle, Ill.: The Open Court Publishing Co., 1942.

Hanson, Dirk. *The New Alchemists*. Boston: Little, Brown & Co., 1982.

Harman, Willis, and Howard Rheingold. *Higher Creativity*. Los Angeles: Jeremy P. Tarcher, Inc., 1984.

Haugeland, John, ed. *Mind Design*. Cambridge, Mass.: MIT Press, 1981.

Hilts, Philip J. *Scientific Temperaments*. New York: Simon & Schuster, 1982.

Hodges, Andrew. *Alan Turing: The Enigma*. New York: Simon & Schuster, 1983.

Hofstader, Douglas R. *Godel, Escher, Bach*. New York: Basic Books, 1979.

Howerton, Paul William, and David C. Weeks, eds. *Vistas in Information Handling*, Vol. 1. Washington: Spartan Books, 1963.

Hull, T.E. *Introduction to Computing*. Englewood Cliffs, N.J.: Prentice-Hall, 1966.

Hunt, Morton. *The Universe Within*. New York: Simon & Schuster, 1982.

Kemeny, J.G., and T.E. Kurtz. *BASIC Instruction Manual*. Hanover, N.H.: Dartmouth College Press, 1964.

Kemeny, John G. *Man and the Computer*. New York: Charles Scribner's Sons, 1972.

Knuth, Donald E. *The Art of Computer Programming, Volume 1, Fundamental Algorithms*. Reading, Mass.: Addison-Wesley Publishing Co., 1968.

Knuth, Donald E., and Luis Trabb Pardo. *Encyclopedia of Computer Science and Technology*. New York: Dekker, 1977.

Kuhn, Thomas S. *The Structure of Scientific Revolution*. Chicago: University of Chicago Press, 1970.

McCorduck, Pamela. *Machines Who Think*. San Francisco: W.H. Freeman & Co., 1979.

Metropolis, N., et al., ed. *A History of Computers in the Twentieth Century*. New York: Academic Press, 1980.

Miller, George, ed. *The Psychology of Communication*. New York: Basic Books, 1967.

Miller, Johnathan. *States of Mind*. New York: Pantheon, 1983.

Muir, Jane. *Of Men and Numbers*. New York: Dodd Mead, 1965.

Nagel, Ernest, and James R. Newman. *Godel's Proof.* New York: New York University Press, 1958.

Nelson, Ted. *The Home Computer Revolution.* Self-published, 1977.

Newton, Isaac. *Philosophiae Naturalis Principia Mathematica.* Berkeley: University of California Press, 1934.

Papert, Seymour. *Mindstorms: Children, Computers, and Powerful Ideas.* New York: Basic Books, 1980.

Peano, Guiseppe. *Formulaire de Mathematiques.* Torino, Italy: Bocca, 1895.

Poincare, Henri. *Science and Method.* Trans. Francis Martland. New York: Dover Books, 1952.

Pratt, Terrence W. *Programming Languages: Design and Implementation.* Englewood Cliffs, N.J.: Prentice-Hall, 1984.

Programmer's Reference Manual, The FORTRAN Automatic Coding System for the IBM 704 EDPM. IBM Corporation, October 15, 1956.

Quine, Willard Van Orman. *Methods of Logic.* New York: Holt, Rinehart, Winston, 1959.

Rheingold, Howard. *Tools for Thought.* New York: Simon & Schuster, 1985.

Rogers, Hartley, Jr. *Theory of Recursive Function and Effective Computability.* New York: McGraw-Hill, 1967.

Russell, Bertrand. *A History of Western Philosophy.* New York: Simon & Schuster, 1972.

Russell, Bertrand. *Human Knowledge: Its Scope and Limits.* New York: Simon & Schuster, 1948.

Russell, Bertrand. *Portraits from Memory.* New York: Simon & Schuster, 1956.

Sammet, Jean. *Programming Languages: History and Fundamentals.* Englewood Cliffs, N.J.: Prentice-Hall, 1969.

Sebeok, T.A., ed. *Style in Language.* New York: John Wiley & Sons, Inc., 1960.

Simon, Herbert A. *The Sciences of the Artificial,* 2nd ed. Cambridge, Mass.: MIT Press, 1981.

Smith, David Canfield, Charles Irby, Ralph Kimball, and Eric Harslem. "The Star User Interface: An Overview," *Office Systems Technology.* El Segundo, Calif.: Xerox Corporation, 1982.

Steen, Lynn Arthur, ed. *Mathematics Today.* New York: Springer-Verlag, 1978.

Specifications for the IBM Mathematical Formula Translating System. IBM Corporation, New York, November 10, 1954.

Teitelman, Warren. *The Cedar Programming Environment: A Midterm Report and Examination.* Xerox Palo Alto Research Center CSL-83-11, June, 1984.

Vygotsky, Lev Semenovich. *Thought and Language.* Cambridge: MIT Press, 1962.

Waddington, C.H. *Tools for Thought.* New York: Basic Books, 1977.

Walter, Russ. *The Secret Guide to Computers.* Boston: Birkhauser Boston, Inc., 1984.

Weissman, Clark. *LISP 1.5 Primer.* Belmont, Calif.: Dickenson Publishing Co., 1967.

Weizenbaum, Joseph. *Computer Power and Human Reason.* San Francisco: W.H. Freeman, 1976.

Wexelblat, Richard L. *History of Programming Languages.* New York: Academic Press, 1981.

Wilder, Raymond L. "The Axiomatic Method." Reprinted in Newman, James R., ed. *The Mathematical Way of Thinking.* New York: Simon & Schuster, 1956.

Wolff, Peter. *Breakthroughs in Mathematics.* New York: New American Library, 1963.

ARTICLES

Abelson, Harold. "A Beginners Guide to Logo." *Byte* (August 1982): 112.

Bacon, Sir Francis. *De augmentis scientarum,* 1623. In Heath, F.G. "The Origins of the Binary Code." *Scientific American* (August 1972): 76-83.

Bobrow, Daniel G., and Bertram Raphael. "New Programming Languages for AI Research." *Computing Surveys* 6, 3 (September 1974).

Borning, Alan. "The Programming Language Aspects of ThingLab, A Constraint-Oriented Simulation Laboratory." *ACM Transactions in Programming Languages and Systems* 3, 4 (October 1981): 353-387.

Burks, Arthur W., Herman H. Goldstine, and John von Neumann. "Preliminary Discussion of the Logical Design of an Electronic Computing Instrument." Original mimeographed report condensed and reprinted in *Datamation* (September-October 1962).

Cherniak, Christopher. "Computational Complexity and the Universal Acceptance of Logic." *Journal of Philosophy* LXXXI, no. 12 (December 1984): 739-758.

Denning, Peter J., and Robert L. Brown. "Operating Systems." *Scientific American* (September 1984): 94-106.

Finzer, William, and Laura Gould. "Programming by Rehearsal." *Byte* (June 1984): 192.

Freiberger, Paul. *InfoWorld* (October 11, 1982): 15-37.

Glinert, Ephraim P., and Steven L. Tanimoto. "PICT: An Interactive Graphical Programming Environment." *IEEE Computer* (November 1984): 7-25.

Gödel, Kurt. "Die Vollständigkeit Der Axiome Des Logischen Funktionenkalkuls." *Monatsh. Math. Phys.* 37 (1930): 349-360.

Gödel, Kurt. "Uber Formal Unentscheidbare Sätze Der Principia Mathematica Und Verwandter Systeme I." *Monatsh. Math. Phys.* 38 (1931): 173-198.

Heath, F.G. "Origins of the Binary Code." *Scientific American* (August 1972): 76-83.

Hilbert, D. "Mathematical Problems." *Bulletin of the American Mathematical Society* 8 (1902): 444.

Holley, Alexander. "The Uncertain Relation Between Science, Engineering, and Art," 1876. Quoted in Morison, Elting. "The Uncertain Relation." *Daedalus* 109, no. 1 (Winter 1980): 179.

Ingalls, Daniel H. "Design Principles Behind Smalltalk." *Byte* (August 1981): 286.

Kay, Alan. "Computer Software." *Scientific American* (September 1984): 53-59.

Kay, Alan, "Microelectronics and the Personal Computer." *Scientific American* (September 1977): 3–13.

Kemeny, John G. "The Case for Computer Literacy." *Daedalus* 112, no. 2 (Spring 1983): 223-224.

Knuth, Donald E. "Algorithms." *Scientific American.* 236, no. 4 (April 1977): 63.

Lawler, R.W. "Designing Computer-Based Microworlds." *Byte.* (August 1982): 142.

Licklider, J.C.R. "Man-Computer Symbiosis." *IRE Transactions on Human Factors in Electronics* HFE-1 (March 1960): 4-11.

Meier, Gisela. "Amazing Grace Hopper." *Micro Discovery.* (July 1983): 30-34.

Patterson, David A. "Microprogramming." *Scientific American* (March 1983); 50-57.

Post, Emil. "Introduction to a General Theory of Elementary Propositions." *American Journal of Mathematics* 43 (1921): 163-185.

Pournelle, Jerry. "User's Column." *Byte*. (April 1983): 330.

Shannon, Claude. "A Chess-Playing Machine." *Scientific American* 182 (February 1950).

Shannon, Claude. "A Mathematical Theory of Information." *Bell System Technical Journal* 27 (1948): 379-423, 623-656.

Shannon, Claude. "A Symbolic Analysis of Relay and Switching Circuits." *Transactions of the American Institute of Electrical Engineers* 57 (1938): 713.

Tesler, Lawrence G. "Programming Languages." *Scientific American* (September 1984): 70.

Turing, Alan. "On Computable Numbers with an Application to the Entscheidungsproblem." *Proceedings of the London Mathematical Society* 42 (1936): 230-265; 43 (1937): 544-546.

Winograd, Terry. "Computer Software for Working with Language." *Scientific American* (September 1984): 131.

Wirth, Niklaus. "Data Structures and Algorithms." *Scientific American* (September 1984): 60-69.

Wirth, Niklaus. "Program Development by Stepwise Refinement." *Communications of the ACM* 14, no. 4 (1971): 221-227.

Wirth, Nicklaus. "The Programming Language Pascal." *Acta Informatica* 1 (1971): 35.

UNPUBLISHED MATERIALS

Barr, Avron, J.S. Bennet, and C.W. Clancey. "Transfer of Expertise: A Theme of AI Research." Working Paper No. HPP-79-11. Stanford University, Heuristic Programming Project (1979): 1.

Block, I.E. *Report on Meeting Held at University of Pennsylvania Computing Center*. April 9, 1959.

Phillips, Charles A. *Summary of Discussions at Conference on Automatic Programming of ADPS for Business-Type Applications*. The Pentagon. May 28-29, 1959.

Smith, David Canfield. *Pygmalion: A Creative Programming Environment*, PhD dissertation, Department of Computer Science, Stanford University (tech report STAN-CS-75-499), 1975.

Index

Abstraction, process of 3, 71-75
Accumulator 102
ACM (American Association for Computing Machinery) 189
"A Conceptual Framework for the Augmentation of Man's Intellect" (Engelbart) 212
ADA 197
Adders 87, 92-94
Address (in computer memory) 90, 101
Aleph-2, Aleph-1, Aleph-0 2
Algebra 37, 42-47
ALGOL 163, 189-192, 217, 245
ALGOL 68 191
Algorithm xvii, 12, 15, 37, 64-69, 75, 111-129, 132-143
al-Khowarazmi 37
Allen, Paul 165
Altair 165
Alto 213, 220
ALU (arithmetic and logic unit) 94, 100
ANSI (American National Standards Institute) 151, 160, 165
ARC (Augmentation Research Center) 212
Archimedes 2
Aristotle 7, 8, 10, 33-38, 42, 61, 63, 240
ARK (Alternate Reality Kit) 228
ARPA (Advanced Research Projects Agency) 177, 211, 217, 230
Array 130, 134

Ars Magna (Lull) 38
Artificial intelligence 74, 121, 127, 161, 167-175, 212, 238-241, 245-248
ASCII code 134
Assembler 73, 103
Assembly language 72, 103-105, 201
Assignment statement 25, 186
"A Symbolic Analysis of Relay and Switching Circuits" (Shannon) 82
Automatic programming 148-150
Axiom of extensionality 58

Backus, John 105, 147-153, 239
Bacon, Sir Francis 8, 10, 75, 126, 223
BACAIC 189
BASIC 18, 25, 73, 114, 117, 134, 161-167, 197
Bateson, Gregory 80
BB&N (Bolt, Beranek & Newman) 177
Bell Laboratories 27
Binary code 76-87, 117
Bit (information measure) 31, 80, 88
Bit mapping 215
Boole, George 40-48, 52-54, 58, 77, 86
Boolean algebra 28, 43-47, 81, 88, 235
Bootstrapping program 108
Borning, Alan 223
Bowles, Kenneth 198

Boxer 187
Bronowski, Jacob 50
Browsers 219, 232
Burns, Robert 69
Byblos 4
Byte (information measure) 89

C 174
Cantor, Georg 2
Cardinal numbers 2, 15
Caricatures 233
Carr, John W. III 159
Cartesian doubt 9
CBL (Common Business Language) 156
Cedar project 243
Chat 240
Chipwits 235
Chomsky, Noam 13, 143
Church, Alonzo 69, 168
Church's Thesis 122
Clascal 221
Class template 219
Clock (computer component) 94
COBOL 137, 153-161, 170, 198
COBOL Journal of Development 160
CODASYL (Committee on Data Systems) 156, 160
Coder 147
Compiler 73, 105-107, 150, 155, 196
Completeness (of a formal system) 61-69
Complexity, algorithmic 124-126
Computability, algorithmic 122-124
Computer language (*see also* programming language) 5, 14
    low level languages 71-109
    high level languages 145-207
    very high level languages 209-248
Computer Power and Human Reason (Weizenbaum) 81
Computer thought 111-143

COMTRAN (Commercial Translator) 155
Conditional expression 169
Conditional interrupt 245
Connotative statements 25
Control logic 87, 94, 99
Control words 25, 120, 166, 197, 245
Copernicus, Nicolai 10
Correctness, algorithmic 126
CPU (central processing unit) 72, 94, 196
CSL (Computer Science Laboratory) 244
Cybernetics 29-32

Dahl, O. J. 143, 217
Dartmouth 161, 168
Data bus 94
Data structures xviii, 15, 46, 75, 88, 90, 95, 11, 127-136, 204, 230
    array 130, 194
    dynamic 129
    field 130
    fixed 129
    heterogenous 130
    homogeneous 129
    list 131, 135, 169-175, 187
    matrix 130
    queue 131
    record 128, 130, 194
    selection operator 130
    set 131, 194
    stack 131, 205-207, 214
    static 129
    tree 132
    variable 129
Data types 194-198, 204, 245
DBMS (data base management system) 160
Decidability (of a formal system) 61-69
Decomposition 142

Deductive reasoning 9, 237, 240, 246
Demon 245
Descartes, René 6-12, 126
Deutsch, Peter 170
Dewey, John 179
Digital Equipment Company 170, 242
Dijkstra, E. W. 143, 166
di Sessa, Andrea 187
Discourse on the Method (Descartes) 7
Dissertio de arte combinatoria (Leibniz) 40

Egyptians 2, 34
Einstein, Albert 52
Elements (Euclid) 47, 50
Emotive language 26
Engelbart, Douglas 212, 242
ENIAC xvi, 95, 98, 139, 146
Equivalence problem 123
Euclid 7, 9, 47-51, 54, 58, 63, 240
Euler 191
Expert systems 239
Extensibility 166, 174, 201-207, 227, 238

FACT 155
Fetch-execute cycle 95
Feurzeig, Wallace 177
Fifth Generation Computer Project 237
FIG (Forth Interest Group) 200
Firmware 100
FLEX computer 217
Flip-flop circuit 88, 94
Flowcharting (flow diagram) 137, 232
FLOW-MATIC 154
Formalist school of mathematics 60
Formal language 35, 52-69
Formal system xvii, 48-69, 72

Formulaire de Mathematiques (Peano) 54
FORTH 131, 174, 198-207, 221
FORTRAN 73, 105, 117, 137, 145-153, 163, 170, 188, 198
FORTRANSIT 189
Frege, Gottlob 58, 61
Functions 147, 183

Galileo 8, 10
GAMM 189
Gates, Bill 165
Generalization, process of 3
Geometrical Researches on the Theory of Parallels (Lobachevski) 51
Geometry
  Euclidean 49
  non-Euclidean 51, 58
Gilbert, Ephraim and Tanimoto, Stephen L. 230
Gödel, Kurt 62-64, 123, 168
Golenischev Papyrus 34
Goldstine, Herman H. 139
GOTO statements 114, 117, 135, 146, 167, 197
Gould, Laura and William Finzer 225
GPL 191
Grammar 15
Graphical editor 225, 234
Grimm, Leslie 235

Half-adder 92
Halting problem 68, 123
Hardware xviii, 30, 72, 83-91, 100, 164, 167, 188, 201, 209, 216
Harris, Kim 200
Hexadecimal 147
Hieroglyphic symbols 4
Hilbert, David 56, 60, 68
Hoare, C. A. R. 143
Homo habilis xv, 3
Honeywell 155

Hopper, Grace 105, 147, 151, 154, 161

IBM 149, 155, 190, 242
IBM 704 Computer 149, 169, 172
I Ching 77
Icons 219, 222-236
Imagination, process of 3
Implementation 165
Incompleteness (of a formal system) 62-69
Incremental compiler 166
Inductive reasoning 10, 223, 240
Infinity 2
Infix notation 172
Information xvii, 27-32, 80, 89, 115
Information Processing Techniques Office 211
Inheritance 219
Instructions xvi, 6, 46, 66, 112, 115-123, 137-143
Instruction set 72, 100
Interface, human-machine 107, 209-215
Interpreter 73, 105-107, 148, 170, 183, 196
I/O (input/output device) 95
IPL-2 (Information Processing Language) 169
IT 151, 189
Iteration 118-122, 180

Jacobson, Roman 24
JOHNNIAC 169

Kay, Alan 25, 217
Kemeny, John G. 161
Kitar al-jabr w'almgabala 37
Kuhn, Thomas 28
Kurtz, Thomas E. 161, 164

Laning, J. H. 148
Lambda calculus 69
Language

assembly language 72, 103-105
comparison of natural language with programming language 19-27, 112, 114
computer language 5, 14, 71-109, 145-207, 209-248
formal language 35, 52-69
functions 24-27
deep structure 2, 15
machine language 18, 72, 99-103, 105, 131, 137, 147
relationship to science 5-12
relationship to thought 1-5, 12, 15, 61, 209-215, 248
spoken 1-4
structure 15-23
written 4, 74
See also Programming Language
Lanier, Jaron 232
Lawler, R. W. 186
Laws of Thought (Boole) 41
Lexical analysis 104
Liar's Paradox 22
Licklider, J. C. R. 210, 229
Light pen 229
Lincoln Laboratory 229
Linguistics
structural school 12
transformational school 13-23
LISP 121, 132, 161, 167-175, 179, 187, 198, 245
List 131, 135, 169-175, 187
Lobachevski, Nicholas 51
Logic 8, 34-69
Logic gates 87-93
Logic language 239
Logicist school of mathematics 60
Logic Theorist 169
Logo 25, 114, 118, 120, 132, 135, 174, 176-187, 217
Lull, Ramon 38

Machine, concept of xv-xx, 47

Machine language 18, 72, 99-103, 105, 131, 137, 147
Machine language interpreter 101
Macintosh 221, 235
Mandala 232-235
MANIAC 146
Mark I 146, 155
Massachusetts Institute of Technology (MIT) 13, 29, 77, 162, 170, 199, 229
MATHMATIC 189
Matrix 130
MBASIC 165
McCarthy, John 168-175, 245
McLuhan, Marshall xv
Mecho 240
Memory (computer) 87-91, 113
Memory cells 90, 205
Memory management 106
Metalingual mode (of language) 26
Metalogic 57-69
Metamathematics 60
Microcode 99-101
Microcomputer 165, 201
Microsoft 165
Minsky, Marvin 169
MITI (Ministry of International Trade and Industry) 237, 242
MITS (Micro Instrumentation and Telemetry System) 165
Modula-2 197
Modules 143, 167, 190, 192-194
Moore, Charles H. 199
Morse, Samuel F.B. 31
Morse Code 31
Mouse 212

NEON 221
Newell, Allen, Simon, Herbert, Shaw, Cliff 169
Newton, Sir Isaac 8, 10, 28, 38, 50
Norwegian Computing Center 217
Nygaard, Kristen 217

Object Code 106
Octal 147
"On Formally Undecidable Propositions of Principia Mathematica and Related Systems" (Gödel) 63
Op code 101
Operand 102
Operating System 71, 106-109, 214
ORBI 240
Organon (Aristotle) 34

Papert, Seymour 177-180
Paradigm shift 28, 241-248
Paradox 22, 26, 48, 57-69
    liar's paradox 22
    paradox of the all-purpose machine xv-xx, 77, 111, 134
    Russell's paradox 59, 63
Parameter stack 206
PARC (Palo Alto Research Center) 213, 217, 222, 225, 228, 242
Parsing
    sentences 16-18
    programs 104
Pascal 25, 73, 118, 143, 167, 188-198, 244
P-complier 196
PDP-1 170
Peano, Guiseppe 54, 58
Pecan 244
Performers 225
Phatic utterances 26
Philosophiae Naturalis Principia Mathematica (Newton) 50
Phoenicians 4, 34
Phonology 16, 23
Piaget, Jean 178, 240
Pict 231
Pictographic symbols 2, 4
Piestrup, Ann 235
Plato 146
Poetic language 25

Pointer 194, 205
Post, Emil 61
Postfix notation 205
Pratt, Terence 151
Predicate calculus 62, 238
Prefix notation 172
*"Preliminary Discussion of the
  Logical Design of an Electronic
  Computing Instrument"* (von
  Neumann et al.) 95
Principia Mathematica (Russell
  and Whitehead) 54, 57, 61-63
PRINT 151
Procedure (Logo) 183
Process control 200
"Program Development by Stepwise
  Refinement" (Wirth) 140
Programming environment 215,
  241-248
Programming language 14, 16,
  20-27, 31, 37, 62, 65, 73,
  97-109, 145-248
  ADA 197
  ALGOL 163, 189-192, 217,
    245
  ALGOL 68 191
  BACAIC 189
  BASIC 18, 25, 73, 114, 117,
    134, 161-167, 197
  Boxer 187
  C 174
  CBL (Common Business
    Language) 156
  Clascal 221
  COBOL 137, 153-161, 170,
    198
  COMTRAN (Commericial
    Translator) 155
  Euler 191
  FACT 155
  FLOW-MATIC 154
  FORTH 131, 174, 198-207,
    221

FORTRAN 73, 105, 117, 137,
  145-153, 163, 170, 188,
  198
FORTRANSIT 189
GPL 191
IPL-2 (Information Processing
  Language) 169
IT 151, 189
LISP 121, 132, 161, 167-175,
  179, 187, 198, 245
Logo 25, 114, 118, 120, 132,
  135, 174, 176-186, 217
Mandala 232-235
MATHMATIC 189
MBASIC 165
Modula-2 197
NEON 221
Pascal 25, 73, 118, 143, 167,
  188-198, 244
Pecan 244
Pict 231
PRINT 151
PROLOG 236-241
Pygmalion 222
Rehearsal World 225-228, 234
Simula 217
Sketchpad 217, 228-230
Smalltalk 215-226
TELCOMP 178
Thinglab 223, 234
Programming Metaphors
  Iconic programming 228-236
  Logic oriented programming
    236-241
  Object oriented programming
    215-228
  Procedural programming
    145-207, 231, 237, 239
  Programming by demonstration
    223
  Programming by description
    (nonprocedural
    programming) 237-241
  Programming by rehearsal
    225-228

Programs xviii, 73, 97,
    111-143, 146, 148, 150,
    158, 161, 163, 175,
    182-187, 192, 204, 238
PROLOG 236-241
Proof theory 48-69
Proteus xix
Pygmalion 222

Queue 131

RAM (random access memory)
    90
RAND Corporation 169
Rather, Elizabeth 200
Recursion 78, 120-122, 132,
    169, 184, 220, 238
Referential statements 25
Registers 90
Rehearsal world 225-228, 234
Reiss, Stephen P. 244
Repetitive algorithms 118-122
Rice's theorem 123
Riemann, Bernhard 52
Robinett, Warren 235
Robot Odyssey 235
Rocky's Boots 235
ROM (read only memory) 100,
    108
Russell, Bertrand 40, 54, 59
Russell paradox 59, 63
Russell, Stephen 170
Rules 237

Sammet, Jean 153, 156
Scientific method 4, 6-12, 51,
    58
Selection algorithms 116-118,
    169
Self-reference (of language) 26
Semantics 16, 19-23, 55
Sentential logic 61
Sequence 128
Sequential algorithm 115
Set 131, 194

Shannon, Claude 28-32, 77, 82
Simula 217
Sketchpad 217, 228-230
Smalltalk 215-226
Smith, David Canfield 222
Smith, Randy 226
Snow, C. P. 12
Software xviii, 30, 33, 87-109,
    164, 188, 209, 216, 242
Software object 217-221
Source code 106
Spreadsheet programs 224
Square of opposition 35, 38, 62
Stack 131, 205-207, 214
Star 213
Stack manipulation operator 206
Stepping variable 186
Stepwise refinement (top-down
    programming) 140-143, 190
Structured programming 118,
    143, 151, 166, 184,
    190-194
Subroutines 152, 166
Sutherland, Ivan 229
Syllogistic logic 8, 34-36, 42,
    45, 237
Symbol systems xvi, 5, 11, 35,
    43-47, 52-57
Syntactic analysis 104
Syntax 16-19, 55

Tail recursion 184
Technology, concept of xvii-xx
TELCOMP 178
"The Magical Number Seven,
    Plus or Minus Two" (Miller)
    213
Theory of types 59
Thinglab 223, 234
Thought
amplification via computers
    176-185, 210-215
computer 111-143
formalized 33-69

relationship to language 1-5, 12, 15, 209, 248
Time, concept of 3
Timesharing 162, 170, 178
Timetable problem 125
Transfinite numbers 2
Transportability 146, 158
Traveling salesman problem 125
Trees 77-80, 132
Trip 225
Truth tables 43, 45-47, 82, 86
Turing, Alan M. 47, 64-69, 77, 123, 147, 168
Turing machines 47, 64-69, 97, 101, 122, 136, 170
Turtle 179-183, 218
TX-2 229

UNIVAC 105, 147, 154
Universal grammar 13
Universalization, process of 4
Universal Turing machine 67-69, 77, 81

Variables 146, 159, 163, 167, 183-187, 192, 201, 219, 230, 237

Virtual computer xviii, 64, 72, 97-109, 129, 146, 148, 215, 237, 239
von Neumann, John 95, 139
von Neumann architecture 95, 216, 236, 247

Wallace Michael 235
Weizenbaum, Joseph 81
WHIRLWIND 148
Whitehead, Alfred North 54
Wiener, Norbert 29
Wilkes, Maurice 99
Winograd, Terry xvi
Wirth, Niklaus 140, 143, 191-198
Word (measure of information) 89
Word (used in FORTH) 202

Xerox Corporation (see PARC)

Zierler, N. 148